DATE DUE

SFPL DEC 17 '80			
JUN 18 1981			
JL 28 '82			
SFPL JAN 21 '89			
SFPL APR 20 '89			
SFPL JAN 27 '91			

DEMCO 38-297

RED STAR RISING AT SEA

SERGEI G. GORSHKOV
Admiral of the Fleet of the Soviet Union

Translated by Theodore A. Neely, Jr.
from a series of articles originally
published in *Morskoi Sbornik*

Edited for publication by Herbert Preston,
Colonel, USMC (Ret.)

Library of Congress Catalogue Card Number
74-82031
ISBN 0-87021-244-9

Printed in the United States of America

Publisher's Preface

The publication of this book is particularly significant now, inasmuch as the navies of the world's two superpowers—the United States and the Soviet Union—now rival each other in their potential capacity to control all or part of the world's oceans.

It is important that English-speaking people have the opportunity to read and consider the words of the leading spokesman of mid-century Soviet naval development, for in those words the reader will find not only an explanation of how the philosophy of Soviet seapower has developed over the last half-century but also a better understanding of the challenge which Soviet naval power poses for the future.

The articles that form the core of this book originally appeared in 1972 and 1973 in *Morskoi Sbornik*, the official journal of the Soviet Navy. The articles were published in translation throughout 1974 in the U. S. Naval Institute *Proceedings*, with commentaries by American admirals. The articles are brought together here with those commentaries, a brief biographical account of Admiral Gorshkov, and an introduction and conclusion by the former Chief of Naval Operations, Admiral Elmo R. Zumwalt, Jr., U. S. Navy (Retired).

Contents

Introduction

By Admiral Elmo R. Zumwalt, Jr., U. S. Navy (Ret.)

There are three points which I think it particularly important to emphasize at the outset to readers of this book.

The first is that what we are seeing in Gorshkov's series is the rationale for decisions already taken by the Soviet hierarchy. Gorshkov is not advocating new departures in Soviet policy. He is recapitulating the arguments which have already proven persuasive in launching the Soviets on a campaign to acquire a naval force—in Gorshkov's words—"second to none." ·

We know that the arguments of Gorshkov's series were presented earlier, in a more limited forum, to the political and military leadership of the Soviet Union. We know as well that the Central Committee of the Communist Party, on the recommendation of its Politbureau, adopted Gorshkov's thoughts on naval expansion as a national goal of the Soviet Union.

These articles, therefore, are doubly important. They reveal to us the arguments which were persuasive with the leaders of the Soviet Union, and to that extent shed light on Soviet priorities. At the same time, they provide important clues about the future direction of Soviet policy. We must study them with that in mind; and profit from what the Soviets have told us about their longer term intentions.

The second point is Gorshkov's emphasis on technology, and the crucial influence it exerts on naval weapons and tactics. Gorshkov has shown himself adept at introducing advanced technology into the Soviet Navy, and in focussing his efforts on those areas where technology promises the highest battle pay-off—electronic warfare, missiles, and advanced propulsion techniques. The large Soviet investment in military R&D presages further rapid technological advance, much of which we will not be aware of until we see the new Soviet systems deployed.

Finally, Gorshkov gives us a clear indication of Soviet mission priorities. In this area he is careful to distinguish between peacetime and wartime missions. As the title of his series suggests, he believes navies can be as important in advancing the state's political objectives in peacetime as they are in defending vital national interests in war.

The wartime mission of the Soviet Navy, Gorshkov

makes clear, is to defeat Western naval forces, thereby denying us the ability to use the seas for our own essential purposes. Over the longer term, Gorshkov's arguments suggest, the Soviet objective is the ability to exert positive control of the seas in all areas of strategic importance.

The peacetime mission of the Soviet Navy has three facets.

The first is to counterbalance the influence which the United States derives from its overseas naval forces, deploying Soviet naval forces in close proximity, in configurations which implicitly threaten preemption of U. S. capabilities. We have seen this technique employed in the Mediterranean, both in the steady-state deployments which the Soviets have maintained there since 1966; and in the rapid augmentation of those forces in crises, which last October brought the Soviet Mediterranean Fleet to a strength of over 90 vessels.

The second function of Soviet peacetime deployments is to solidify the image of the Soviet Union as a superpower with global interests, capable of employing military power anywhere those interests may require. In this respect it supports Gromyko's description of the U.S.S.R. as a state with the right to influence the outcome of all important international issues, wherever they may occur.

The third objective of Soviet peacetime deployments is to exert pressures in support of Soviet political goals in areas of particular importance to the U.S.S.R. The expanding Soviet presence off the coast of Norway is an example. The Soviet Navy has already achieved important psychological gains by persuading large segments of the Norwegian public that their country is now "behind the U.S.S.R.'s front line."

The growing Soviet presence in the Indian Ocean provides another illustration. Here the Soviet Navy supports a variety of political objectives, including the isolation of the People's Republic of China; the encouragement of radical nationalist regimes along the Arabian Peninsula and the East African littoral; and the enhancement of Soviet influence with the oil-importing nations, who cannot help but observe that Soviet capabilities to operate along the critical Indian Ocean oil routes imply an ability to jeopardize their own economic viability, should the Soviets choose to do so.

In reading Gorshkov, one almost senses that he feels the peacetime role of Soviet naval forces is the more important of the two—in terms of the benefits it can bring the U.S.S.R. Gorshkov clearly believes that the Navy can help attain a variety of important political objectives for the U.S.S.R., without having to fire a shot. In this respect naval power is unique among the several forms of military power at the disposal of the Soviet leadership; and therein lies one of the most telling arguments Gorshkov advances for a navy "second to none."

The real significance of Gorshkov's series, in my judgment, is what it tells us about the sophistication of the Soviet leadership. In recent years we have been impressed by the growing finesse, subtlety, and effectiveness with which the Soviets have pursued their external goals. They have shown the ability to profit from experience, and to adapt Western techniques to their own needs. Nowhere is this more evident than in their acceptance of the case for a maritime strategy. Having established themselves as the dominant power on the Eurasian land mass and overcome U. S. superiority in intercontinental strategic capabilities, the Soviets have now turned to the oceans with the objective of establishing their superiority in this one remaining area of traditional Western predominance.

If they accomplish this, we will be confronted with the unprecedented situation of Soviet superiority in all facets of military power. Under these circumstances, past Soviet behavior will be an unreliable guide to the future; and we can expect vigorous Soviet action to derive the maximum political benefit from this fundamentally altered situation.

I need not belabor the point that this would be an extraordinarily dangerous situation for the rest of the world—fraught with the potential for Soviet miscalculation, and marked by the steady erosion of Western confidence and political will. It would greatly reduce the possibility of acceptable negotiated solutions to our political differences with the Soviets, and would return the superpowers to a posture of confrontation or force-negotiated solutions unfavorable to the United States; for, as our political leaders have emphasized, military equilibrium is the essential foundation of any policy directed at the relaxation of East-West tensions.

This dangerous situation need not come to pass, however. We are already embarked on programs which, when carried to completion, will restore confidence in our ability to use the seas for our own essential political, economic, and military purposes.

In his own way, Admiral Gorshkov has made a unique contribution to the success of those programs by so clearly articulating the way in which the Soviets intend to use the seas to advance their own ambitions.

The lesson is one which we cannot ignore. It is with that thought in mind that I have encouraged the broadest possible dissemination of Admiral Gorshkov's views, and asked the Naval Institute to make available this volume of the Gorshkov articles, together with informed commentary on them.

I hope you will find the series as thought-provoking as I have.

Navies in War and in Peace

By Admiral of the Fleet of the Soviet Union S. G. Gorshkov

With Commentary following the article by
Rear Admiral George H. Miller, U. S. Navy (Retired)

EDITOR'S NOTE: *Admiral Gorshkov has been Commander-in-Chief of the Soviet Navy for 18 years. He is a Deputy Minister of Defense and a full member of the Central Committee of the Communist Party.*

What follows is a translation of an article which appeared in Morskoi Sbornik No. 2, 1972, *having been approved for publication in the Soviet Union on 28 January 1972. Plainly, the thoughts and beliefs which appear in this article—and those which will be published on these pages over the next ten months—are views which Admiral Gorshkov wishes to share with the other officers in his navy. For that reason alone, they are considered to be of profound interest to the officers of his country's principal rival at sea, the United States Navy.*

For many centuries the ocean expanses have not only been a convenient means of communication between continents and between the suppliers of products vitally essential to mankind, but also an arena of fierce struggle and military conflicts. The scale of utilizing the water medium for military aims, i.e., for the defense of one's own country and to seize overseas possessions, has grown in relation to man's knowledge and mastery of the ocean. At the present time, in an era of far-reaching scientific discoveries and the utilization of them for military needs, the capabilities for conducting combat operations on the oceanic expanses have increased incredibly, while the naval arms race abroad, and the creation of diverse means of naval combat have reached unprecedentedly imposing scales.

The hallmark of naval forces is their high degree of maneuverability, and ability to concentrate secretly and to form powerful groupings which are of surprise to the enemy. At the same time, naval forces are more stable against the effects of nuclear weaponry than land forces. All of this has catapulted the navies into the front ranks of the diverse, modern means of armed combat. Their employment in nuclear-missile warfare is related to the introduction of much of what is new in tactics and operational skills, in ship design, and in the outfitting of ships with equipment and armament.

The qualitative transformations which have taken place in naval forces have also changed the approach to evaluating the relative might of navies and their combat groupings. We have had to cease comparing the number of warships of one type or another and their total displacement (or the number of guns in a salvo, or the weight of this salvo), and turn to a more complex, but also more correct appraisal of the striking

General quarters, Russian style, in a peacetime drill sharpens the training of the Red Banner Fleet deployed in the Baltic.

and defensive power of ships, based on a mathematical analysis of their capabilities and qualitative characteristics.

The military technical revolution is constantly introducing new things in all areas of military affairs, but the final goals of naval warfare remain the same: the defeat of the enemy and the destruction of his vital forces and materiel (i.e., his ships with their crews and weapons stores, and weapons or shore objectives located within range). Therefore, combat operations at sea, just as on land, by obeying the general laws of the dialectic which are constantly in effect, cannot be conducted separately from the goals of that policy which led to the war. Therefore, in today's context it is interesting to trace, from a historical standpoint, the dialectical relationship between the development of naval forces and the state policy goals which they were intended to serve.

V. I. Lenin pointed out that "Every war is inseparably linked with the political system from which it stems. That very policy which a certain power and a certain class within this power conducted for a long time prior to a war, inevitably and unavoidably will be continued by this same class during a war, changing only the form of action."[1] And further, "Policy is reason, while war is only the instrument, and not the opposite. Consequently, it only remains to subordinate the military point of view to the political."[2]

The basic and sole means of waging armed conflict between states has always been the army and navy, which in peacetime have continued to serve as the instrument or weapon of state policies. Many examples from history attest to the fact that in the age of feudalism and capitalism all problems of foreign policy were always decided on the basis of, and taking into account, the military power of the "negotiating" sides, and that the potential military might of one state or another, built up in accordance with its economic capabilities and political orientation, permitted it to conduct a policy advantageous to itself to the detriment of other states not possessing corresponding military power.

The development of armed forces is linked in the most direct manner to the history of social-economic systems, and to the methods of material production characteristic of them. The flourishing or decline of them is determined by the process of the formation or decay or one social system or another. Thus, these periods when one social-economic system was being replaced by another, more progressive system have given considerable impetus to progress in the military area.

Technical discoveries have always had a revolutionizing effect on the development of armed forces and on the art of employing them. This demonstrates the pattern of the influence on the military field of the society's economic development and the growth of its productive forces. In this connection, V. I. Lenin wrote: "Military tactics depend on the level of development of military equipment. . ."[3]

Such highly important factors as the social and political system, the social composition of the people from whom the armed forces are drawn, the extent of combat training, the level of knowledge, and the moral make-up of the personnel also affect the condition of the armed forces and the level of the art of their employment. In turn, the above qualities depend on the character of the leaders of the fighting men.

Marxism considers the geographic environment, which also influences the character and direction of the development of armed forces, to be one of the constant and invariable conditions in the development of human society. Among the many elements embraced by the concept of the geographical environment and affecting the development of mankind, and, consequently, also of the armed forces of states, are the seas and oceans. In solving problems of commerce, of reliable routes of communication, of relationships between peoples, and of the fishing and maritime industries, men back in ancient history had already opened up individual littoral areas of the seas and oceans. The maritime location of many countries fostered the development in them of specific areas of industry (e.g., shipbuilding, the catching and processing of fish and marine animals, etc.) which had a beneficial effect on the overall progress of these countries that, naturally, also left an impression on the development of the armed forces of the states which, to one degree or another, were engaged in the construction of navies and to a greater or lesser degree employed them in wars.

In different historical eras the above factors have had a definite effect on the character and structure of the armed forces which were made up of various components. Without resorting to a detailed examination of the changes in the structure of the armed forces of states on a historical plane, let us simply note that all maritime countries, without exception, usually have had (or strove to have) both ground forces and a navy. Ápropos of this, Peter I said: "Every potentate who has only ground forces has only one hand; yet whoever has a navy too, has both hands." The role and importance of each of them, at the level of development of technology and the economic capabilities which existed, were always determined by the unfolding political

[1]V. I. Lenin. *Poln. sobr. soch.* (Complete Collected Works), Vol. 32, p. 9.

[2]*Leninskiy sbornik* (Collection of Lenin's Articles) XII, 2nd Ed., 1931, p. 437.

[3]V. I. Lenin. *op. cit.,* Vol. 13, p. 374.

strategic situation and the mutual positions of the states or nature of the coalitions. In some stages of the history of states, ground forces have played the main role, and in others, the navy.

The place and role of each of the branches of a country's armed forces can change both in peacetime and in war depending on technical reorganization, on the enemy being confronted, the geographical conditions, etc. History presents many examples of this. From them we may recall the growth of the role of the Navy in the Northern War of 1700–1721, when Russia transferred operations from her own territory to the territory of the enemy, thereby forcing him to sign a peace treaty. Sometimes, however, wars which began with the Navy being predominantly important were ended by the overwhelming actions of the Army (for example, the Russo-Japanese War of 1904–1905). Clearly, in all cases, one aspect remains unchanged: the results of the victory in a campaign or war can only be secured by ground forces capable of confirming the reality of it by their actual presence.

Moreover, the experience of history attests to the fact that each branch of the armed forces makes its own certain and always discernible contribution to victory. To achieve victory, the presence of all branches of armed forces, properly organized, equipped, and trained, is essential. Each of them has its own specific features, sphere of employment, and conditions for concerted action. The skillful (or on the other hand, the unskillful) employment and the consideration of these specific features often determine the success (or failure) of operations, campaigns, or even the war as a whole.

In the modern context, in speaking of the military might of states, it is a matter of harmoniously combining all branches of developed and rationally balanced armed forces, and it is precisely because of this that the principle of cooperation among all branches of the armed forces is the basis of Soviet military doctrine. Only by coordinating their efforts can victory be achieved.

As early as 1921, M. V. Frunze wrote about this in works devoted to the building up of the Red Army. The idea of the decisive importance of coordinated actions by the Army and Navy in all areas of armed combat was vividly expressed in his work "A Single Military Doctrine and the Red Army."

An analysis of the employment of various branches of armed forces in time of war, or in peacetime, is of definite interest from the point of view of both the development of the art of war and the knowledge by the command personnel, of the specific features with which each of the branches of the armed forces is imbued.

Taking into account that such an understanding fosters the development of a unity of operational views in the command personnel of the armed forces, and is an indispensable and most important condition for skill in acting in concert, let us examine those questions applicable to the Navy, both in the historical and problem aspects. In this connection, we do not intend to cover the history of the naval art, much less define the prospects for the development of naval forces. We intend only to express a few thoughts about the role and place of navies in various historical eras, and at different stages in the development of military equipment, and of the art of war, in order, on this basis, to determine the trends and principles of the change in the role and position of navies in wars, and also in their employment in peacetime as an instrument of state policy. In this connection, the focus of attention on the Navy does not in any way imply any sort of unique importance of naval forces in modern armed combat, but stems from the above mentioned considerations.

Proceeding from the special features of the Navy as a military factor which can be used also in peacetime for purposes of demonstrating the economic and military power of states beyond their borders, and from the fact that over a period of many centuries it has been the solitary branch of armed forces capable of protecting the interests of a country beyond its borders, in our view it is useful to examine questions related to this specific feature of naval forces as a real component part of the military organization of a state.

In examining these questions, one should also take into account the ever growing interest in oceanic problems of various social quarters from different aspects—economic, political, and military—and in their dialectical relationship. In tracing the direct dependence of mankind on the World Ocean over the entire course of its centuries of history, it is impossible not to note how the ability of peoples to learn to appreciate the ocean, and to use it for their own needs, directly affects the growth of the political prestige of the country and its economic and military power.

Times Distant, Yet Important for Understanding The Role of Navies

Navies have always played a great role in strengthening the independence of states whose territories are washed by seas and oceans, since they were an important instrument of policy. Naval might has been one of the factors which has enabled individual states to advance into the ranks of the great powers. Moreover, history shows that those states which do not have naval forces at their disposal have not been able

to hold the status of a great power for very long.

And, it cannot be otherwise, for the sphere of naval operations are the seas and oceans which occupy seven-tenths of the surface of our planet. The continents are essentially gigantic islands whose total area is barely 150,000,000 square kilometers. They are surrounded, connected with one another, and kept in many respects (in particular, with regard to climate) in a constant state of dependence on the World Ocean, whose surface is equal to 350,000,000 square kilometers.

The seas and oceans serve as an inexhaustible source of diverse food resources, industrial raw materials, and energy. The most important and most economically advantageous routes of communications between countries, through which trade and other ties between peoples are carried out, pass through the seas and oceans. All of this determines the special role of the seas and oceans in the economy of states.

The development of maritime states has turned out to be so closely connected with the sea that, as a rule, their capitals and largest cities have grown up on the coasts. Seven of today's ten largest cities of the world are located on the shores of seas and oceans. The building-up, in the maritime countries, of many areas of industry and the economy dependent on the sea, which has brought about higher industrial development in these countries, has fostered the overall growth of the economy of maritime countries and the rate of growth. Therefore, it is not by accident that civilization, as a rule, originated and developed most often on the shores of seas and oceans. It is also not accidental that countries whose populations have been connected with sea-faring have become economically strong earlier than others. Among these we may cite in various periods in history, Spain, England, Holland, France, Portugal, Turkey, and the U.S.A. All of the modern great powers are maritime states.

At the same time, for a long time wars have been waged not only on land, but also on the watery expanses, at first on rivers and lakes and in coastal areas of the seas, and later on the seas and oceans. Military necessity, the development of an economy related to the sea, and political conflict have always, and on an ever increasing scale, forced states to build, possess, and maintain naval forces on a modern level within the overall system of armed forces. At a certain stage of development, many states (primarily Holland, Spain, England, France, Japan, and the U.S.A.) have formulated their military strategy primarily on the basis of sea power.

Every social-economic system has built up armed forces, including navies, corresponding to its economic and technical capabilities. Thus, in the slave-holding society, galleys were the basis of the navies. In the era of feudalism, sailing ships appeared, which were developed more fully up to the moment of capitalism's entry into the world arena.

The scientific technical revolution of that day led, in the mid-19th century, to the following fundamental change in the material resources and equipment of naval forces—to the creation of the steam fleet, and lateral to undersea forces. And finally, recently even more profound and revolutionary changes have taken place in connection with the construction of the nuclear-powered navy of the nuclear-missile era.

These stages of naval development were not just stages in the technical improvement of warships. At the same time as the material resources and equipment were being altered, changes were also taking place in its position within the system of armed forces, in its basic mission, and in its role in the policy of the state in peacetime and in military operations at sea.

Even in ancient times, in solving problems concerning trade, routes of communications, ties between people, and of the fishing and marine industries, mankind developed several coastal areas of the seas and oceans. Parallel to this, knowledge was accumulated and expanded, at first about the individual regions of the earth; and later about the entire planet, including the World Ocean. It is difficult to overestimate the role of the Navy in this.

At the same time, from the era of the slave-holding society even up to our day, navies have been employed in numerous wars as the most important (and often the only) means of supporting the transport of military cargoes and land forces or the invasion by troops of the enemy territory, as well as to protect their own sea routes and to attack the enemy's merchant ships.

In the 16th to 17th centuries, one of the most important periods in the history of mankind began—the era of great geographical discoveries, the era of the initial accumulation of capital, and the development of capitalism. The major countries of Western Europe converted their navies into one of the instruments of the initial accumulation of capital: they were used to seize colonies, for the enslavement of peoples of entire continents, and to plunder them, and as the agents for the fierce struggles between rivals in the plundering of colonies, and also for control in the colonies and of the sea routes.

A contingent from the SAM-Kotlin class destroyer Skrytny *parades at Massawa to celebrate Ethiopian Navy Days on 9 February 1973 and demonstrates Soviet understanding of the Navy role in peacetime as an instrument of state policy as well as particular Soviet interest in the geographical crossroads, Mediterranean-Suez-Arabian Sea.*

ROYAL NAVY

"The discovery of gold and silver mines in America, the eradication, enslavement, and the burning alive of the natives in pits, the first steps toward conquering and plundering East India, and the transformation of Africa into a preserve for hunting blacks—this was the dawning of the capitalist era of production." [4]

Spain and Portugal were the first to rush to discover new lands and colonize them. Sailing expeditions by Columbus, Magellan, Vasco da Gama, and other seafarers not only opened the American continent, extended the water route around Africa to India and China, and discovered many Pacific Ocean islands, but also initiated the colonization of these regions and countries. The English, French, and Dutch joined the Spanish and Portuguese in participating in the geographical discoveries and in the colonization of the new lands.

In the 16th century it seemed that Spain had firmly established a position as a great power, possessing vast colonies. But due to political backwardness and the inability to compete with rapidly developing England, she was not able to exploit the riches plundered from the colonies, to rapidly develop her economy and her industry, and consequently, to build up armed forces, and particularly a navy, which were modern for that day. Soon after the defeat of the "unbeatable armada" by the more modern English Fleet, Spain, being in no condition to protect her overseas possessions, lost them and was gradually transformed from a great power into a third-rate state.

In the middle of the 17th century, Holland, which had taken the capitalist path of development earlier than the others, and had the strongest navy in the world at its disposal, became the largest colonial power and reached the apex of its power. But soon England, where industrial capital played the leading role as opposed to trade capital which held sway in Holland, became its main rival. The struggle between these countries became the hottest in several wars which history has named the Anglo-Dutch wars. The North Sea was the main arena for their struggles. After losing several naval battles and after attacks by the English from land, Holland acknowledged defeat and became a second-rate colonial power. Its fate was sealed by the victory of the industrial capital of England over Holland's trade capital, which was manifested militarily in the superiority of the English Fleet (or, in the final analysis, in the naval might of England).

Karl Marx wrote about this in this manner: ". . .Trade domination is now already related to the greater or lesser predominance of the conditions of the existence of major industry. It pays to compare, for example, England and Holland. The history of the fall of Holland as the dominant trade nation is a history of the subordination of trade capital to industrial capital." [5]

England also often used her Navy for direct enrichment. It is sufficient to recall that many English ships and merchantmen in the service of the King acted as pirates: they robbed the merchant ships of other countries, seized them, and dragged them away into English ports. Thus, instead of a consumer, the Navy became a source of enrichment to the state.

At the beginning of the 18th century, France also took the path of capitalist development. Through the enslavement of overseas countries, in which the Navy played an important role, she was also transformed into a vast colonial empire possessing Canada, large territories in the Mississippi Valley, several West Indian islands, part of India, and broad regions in Africa. The core of England's policy was to attain the position of "Mistress of the Seas", personifying a world economic and political power; she chose to use every possible way to bring down her rivals at sea to the level of the states which were incapable of opposing her Navy as one way of achieving this goal. At this time the struggle in the world arena for economic hegemony, colonial possessions, and domination in world trade shifted to the sphere of rivalry between England and France. The culmination of this struggle was the so-called Seven Years' War, in which almost all of the states of Europe were involved. "England and France fought over colonies in the Seven Years' War, i.e., they waged an imperialistic war. . ." [6]

The principal events at that time unfolded at sea, as a result of which the navies played the most important role. The outcome of the battles between the English and French Fleets played a decisive role in achieving the political goals of this war. As a result of their hostilities, France, having lost any hope of domination, or even a predominant position on the sea and having lost control over the sea lanes, was forced to relinquish North America and India to England.

In the middle of the 18th century, having surpassed the other countries in economic development and possessing a developed industry and numerous colonies, England became the first world power. Backed by a powerful economy which provided England the supremacy of having the strongest fleet on the World Ocean, she assumed the leading position among the capitalist countries and held it for almost two centuries.

The desire of the British capitalists to hinder the development of industries in the colonies by every

[4] K. Marx. *Kapital*, Vol. 1, 1949, p. 754.

[5] K. Marx. *op. cit.*, Vol. 3, 1954, p. 345.
[6] V. I. Lenin, *op. cit.*, Vol. 30, p. 7.

means, in order to keep them as mere suppliers of raw materials and as consumers of the goods of British industry, produced the war for independence of the more developed of its North American colonies. The navies of England's former rivals, France, Holland, and Spain, acted on the colonies' behalf. The position of Russia, which declared a so called "armed neutrality", supported by the power of the Russian Navy, did not permit England to blockade America, also played a positive role for the Americans. The "mistress of the seas" had to fight a war under conditions in which her Navy was considerably inferior to the united fleet of the enemies. After England had lost several battles on land, considering the unfavorable relative strength of the forces on the sea which prevented unhindered supplying of reinforcements via the ocean, she was forced to recognize the independence of the United States of North America.

Despite the fact that the main missions in the war for independence were executed by the armies, it once more affirmed the growing influence of naval forces on the course and outcome of armed conflicts fought on land. In this war, naval operations were shifted from European waters to distant ocean regions which sharply increased the importance of communications, and problems of defending and hindering them in support of military actions on land arose on such a scale for the first time.

The new conditions of naval combat operations imposed higher demands on the seakeeping ability of the warships and on their combat stability. In connection with this, their dimensions were increased, designs were changed, armament strengthened, and subsequently armor made its appearance. The considerable growth in the capabilities of the rapidly developing capitalist industry fostered the building up of warship inventory, taking the new demands into account. All of this speeded up naval development, and at the turn of the 19th century permitted the naval role in political struggles and in military operations to be enhanced even further.

The main organizing force of the wars in the above period was the English bourgeoisie, which intended to seize France's remaining colonial possessions. In this connection, England tried to transfer the weight of the battles on the continent to her European allies, while limiting her participation in the wars mainly to operations at sea and against France's maritime territories.

It should be noted that the large bourgeoisie which came to power in France after the Thermidorean coup, also made it a primary task to reduce England's colonial power. Bonaparte's expedition into Egypt was undertaken for this purpose and with the future goal of seizing India. The French troops, which were transported across the sea unbeknownst to the English, began successful combat operations in Egypt. Within just two and a half months the English Fleet, under the command of Nelson, found the French warships anchored in Aboukir Bay and defeated them. The destruction of the French Fleet primarily affected the combat capability of that part of the army which was in Egypt and which turned out to be cut off from its main supply bases located in Europe. Moreover, it also affected the operations of the main forces of the French Army which, within six months of the defeat of the French Fleet at Aboukir, surrendered to the enemy in a few months that which Bonaparte had won in his day in dozens of victorious battles. [7]

Thus, the weakness of the French Fleet became one of the main reasons for the failure of the plans for the conquest of Egypt, the passage to India, and the curtailing of English colonial power, even though France had the necessary ground forces at its disposal.

Continuing the struggle, Napoleon decided to land a large landing force directly on the British Islands, for which 2,343 diverse transport ships were readied. It seemed that a fatal threat hung over England. However, the preparation for the invasion was delayed. An attack, initiated by Russian troops under the command of Kutuzov, forced Napoleon to abandon entirely the landing of a force in England.

On 21 October 1805 in the Atlantic Ocean off the coast of Spain, the battle of Trafalgar took place in which the English, under the command of Nelson, inflicted a decisive defeat on the Franco-Spanish Fleet. The significance of this battle, as well as the role of the English Fleet in the struggle with Napoleonic France, were actually great, but were exaggerated to an even greater degree by a Western European historiographer who asserted that "at Trafalgar not only the greatest naval victory was won, but also the greatest and most remarkable victory of all those won on land and at sea in the course of the entire revolutionary war. No single victory nor any series of victories by Napoleon had such an effect on Europe." [8]

One cannot agree with this. As is well known, the struggle against Napoleon lasted many years and the main and decisive role in it was played by Russia, which destroyed the French Army in the Patriotic War of 1812. The victory gained by Russia actually had a greater effect on the political situation in Europe.

As for the Battle of Trafalgar, with respect to its consequences, it, of course, was not an ordinary military clash of fleets. After the series of defeats of the French Fleet, its final rout in this battle demonstrated France's

[7] Ye. V. Tarle. Napoleon, Izd-vo AN SSSR, 1957, p. 74.
[8] Fyffe's History of Modern Europe, Vol. 1, p. 281.

inability to carry on a battle at sea with an enemy having a more modern fleet consisting of better quality ships, manned by more highly trained personnel, and employing tactics which were new for that time. The main result of the victory achieved in the naval engagement was that the home country and the British colonies became practically invunerable to attacks from the direction of the sea. England was able to deprive the enemy of the weapon which was most dangerous for her—the navy. Only a navy at that time could directly threaten the home country and the security of the communications connecting England with the colonies which supplied the raw materials for her industry and food products for the population. The liquidation of the threat from the sea freed the hands of the English bourgeoisie to organize and finance new alliances to continue the struggle with Napoleonic France. France, however, was forced to refrain once and for all from combat operations at sea and to seek other ways not connected with the sea to combat her main enemy.

Thus, the course of the war at sea and the gaining of domination by the English Navy had a great effect on the further policy of the belligerents.

From all that has been said, it follows that from the dawning of the capitalist era, the navies of the Western states have represented not only a part of the armed forces, which were employed in war in the naval theaters, but also a weapon of state policy in peacetime, which permitted them to enslave underdeveloped peo-

ples and countries overseas and to transform them into their own colonies. The fleets of the Western European powers travelled the path from "privateers in the service of the King" to regular naval forces which received an organized structure and official operational tactics. The employment of this naval force in wars, especially when it was the main force in achieving the goals of the war, had a considerable influence on state policy, which was determined and conducted taking into account the disposition of the forces at sea at certain times.

Maritime states having great economic capabilities have widely used their naval forces in peacetime to put pressure on their enemies, as a type of military demonstration, as threats of interrupting sea communications, and as a hinderance to ocean commerce.

Navies have served these states as an important means of further enrichment and of extending expansion and colonization.

In addition, navies have also carried out the pleasant mission of being discoverers. Naval ships of the great powers, including Russia, have carried out wide-scale oceanographic studies and have made an inestimable contribution to the science of geography. This tradition of mariners (including also naval mariners) still continues even today, when the "blank spots" in the ocean are becoming fewer and fewer, yet the knowledge of the secrets of the ocean represents a very great scientific task even today.

By Rear Admiral George H. Miller, U. S. Navy (Retired)

After battleship, cruiser, and destroyer service prior to World War II and command of the USS *Brennan* (DE 13) in 1943, Read Admiral Miller lectured on seapower and maritime strategy while serving as plans officer at the Naval War College from 1947 to 1949. He was the Navy member of the joint strategic survey council, Joint Chiefs of Staff, from 1960 to 1962, and director of the Navy's Long Range Objectives Group from 1964 to 1967. From 1967 to 1970 he served as Director of Strategic Offensive and Defensive Systems on the staff of the Chief of Naval Operations. Admiral Miller is now the Naval Advisor to the Assistant Secretary of Commerce for Maritime Affairs.

Since the early 1950s, the world has watched the Soviet Union build up its merchant and combat navies and break out into the Great Oceans in a comprehensive program of political, commercial and coercive penetration of less developed areas. Their overall approach is an updated version of that taken by the more successful, durable great powers of history. Particular effort has been funneled into three important geographic crossroads: Mediterranean-Suez-Arabian Sea; Southeast Asia-Straits of Malacca; and the Caribbean. Soviet actions appear to reflect systematic exploitation of strategic geography and the lessons of history to further their overseas interests.

Now we have the words of Admiral of the Fleet of the Soviet Union S. G. Gorshkov to confirm these carefully planned and executed actions.

In the opening paragraphs of this, the first of his 11 articles, Admiral Gorshkov points to the historic importance of the oceans in human affairs: communications between continents, between suppliers of products vitally essential to mankind; utilizing the water medium for peaceful purposes, for defense of one's own country and to seize overseas possessions. He calls attention to the fact that naval forces have a high degree of maneuverability; they can form powerful groups secretly which are of "surprise to the enemy."

Admiral Gorshkov and his countrymen know something about surprise attack. The Japanese fleet opened the Russo-Japanese War in 1904 with a surprise attack on Port Arthur. In 1941, while German and Soviet leaders talked and signed treaties of friendship, cooperation and détente, the German army deployed secretly and launched the most devastating surprise attack in Russian history. The Soviet leadership remembers.

Admiral Gorshkov rejects the time-honored political and budget game of comparing numbers of ships of one type or another, in comparing relative naval strength. He suggests a more complex and accurate method of appraisal.

Final goals of armed conflict at sea are still regarded by the Admiral, as defeat of the enemy and destruction of his vital forces and material. Targets specifically listed for destruction are ships with their crews and provisions, and weapons or shore objectives within range.

Lenin is quoted on the inseparable link between war and the political system from which it stems. He points out that national policy is the controlling factor; war is only a weapon. On the basis of what Leninism has achieved in the past 50 years, one might suggest that Lenin himself may be classed among the most successful strategists of recent history. His writings are of importance to those Americans who wish to know more about their principal competitors.

Admiral Gorshkov highlights the role of geography, and particularly the seas and the oceans, in influencing the character and direction of development of the armed forces, as well as human society. He discusses armed forces under the groupings Army and Navy, and he suggests how the place and role of each of the branches does change in peacetime and in war.

He points to "the special feature of the Navy as a military factor which can be used in peacetime for purposes of demonstrating the economic and military might of states beyond their borders. . . . it has been the solitary form of armed forces capable of protecting the interests of a country overseas". No comment is made on the stationing of land forces on foreign soil in peacetime.

Admiral Gorshkov says, ". . . it is impossible not to note how man's ability to comprehend the ocean and to use it for his own needs directly affects the growth of the political prestige of the country and its economic and military might".

In a very brief summary of "distant past" history, the author begins with this paragraph: "Navies have always played a great role in strengthening the independence of states whose territories are washed by seas and oceans since they were an important political weapon. Naval might has been one of the factors which has enabled certain states to advance into the ranks of the great powers. Moreover, history shows that states which do not have naval forces at their disposal have not been able to hold the status of a great power for a long time".

He notes how civilization developed and flourished most often on the shores of seas and oceans; and how the large countries of Western Europe used their fleets ". . . to seize colonies, for the enslavement of peoples of entire continents and to plunder them. . . ."

The Soviets of course are also using their maritime fleets as a "weapon of state policy" for peacetime penetration of less developed areas. However, they package their own operations with more internationally palatable phraseology such as Trade Missions, Wars of National Liberation, and Peoples Democratic Republics.

It is important to remember that the advice and influence of Soviet maritime leadership are injected personally and directly at the highest political and security levels of the Soviet government.

Admiral Gorshkov is without doubt one of the foremost authorities on naval strategy of modern times. His writings should be studied as assiduously as European statesmen studied Alfred Thayer Mahan's works during the years preceding World War I. They are of considerable importance in determining the nature and scope of the big-power competition to be expected in the years to come.

One can find very little if any material in this first installment which is not important. All of it is deadly serious.

Russia's Road to the Sea, Peter I to Napoleon

With Commentary following the article by
Rear Admiral E. M. Eller, U. S. Navy (Retired)

EDITOR'S NOTE: *This article, by the man who has com-manded the Soviet Navy for the past 18 years, was cleared for publication in the Soviet Union on 25 February 1972. In this, the second of an 11-chapter series, Admiral Gorshkov traces his countrymen's immemorial, lemming-like compulsion to reach the sea. Restrained, but never fully, by ancient and/or modern enemies, e.g., the Swedes and the Turks, and often constrained by either short-sighted tsars or commissars, the heirs of Peter the Great today assert their "undisputable and legal right to have warships in the Mediterranean Sea"—which may or may not put them on a collision course with the U. S. Navy.*

Due to a series of political and historical reasons, the development of the Navy of Russia, the largest continental power in the world, transpired in a very unique manner.

Without a strong Navy, Russia had been unable to join the ranks of the great powers. However, at various stages in history her leaders often did not understand the role of the Navy within the system of the country's armed forces and underestimated its capabilities. To a

Western historians have long believed that the genesis of the Russian Navy can be traced to one man and one ship—Peter the Great and the vessel he built in 1693—a statue and replica of which occupy a place of honor in the Naval Museum at Leningrad. Admiral Gorshkov suggests the Navy had its beginnings ten centuries earlier.

considerable degree this was fostered by many centuries of propaganda conducted by states that were hostile toward Russia, headed by England, which strived to prove that such a large continental power as Russia could not have interests at sea. This psychological coercion began when the Russian Navy under Peter I became one of the strongest navies in the world, and England became seriously alarmed with regard to her title of "Mistress of the Seas."

It must be acknowledged that the propaganda which was inimical to our Motherland had its results. It penetrated into Russia and often found ardent support-ers among influential Tsarist high officials, who held the view that the country did not need a powerful Navy and that expenditures for its construction and for maintaining it at the required state of readiness should be cut in every possible way. Thus, in particular,

War Minister Kuropatkin wrote in his diary prior to the Russo-Japanese war: "Yesterday with Witte . . . we rapidly convinced His Majesty of the need to halt expenditures for the Navy and the Far East."[1]

The hostile propaganda continually promulgated the idea that Russia is not a maritime country, but rather a continental one, and therefore she does not need a Navy. And if she indeed does need one, then it is only to handle modest coastal defense missions. These ideas were based on the slanderous assertion that the Russians are not a seagoing nation, but rather a dry-land nation, that the sea is alien to them, and that they are not good at seafaring.

Our country, without doubt, has been and is the largest continental power in the world. However, at the same time it has been, and remains, a great sea-power. It is enough to recall that the length of the maritime borders of Russia is almost twice that of the coastline of the United States of America and almost 15 times that of France. The portion of the maritime borders of Russia, the U.S.A., and France are about the same—about two-thirds of the total national borders—while for Germany (up to World War II), it was one-third. Yet no one reproached Germany for the fact that, while a continental power, it was striving to have a large Navy.

And today there is widespread propaganda abroad, produced by American ideologists, asserting that the Soviet state does not need a powerful Navy. An example of this is President Nixon's speech of 4 August 1970 in which he stated: "That which the Soviet Union needs in the way of military preparations differs from what we need. The U.S.S.R. is a land power . . . We, however, are primarily a seapower, and our needs are therefore different."[2]

One hardly has to say that Nixon's speech, which is a modern-day version of the old attempts by English politicians to show Russia's lack of need for a strong Navy, bears no relationship to the actual state of affairs and contradicts the interests of our state both past and present.

The opponents of Russian seapower have widely used (and are widely using) falsification of her military history. In particular, they assert that all of Russia's victories have been gained only by the Army, and that she can be powerful only by strengthening the Army at the expense of the Navy. For example, the same Kuropatkin reported to the Tsar in 1900: "The lessons of history have taught us to follow the same path

which our forefathers took, and to see Russia's main force to be her land Army . . ."[3]

Actually, as is well known, both the Army and the Navy have actively participated in all of the wars which Russia has waged. Wars without the participation of naval forces have been very few. Thus, in the 200 years preceding the First World War, Tsarism waged 33 wars,[4] and the Navy failed to participate in only two of them (the Hungarian Campaign of 1849 and the Akhaltekinsk Expedition of 1877–1879).

The narrowness of the thinking and the intellectual limitations of the Tsarist satraps of Kuropatkin's type and his successor, Vannovskiy, did not pass Russia by without leaving a trace. Their reactionary ideas in opposing a Navy did noticeable damage to the coordinated development of the armed forces, and, consequently, to the defensive capability of the country.

An examination of the role of the Navy in the centuries-old history of Russia leads to the main conclusion that in all stages of the life of the country, she had need of a powerful Navy as an integral part of her armed forces commensurate with the interests of a world power. And therefore Russia repeatedly attempted to build up her Navy even prior to Peter I (for example, the privateer Fleet of Ivan The Terrible in the Baltic).

The development and employment of the Russian Navy undoubtedly was greatly determined by the fact that Russia was the largest continental country in the world. The defense of her borders in wars with contiguous land enemies took place mainly with the aid of armies, which created the preconditions for the underestimates of the Navy by Tsarist high officials. As a result of this and a series of other reasons (among these not the least of which was the economy) the Navy of the Motherland developed rather unevenly. Surges in the naval might of Russia gave way to declines. And each time, a reduction in her seapower evoked new difficulties in the historical path of the state and led to serious consequences. Thus, the outcome of the Crimean War of 1854–1856 was predetermined by the economic superiority of the English and French as expressed in the better armament of the armies and in the superiority of their fleets. The underrating by the Tsarist government of the role of the Navy led to the fact that under the conditions of the peace treaty of 1856 Russia was prohibited from having a Fleet in the Black Sea.

[1] A. I. Sorokin. *Russko yaponskaya voyna 1904–1905. Voyennoistoricheskiy ocherk* (The Russo-Japanese War 1904–1905. Military Historical Essays), Voyenizdat, 1956, p. 19.

[2] The Washington Post, 5 August 1970.

[3] *Itogi voyny. Otchet general-ad"yutanta Kuropatkina* (Results of the War. Report of Kuropatkin's Adjutant General), Vol. 4, Warsaw, 1906, Tipografiya Okruzhnogo shtaba, p. 68.

[4] Shatsillo, K. F., *Russkiy imperialism i razvitiye flota nakanune pervoy mirovoy voyny* (Russian Imperialism and the development of the Navy on the Eve of WW I), Izd-vo Nauka, 1968, p. 12.

The lessons of this war were not studied by the autocracy. In the war with Turkey in 1877–1878, the appearance in the straits of English ships forced the victorious Russian Army, which was crushing the enemy before it and which was already standing at the walls of Constantinople, to flee without achieving one of the main goals of the war—free access to the Mediterranean Sea. In this case, errors by the Tsarist government with regard to questions of building up the Navy were one of the reasons for the fact that Russia, having begun a "semiwar" in 1877, could only conclude it with a "semipeace."[5] While at the same time England, without participating in this war, and by making only a demonstration of naval might, "was permitted to occupy the island of Cyprus . . . England thereby came into possession of the most important strategic point in the eastern Mediterranean."[6]

The weakness of the Russian Navy, which was revealed in the course of the 1877–1878 War, greatly alarmed public opinion in Russia. As a result, in 1878 a Voluntary Navy, created by public contributions, was founded in the country: from April through September, broad sectors of the population donated several million rubles to its construction. The work of the cruisers of the Voluntary Navy began with the transporting of Russian troops who had participated in this war from Turkey to the Homeland. Such was the reply of a wide sector of Russian society to the underrating of the role of the Navy by the Tsarist government.

After the war with Turkey, somewhat greater effort was devoted to the strengthening of the country's naval power than prior to it. With regard to building up the Navy, this was expressed mainly in an increase in the number of ships. However, the necessary attention was not given to the qualitative side of the armament and also to the training of the personnel, which had a considerable effect on the results of the employment of the Navy in the Russo-Japanese War of 1904–1905.

In addition to the fundamental economic and political causes, the inactivity of the Russian Navy at the outbreak of the Russo-Japanese War and later its defeat could not have failed to have, according to V. I. Lenin's analysis in the article "The Fall of Port Arthur," a decisive influence on the grave outcome for Tsarism in this war.

In the period of decline, the Navy of the Homeland became inactive (particularly after the Industrial Revolution when the general lagging of Russia in comparison with the other large countries was vividly displayed). This was indicative of the gradual loss by Tsarist Russia of the position of a great power following an independent and sovereign policy and of her transformation into a supplier of cannon fodder to the imperialist plunderers fighting for interests which were alien to the Russian people.

The considerable difficulties for Russian seapower stemmed from her geographical position, which required having an independent fleet capable of ensuring the performance of missions confronting it in each of the far-flung naval theaters. Nonetheless, despite this, the Navy wrote many remarkable heroic pages in the history of the Motherland and played an important role in the fate of the state.

The history of the Russian Navy usually begins with the era of Peter I. In characterizing this era, Karl Marx said that one cannot imagine a great nation so shut off from the sea as Russia prior to Peter I. "Not a single great nation has ever existed or has been able to exist in such an inner-continental position as the state of Peter the Great did initially; no nation has stood by in such a manner to watch her shores and river mouths being wrested away from her. Russia could not leave the mouth of the Neva, the solitary path for delivering the products of the Russian North into the hands of the Swedes."[7]

Russia's struggle for outlets to the sea required the building of an army and a powerful navy with all urgency. Therefore the construction of the Navy under Peter I was the logical continuation of the preceeding development of the Russian state and the actual recognition of the rebirth, under the new conditions, of the qualities of a seagoing people inherent in Russians since ancient times.

Actually, beginning as early as the 7th century, our forefathers engaged in armed combat on the Black, Mediterranean, and Caspian Seas (it was precisely at this time when the birth of the Russian naval art began). In the early 9th century, the feats of the Russians were widely known. History recalls the cruise of Oleg through the Black Sea to Constantinople with 2,000 ships carrying 80,000 warriors, and the sea cruises of Igor and Svyatoslav, and others. The voyages of the Russian princes overseas have received sufficient coverage in domestic historical literature.

Beginning in the 9th and 10th centuries "Russian ships sailed the Black . . . and Baltic Seas,"[8] "at the end of the 11th century the shores of the Gulf of Finland became part of the Novgorod possessions,"[9]

---

[5] *Diplomaticheskiy slovar'* (Diplomatic Dictionary), Vol. 1, Gospolitizdat, 1960, p. 402.

[6] *Vsemirnaya istoriya* (World History), Vol. VII, Izd-vo AN SSSR 1960, p. 175.

[7] K. Marx. *Taynaya diplomatiya XVIII v.* (Secret Diplomacy of the 18th Century).

[8] *Vsemirnaya istoriya* (World History), Vol. III, 1951, p. 251.

[9] *Istoriya voyenno-morskogo iskusstva* (The History of the Naval Art), Vol. I, 1953, p. 81.

and by this time "the Russians knew the sea route around Europe via the Varanger and North Seas, along the shores of France and Spain, through the Mediterranean Sea to Constantinople." [10] In the 13th century after a prolonged and arduous struggle with the Swedes and the Livonian Order of Knights, Novgorod began to play an important role in commerce on the Baltic Sea and entered the Hanseatic League of maritime commercial cities. In the 12th century, the Russians engaged in maritime industry and trade on the White Sea, penetrated into the Pechora territory, and in the 15th and 16th centuries they sailed to Grumant (Spitzbergen), Novaya Zemlya, and to the Kara Sea.

Many foreign researchers have also written of the Russian navymen of that day. Thus, the English researcher Fred Jane pointed out: "This (the Russian) Navy can claim an older origin than the British Navy. One hundred years before Alfred built the first English naval ships, the Russians were already engaged in far off sea battles, and one thousand years ago the Russians were considered to be the best navymen of their time." [11]

The fatal invasion of the Tatars destroyed Russian seapower on the southern seas and for a long time separated Russia from the Black and Caspian Seas. She retained in her hands only the shores of the White Sea and a small section of the coast of the Gulf of Finland at the mouths of the Neva and Narva Rivers, where the people of Novgorod steadfastly opposed the enemies which were striving to completely cut them off from the Baltic Sea.

As a result of the prolonged, yet unsuccessful struggle for an outlet to the Baltic Sea, Russia, by the Peace Treaty of Stolbovo (1617), was completely cut off from the Baltic coast. The Swedish King Gustavus Adolphus called this peace one of the "Gods' greatest good deeds", and stated that it would be difficult for the Russian people to surmount the obstacle which had been set up. [12]

The Tatar yoke and the Polish and Swedish interventions following it held back Russia's development for almost five decades. The difficult period for Russia also affected the development of her Navy and maritime commerce (it was reduced to almost nothing). The Western countries, however, which were not subjected to such serious tests and which were protected from the Tatar invasion by the Slavs, developed rapidly

and built mighty fleets which were used to conquer colonies and to expand maritime commerce.

However, the activity of the Russians, which had been checked on the southern and Baltic seas, continued in the north, where almost the entire shore from Pechora to the Sea of Okhotsk was explored, and the first information concerning Sakhalin and the Shantar Islands was obtained. In the south, despite the opposition of powerful enemies, the Don and Ukrainian cossacks reached the sea from the Dnieper and Don Rivers. The reunification of the Ukraine with Russia also had a great effect on the development of the Russian state.

Russia had not resigned herself to being cut off from the seas and continually waged a struggle for egress to them. In the situation which developed at the turn of the 16th century, the further development of the state and its economy could have proceeded only with the re-establishment of outlets to the sea. Yet this could be achieved only by the military route for which, in addition to a strong army, a navy was also required. The backward country had to surmount exceptional hardships to solve such a problem in a short time.

It was resolved to begin the breakthrough to the sea with the taking of Azov, which would relieve Russia from the threat of the Turko-Tatar attacks. The international situation and the system of military and political alliances (Russia, Poland, and Austro-Hungary against Turkey) affirmed the correctness of the choice of this direction. However, as the First Azov Campaign (1695) showed, the *strelets* troops [soldiers in the Russian Army in the 16th and 17th centuries—Ed.] turned out to be poorly suited to waging a large war, and the Army alone, without the aid of a fleet, was in no condition to capture the fortress, which received constant aid from the sea. Already by the spring of 1696 the construction of ships permitted the Navy to join the siege of Azov and by joint operations with the Army to capture it. It should be noted that the concerted operations of the young Russian land and sea forces in the taking of this fortress were favorably distinguished from similar but unsuccessful attempts of the British to capture Quebec (1691) and Saint Pierre (1693).

It is true that the capture of Azov did not solve the question of the return of outlets to the sea for free maritime commerce. A difficult struggle had to be won with one of the strongest powers—Sweden—which was dominant in Northern Europe. For this, Russia had to have not only a modern Army but also a no less modern Navy, without which it was impossible to achieve success in the struggle on the Baltic Sea. The first step in this direction was the transport, in 1702, of two warships which were built in Arkhangelsk from

---

[10] *Morskoy Atlas. Opisaniye k kartam* (Naval Atlas. Description of the Charts), Vol. III, Part 1, pp. 54–55.

[11] Jane, Fred. T., The Imperial Russian Fleet. Its Past, Present, and Future., London, 1904, p. 10.

[12] N. P. Lyshin, *Stolbovskiy dogovor i peregovory emv predshestvovavshiye* (The Stolbovo Treaty and the Talks Preceeding It), St. Petersburg, 1857, p. 58.

the village of Nyukhch (White Sea) to Novenets (Onezhskoye Ozero). They were delivered by portaging them over "His Majesty's Road," which stretched 160 verst [a Russian unit of measurement equal to .06629 miles—Ed.] through dense forests and swamps.

The appearance of a Russian Fleet in the Baltic had an immediate effect on the combat operations for an outlet to the sea at the mouth of the Neva and for possession of the island of Kotlin, and also on the success of the defense of St. Petersburg, which had been recently founded. By 1705, when the Swedes undertook a combined attack of land and sea forces against the city, Peter's Navy already numbered 11 frigates and 107 more light craft (mainly galleys). Encountering opposition by the Russian Army and Navy, the Swedish attack failed.

One of the most important dates in Russian history is 27 June 1709—on this day the victorious Battle of Poltava took place, signifying the end of Sweden as a great power. However, the aims of this war were not achieved. Twelve more long years of intense struggle were required to achieve them.

In order to clear the Gulf of Finland of hostile warships they had to possess Vyborg, to remove the direct threat to Petersburg, and to open the path for

With ships such as those seen above under construction at St. Petersburg's Admiralty Shipyard on the Neva, Peter pressed the Great Northern War to its successful conclusion on 30 August 1721. When Sweden signed the treaty of Nystadt, thus surrendering to Russia both the pick of the Baltic provinces and hegemony of the north, jubilant Russians bestowed on Peter the title "Father of the Fatherland, Peter the Great, and Emperor of all Russia."

the Russian Fleet to the Finnish skerries. An attempt to solve the problem with some ground forces did not lead to success. Vyborg was taken later by closely coordinated operations by land and naval forces. It was followed by Riga, Pernov, Arensburg, the Moon Sound Islands, and Revel. The Navy gradually became the most important factor in the continuing struggle. As a result of joint operations of the ships and the troops landed from them, in the summer of 1713 Helsingfors [Helsinki] and Abo were captured, which created the direct threat of the seizure of the coast of Sweden and its capital. Yet, despite this, the Swedes did not consider themselves beaten, because they were confident that their ships of the line would be able to destroy the Russian Navy and to prevent the transit of landing forces across the Gulf of Bothnia.

The Hanko victory was the "first important victory (of Russia) at sea which raised the spirits in the Army and Navy and made them believe in their own power. Peter the Great, who equated the Hanko victory with the one at Poltava, awarded all of its participants with a medal struck in honor of the triumph."[13] This victory opened the way to the shores of Sweden and consequently to Stockholm to the Russian Navy and Army. "Both hands of the Russian potentate" had given Russia a glorious victory, which was of vast significance to her.

England and France, and subsequently also other states, fearing the strengthening of Russia and the complete defeat of Sweden, wove every type of intrigue against Russia and put pressure on her. However, Peter I did not give up his intentions to consolidate the shores of the Baltic Sea taken by him for Russia with the aid of a battle-proven Army and Navy, which became the real force supporting the independence of the state's policy. The Russian Baltic Fleet continued to grow. According to the general consensus there were only two powerful navies in the world at that time— the English and the Russian Navies.

Attempts to restrain Russia in her desire to reach the sea were not limited to intrigues and diplomatic pressure by foreign states: in the summer of 1719 England introduced her ships into the Baltic Sea. Inspired by this, the Swedes undertook active naval operations. However, in a naval battle off Ezel [Saare] Island on 24 May 1719 the Russian line forces under the command of N. A. Senyavin defeated the Swedish squadron and captured three ships (including the flagship), and in July and August, galleys under the cover of ships of the line landed large landing parties in the area of Stockholm.

At the end of 1719 England concluded a military alliance with Sweden, directed against Russia, which inspired the Swedes to continue the war.[14] In 1720, large English naval forces again entered the Baltic Sea. However, the Russian Fleet, operating actively off of the Swedish coast, won a victory over the Swedes in a battle off Grengam Island. In 1721, despite the presence in the Baltic Sea of the English, the Russian pressure on the Swedes continually grew. On 30 August 1721, Sweden was forced to sign a peace treaty with Russia according to which it relinquished forever the areas of the Baltic coast taken by the Russian troops. This treaty was clear evidence of the importance of a Navy operating in concert with ground troops to achieve the goals of a war. Even the interference of England and other states could not ruin the results of the Poltava victory and prevent Russia from becoming firmly established on the Baltic shores.

Thus, the Navy fulfilled an important role in Russia's long and difficult struggle, initiated to re-establish outlets to the seas ensuring the development of her economy and freedom of overseas trade. Following the victory of the Russian Army at Poltava, the Navy smashed the Swedish naval power in battles at Hanko, Ezel, and Grengam, and forced it to relinquish forever the land captured by the Russians on the shores of the Baltic Sea.

On the medal struck in honor of the victory over Sweden it is written: "The end of this war through such a peace was obtained by no one other than the Navy, for it was impossible to achieve anything by land."

Although the Navy still remained a formidable force, signs of deterioration began to appear more and more after the death of Peter I. Ships, being maintained ever more poorly, fell into decay and were not replaced by new ones in time, since shipbuilding had slowed down. Russia lost her importance as a great seapower.

Russia's participation in the Seven Year's War (1756–1763) evoked a timely increase in attention to the Navy, which blockaded the Prussian coast, acted in concert with the Army in taking Memel and Kolberg, and provided sea transportation.

For Russia, the problem of the return of her outlets to the southern seas which had been taken from her still remained, and this required the restoration of the Navy and an increase in its role within the system of armed forces. In 1769, the construction of warships was renewed in the Petrovsk shipyards, and as early as the Russo-Turkish War of 1768 to 1774 the young Black Sea Fleet, under the command of A. N. Senyavin,

---

[13] *Voyennaya entsiklopediya* (Military Encyclopedia), Vol. VII, St. Petersburg, 1912, p. 175.

[14] Tarle, Ye. B., *Russkiy flot i vneshnyaya politika Petra I,* (The Russian Navy and the Foreign Policy of Peter I), Voyenizdat, 1949, p. 83.

opened the country's way from the Sea of Azov to the Black Sea, won a series of glorious victories over the more numerous Turkish Fleet, and smashed the landing of its landing force in the Crimea, which aided the establishment of Russia on the shores of the Black Sea.

At the same time, the expansion of the Russian state was taking place toward the East for access to the Pacific Ocean. In the 17th and 18th centuries, the Russians first explored the vast territories of Siberia and the Far East and later Northwest America surprisingly rapidly. The results of these explorations are among the geographical discoveries of world-wide importance. Bering's expedition was organized by Peter I. It was followed by the expeditions of Malygin, Chelyuskin, the Laptev brothers, and others. They explored the shores of Siberia, Kamchatka, Alaska, the Aleutian and Kurile Islands, Sakhalin, and the Sea of Okhotsk, and pioneered Petropavlovsk-Kamchatka.

In the course of the long-time struggle for egress to the sea, Russia managed to build a powerful Navy and her own shipbuilding industry, possessing great potential capabilities. The talent of the Russian officers and admirals was crystallized in an advanced naval art and shipbuilding science. The glorious traditions of the Russian naval school, which gave the world and the Homeland such prominent naval leaders as Spiridov, Ushakov, Senyavin, Lazarev, Nakhimov, and Makarov, and such remarkable shipbuilders as Sklyayev, Vereshchagin, Kurochkin, Yershov, Titov, Bubnov, and Krylov, have been preserved for ages and are being multiplied by Soviet navymen.

The Russians in the Mediterranean Sea

The ancestors of the Russian people appeared for the first time in their ships in the Mediterranean Sea as early as the 6th and 7th centuries. More than once they participated with the Byzantine Fleet in combat operations off the coasts of Italy, Sicily, Crete, and Cyprus. In the following centuries, cruises by Russian ships to the Aegean Sea and to the shores of Asia Minor continued. Owing to these cruises, political, cultural, and trade relations were maintained with the peoples of the Mediterranean countries. Later, the Russian Navy, in supporting the security of its own country from the southwest, did not lose a single battle in the Mediterranean Sea, and the remarkable victories in this region brought it world acclaim.

A brilliant page in history was written by the Baltic Fleet squadron, under the command of Admiral G. A. Spiridov, which was located in the Mediterranean Sea in the period 1769 to 1774. This expedition was intended to support the making of major political moves by Russia by threatening Turkey from the sea and by supporting the uprising of the Balkan peoples enslaved by the Turks. The Baltic squadron, consisting of 10 ships of the line and other combatants, were entrusted with unprecedented missions, which until then were considered inconceivable by many. In a letter to Orlov, the Commander in Chief of the Russian forces in the Mediterranean Sea, Catherine II analyzed this cruise in this manner: "All of Europe is marvelling at your feat and is looking at you with expectation." And the squadron brilliantly justified the hopes placed on it. Over a period of several years, in conducting military operations far from its own shores, it destroyed the Turkish Fleet in battles at Khios and Cesme, blockaded the Dardanelles, interrupted the sea communications of the enemy, landed numerous landing forces, thereby drawing the enemy's forces away from the main northern Black Sea area, and captured 20 islands in the Aegean Sea and several coastal cities, including also some on the coast of Cyprus. The Turks, who were constantly in fear of an attack against Constantinople from the south by the Russian Navy, were forced to maintain considerable army forces and the main part of the Navy in readiness to repel this threat.

The stay of the Russian Fleet in the Mediterranean Sea is an outstanding example of autonomous operations by a large naval formation completely cut off from its home ports, which increased the international prestige of Russia and evoked warm sympathy toward her by all the peoples of the Mediterranean Sea basin.

However, the countries hostile to Russia, above all England, still prevented the Russians from achieving full freedom of passage from the Black Sea into the Mediterranean. Only successful actions by the Russian Army and Navy from the north and from the south forced the Turks to conclude a peace, according to which Russia received land between the Bug and the Dnieper and finally established herself on the Sea of Azov and an outlet from it to the Black Sea. The Crimea was recognized as being an independent state by Turkey and subsequently joined Russia. However, the most important thing was that Russia acquired the right to free commercial navigation in the Black Sea with the right of transit into the Mediterranean.

Turkey did not resign itself to the results of the war. The rapid political rise of Russia had evoked irritation among the states hostile to her, which supported Turkey in every possible way in its attempts to compel the Russians by force to give up their territorial acquisitions in the south.

In August 1787, Turkey again initiated military operations against Russia, thereby forcing the drawing off of the Russian ground forces to the southern borders of the state. Taking advantage of this, Sweden, whose leaders still nourished hopes of wresting Baltic areas from Russia, in the summer of 1788 initiated military actions without declaring war, putting Petersburg in a critical position. The Swedish King, Gustav III, intended to seize the border fortresses by decisive attacks, defeat the Russian Navy, land a landing force on the southern coast of the Gulf of Finland, and seize Petersburg. The main burden in the struggle for the security of the capital lay on the Baltic Fleet, which successfully defended our shores and, after a series of victories at sea, together with the Army, expelled the enemies from the borders of Russia. Clearly, had there not been a strong Navy, the ground forces would have been unable to rapidly cope with such a danger due to their insufficient strength.

The states supporting Turkey and Sweden in this war shifted from diplomatic pressure to threats: England introduced her Navy into the Black and Baltic Seas, and Prussia concentrated troops on the Russian borders. Yet the military actions in the south turned out favorably for Russia. The Black Sea Fleet under the command of F. F. Ushakov inflicted a defeat on the Turkish line fleet in 1790 at Kerch and off the island of Tendra, and in 1791 it finally routed it off of Cape Caliacra. Thus, the Turkish Fleet was expelled from the Black Sea and its Army, deprived of ship support, soon reduced its resistance. In 1792, peace was concluded in Yassakh according to which the Black Sea coast from the Dniester to Novorossiysk went to Russia.

During this war, Russia was unable to dispatch a squadron to the Mediterranean Sea due to the need to conduct combat operations in the Baltic and Black Seas. However, by taking advantage of the sympathy of the Mediterranean peoples, the Russians were able to rapidly outfit privateer detachments of Greek ships, and both at Trieste and Syracuse they created privateer squadrons which, by interrupting the enemy's shipping and attacking his coastal bases, diverted considerable Turkish land and naval forces from the main, Black Sea theater. This essentially created a second front for the Turkish Army, which undoubtedly had a considerable effect on the course and outcome of the struggle in the main area.

The international situation at the turn of the 19th century was extremely complex. After a bourgeois revolution, France waged a fierce struggle with England, which had already been a capitalist society for a long time, and which had seized the main colonial regions. Serious disputes arose between France and Russia, who were striving to take advantage of the legacy of the disintegrating German empire. In this period, Engels pointed out, it was only a question of whether the weak German states would form a French or Russian Confederation of the Rhine. The stratagems in the situation led to sudden sharp turns in the policies of the major countries of Europe and to changes in the directions of their main military efforts.

From 1797 to 1800, Russia, allied with England, Austria, and Turkey, conducted military operations against France. The Russian Army led by A. V. Suvorov displayed wonderful heroism in Switzerland and northern Italy. The Russian squadron in the Mediterranean Sea, under the command of F. F. Ushakov, freed the Ionian Islands from French domination, and later took an active part in driving the French out of Italy. One of the most brilliant deeds of the Navy was taking the strong fortress of Corfu in 1799 after a three month siege. Having received news of this Suvorov said: "Our Peter the Great lives. What he said upon beating the Swedish Fleet off of the Aland Islands in 1714 is, namely, that nature made only one Russia: she has no rivals—that we now see too. Hurrah! To the Russian Navy! . . . Now I say to myself: Why wasn't I at Corfu, even as a Warrant Officer?" [15]

It should be recalled for comparison that at this same time the English Fleet under the command of Admiral Nelson was conducting a siege for the second year of the weaker fortress of La Valletta on Malta and was unable to take it.

The political consequences of the victory of the Russian Navy in the Mediterranean Sea were very significant. Napoleon felt that the Ionian Islands were the most important jump-off position for military actions against Egypt, the Balkans, Constantinople, and the south of Russia. Therefore the expelling of the French from the Ionian Archipelago radically altered the situation in the Mediterranean Sea. Thus, the Navy was the most powerful weapon of the foreign policy of Russia, who by the actions of her Navy drew Italy, Sardinia, and even Tunisia into her own sphere of influence.

Despite the vast contribution of the Russian Navy in changing the political situation in Europe, Western European and American historians even today with the light hand of Mahan continue to ignore Ushakov in every way and refer to him merely as a conscientious pupil of Nelson's, supposedly due to which he achieved success. However, a simple comparison of dates of the largest battles conducted under the leadership of these two famous admirals shows that the main naval victories of Ushakov were won considerably before Nelson was able to display his talent as a naval leader.[16]

The flourishing of the naval art in Russia in the

---

[15] *Istoriya russkoy armii i flota* (The History of the Russian Army and Navy), Vol. IX, Moscow, 1913, p. 57.

[16] F. F. Ushakov's victories: at Kerch in 1790; at Tendra in 1790; at Caliacra in 1791; and the taking of Corfu in 1799. Nelson's victories: at Abukir in 1798; and at Trafalgar in 1805.

second half of the 18th century coincided with the furious development of the Russian art of war as a whole. Thanks to A. V. Suvorov, the Russian Army considerably increased its glorious combat traditions. F. F. Ushakov performed the same service for the Navy.

After the main forces of Ushakov's squadron had left the Mediterranean Sea, part of the ships and naval infantry remained there in order to ensure the safety of the Ionian Islands. Yet within only a few years Russia again began to concentrate naval forces here under the command of Admiral D. N. Senyavin to counter new attempts by the French to carry out takeovers in the Balkans and also to protect the Ionian Islands as bases for the Russian Navy in the Mediterranean.

Naval operations in this period were prosecuted in a very complex and rapidly changing military and political situation. At the end of 1806, Turkey, at the urging of Napoleon, declared war on Russia, which completely changed the mission of the Russian Mediterranean squadron, whose main goal became operations against Turkey from the south together with the allied English Navy. However, the true intentions of England boiled down to not allowing free passage of Russian ships through the Black Sea straits, thus ensuring complete sway for her ships in the Mediterranean Sea. As a result, Senyavin was forced to limit the squadron's mission to blockading the Dardanelles. Nevertheless, in a battle off the Dardanelles and in the battle at Aphantos, it routed the Turkish Fleet.

At the same time as the Russian Fleet was winning brilliant victories in the Aegean Sea, peace talks were underway in Neman between Napoleon and Alexander I. On 25 June 1807, within a week after the Aphantos battle, the Peace Treaty of Tilsit was signed which sharply altered the foreign policy of the Tsarist government which shifted to an alliance with Napoleon. Russia received a breathing space, which was purchased at an extremely expensive price: Napoleon's territorial

seizures in Western Europe were recognized, Russia was obliged to participate in the continental blockade of England, starting a war with her, she had to accede to France and Turkey all the strategic positions won by her by that time in the Mediterranean Sea, to withdraw all of her forces, and to put a squadron under complete French authority.

This sharp turn in Russia's foreign policy created an exceedingly difficult situation for the Mediterranean squadron. And it was only after almost 20 years that it again appeared in the Mediterranean on the pleasant mission of rendering aid to the Greek people.

In 1827 the Russian squadron under the command of Admiral L. P. Geyden, together with the English and French squadrons, was supposed to force the Turkish occupation forces in Greece to cease exterminating the population which was fighting for national independence. Joint operations of the allied fleets began with the famous battle of Navarino (October 1827) in which the more numerous Turkish Fleet was completely crushed. In the Russo-Turkish War of 1828–1829 a Russian squadron under the command of Admiral P. I. Rikord tightly blockaded the Dardanelles and the Turkish coast from the south.

Later the Russian Navy did not conduct combat operations in the Mediterranean Sea, although its forces, right up to the squadrons of steam vessels, were regularly located there.

Thus, in summing up what has been said, we clearly see that the Mediterranean Sea, which is located close

Through bold use of mines, coupled with such unnerving assaults as this night attack by seven torpedo boats, the Russian Navy was able, in the war of 1877–1878, to reduce to impotence a Turkish fleet which was one of the most modern in the world.

to the southwestern borders of Russia, beginning with the period of the sailing fleets, was the region having a most important significance for her defense. Russian squadrons conducted combat operations there not to seize foreign territories or enslave peoples, but for the sake of ensuring the security of their own country. This was a struggle of forces on the foremost line of defense of the country when threats of aggression arose from the southwest.

The operation of the Russian Navy in the Mediterranean Sea, which was of an exceedingly active nature, each time led to results which had a very significant effect on the overall course and outcome of the armed defense of the country from aggression from the southwest. Thus, in 1770–1774, the Navy rendered most important aid on the strategic plane, not only in the defense of the southwestern regions of the country, but also by diverting large enemy forces toward itself, and directly aided the Russian Army in achieving remarkable victories on the Danube front. And the timely movement of naval forces to the Mediterranean Sea and their brilliant victories played a great role in the conclusion of an exceptionally favorable peace treaty for Russia in the war of 1768 to 1774.[17]

The combat operations of Admiral F. F. Ushakov's squadron in the Mediterranean Sea from 1798 to 1800 had the goal of heading off the imminent aggression of Napoleonic France against Russia from the southwest. At that time the situation was crystallizing in such a manner that the capture by the French of the region of the Ionian Archipelago, which represented a first rate position for the subsequent development of military operations capable of having an effect on the course of Suvorov's campaign in Italy, forced Russia, while not expecting a direct attack, to send naval forces into the Mediterranean. The victorious actions of the Navy led to a radical change in the situation not only in the Mediterranean Sea, but also on its entire coastline, which was of inestimable aid to Suvorov's Army and aided in achieving the goals of the armed struggle of the state.

The presence of the Russian Fleet under the command of D. N. Senyavin in the Mediterranean Sea in 1806–1807 also had as its objective strategic cooperation with the Russian Army battling with the troops of Napoleonic France, which was allied with Turkey. And also in this case our Fleet achieved its goal, delivering a series of crushing defeats to the Turkish Fleet at sea and to the French troops in the Balkans.

As is seen, historically it has turned out that when a threat arises of enemy encroachment on the territory of Russia from the southwest, the Russian Navy has been moved into the Mediterranean Sea where it has successfully executed major strategic missions in defending the country's borders from aggression. In other words, our Navy has shown the whole world that the Mediterranean Sea is not anyone's preserve or a closed lake and that Russia is a Mediterranean power. The location of her forces in these waters is based not only on geographical conditions (the proximity of the Black Sea to the Mediterranean theater), but also the age-old need for the Russian Navy to stay there.

Today, when the capabilities of the imperialist aggressors to attack the Soviet Union directly from the Mediterranean Sea have increased extraordinarily, this region has assumed especially important significance in the defense of our Homeland. The constant presence there of the U. S. Sixth Fleet, with aircraft carriers and missile-carrying submarines, has as its basic mission a surprise attack against the Soviet Union and the countries of the Socialist community. The U. S. Navy command openly states that the missiles of the nuclear-powered submarines and the carrier aircraft from the Mediterranean Sea are aimed at objectives in the U.S.S.R. and the states of Eastern Europe and are in a constant state of readiness to deliver nuclear strikes against them.[18]

It is natural that in response to the direct threat, the Soviet Union is forced to undertake defensive measures and implement its undisputable and legal right to have warships in the Mediterranean Sea. They are there not to threaten peace-loving peoples, and not to implement any sort of expansionist desires, which are alien to the very nature of our Socialist state, but in order to nip aggression in the very bud, should the imperialists attempt to undertake it from this region.

And if our enemies more and more often look at the Soviet Navy and see it as a hindrance to their adventures, this means that it is accomplishing the mission assigned to it.

For several years, the Western bourgeois press, and state and military figures have been conducting a high-flown propaganda campaign with regard to the stay of Soviet warships in the Mediterranean Sea. A majority of the statements, having the goal of deceiving public opinion, are colored by false assertions that the Soviet Union is sending warships to the Mediterranean Sea supposedly to put pressure on individual states of this region, to conduct "gunboat diplomacy," to threaten

---

[17] Keep in mind the Kuchuk-Kaynardzha Treaty concluded by Russia and Turkey on 10 (21) July 1774, according to which Russia acquired the land between the Bug and the Dnieper, finally established herself on the Sea of Azov and outlets for herself to the Black Sea, and received the right of free commercial navigation in the Black Sea and an outlet to the Mediterranean Sea. The Crimea was recognized as a state independent of Turkey.

[18] Newsweek, 19 July 1971.

the southern flank of NATO, etc. They write and say that the "political influence of the Russians in this strategically important sea is directly proportional to the numerical strength of their Fleet."[19] Admiral C. Duncan, an American who is Supreme Commander-in-Chief of the NATO Forces in the Atlantic, recently asserted that the most dramatic challenge that NATO is running up against is the fact that the Russians have put to sea.[20] Such statements are an attempt to ascribe to the Soviet Union intentions which are completely alien to it. Our influence in this region (as well as throughout the world) is growing, primarily owing to the policy of peace and friendship being conducted by the Soviet state.

Undoubtedly the strengthening of the prestige of the U.S.S.R. in the opinion of the Mediterranean peoples is also being fostered by the comparison by them of the policy of our state with U. S. policy. The most important instrument of American policy in the Mediterranean is the Sixth Fleet, which has repeatedly interfered in the internal affairs of the Mediterranean states and has supported aggressors in their actions against freedom-loving peoples. Such actions characterize U. S.

[19] Newsweek, 19 July 1971.

[20] Associated Press, 13 December 1971.

policy as a clearly expansionary, antidemocratic, and policeman policy.

In contrast to the Sixth Fleet, the Soviet Navy has not once interfered in the internal affairs of the Mediterranean states and has not committed any sort of aggression against them. The presence of our warships in the Mediterranean Sea constantly prevents the disturbance of the peaceful atmosphere in this region and plays a deterrent role. As early as 1968 a TASS statement pointed out: "The Soviet Union as a Black Sea power, and, consequently, a Mediterranean power, is exercising its indisputable right to have a presence in this region. Soviet naval ships are in the Mediterranean not to create a threat to any people or state. Their mission is to promote the cause of stability and peace in the Mediterranean Sea region."

At the 24th CPSU Congress, L. I. Brezhnev said: ". . . Attempts to ascribe to the Soviet Union intentions that are alien to it do not deceive the people. With full responsibility we declare: we have no territorial pretensions whatsoever, we threaten no one and we intend to attack no one; we stand for free and independent development of all peoples. . . . In contrast to the aggressive policy of imperialism, the Soviet Union presents a policy of active defense of peace and the strengthening of international security.

Commentary

By Rear Admiral E. M. Eller, U. S. Navy (Retired)

A graduate of the Naval Academy in 1925, Admiral Eller served in the Pacific during most of World War II and, in 1946, assumed the duties of Director of Public Information, Navy Department, Washington, D.C. After graduating from the National War College and serving on the Joint Staff of the Joint Chiefs of Staff, he commanded the Middle East Force, 1950-1951. After his retirement in 1954, Admiral Eller became Director of Engineering at Bucknell University, a position which he held until 1956 when recalled to active duty as Director of Naval History Division, Navy Department. Since his retirement in 1970 he has been spending his time writing, including his recent book *The Soviet Sea Challenge*. Admiral Eller is a three-time winner of the Naval Institute's Prize Essay Contest. He has received honorable mention in the Contest on three other occasions and has been a frequent contributor to the *Proceedings*.

Admiral Gorshkov well understands the magic advantages which control of the sea bring a nation. Writing with clarity of perception and skill in slanted argument, he drives home the correct conclusion that the U.S.S.R. needs great power afloat to force the world into Communism. Without this force, she cannot insure successful insurgencies. Neither can she expand and dominate the world.

He sings the propaganda song of friendship and support of "peace-loving people." Yet throughout, his historical examples demonstrate to the Party that a strong Navy has helped bring vast territorial gains—and today opens to the world as "the most powerful weapon of Russia's foreign policy."

The shrewd leader of the Red Navy not only perceives the importance of seapower himself, but obviously has so convinced the leaders who count in the Politburo. Pronouncements like this group of significant articles are not made lightly in the U.S.S.R. They speak the party line, so we should listen carefully. With Gorshkov showing the way, the Kremlin has concentrated immense resources into all elements of maritime strength. The results are frightening. Almost overnight the Soviets have rushed ahead to pass the United States and to become Number One on the oceans. These articles help show why.

As a professional naval officer, Admiral Gorshkov says strikingly little about tactics, training, naval weapons, leadership, and other essentials of the naval art. Clearly writing to inform, and to convince doubters, he concentrates on the military and political benefits to the country of a strong Navy.

Like the others, this second article has a facade of party line ideology. Yet the points Gorshkov drives home show understanding of the historical importance of seapower, astute thinking, and clever presentation to gain acceptance from the land-minded hierarchy:

▶ *He blocks opposition to naval power by accurately showing that "The Motherland" could not "join the ranks of great powers" without a strong Navy.* Russia's past setbacks and failure to win territorial gains in war, he says, came usually because she lacked the necessary fleet. Many examples drive home the point and the effect upon the "historical path of the state."

▶ *Russia suffered in the past because Tsarist leaders swallowed hostile foreign propaganda (led by Britain and now the United States) that she is not a maritime country and therefore does not need the sea.* Thus, if any Soviet leaders today oppose the aggressive build-up in all facets of seapower, they become suspect dupes of foreign anticommunist propagandists.

▶ *The U.S.S.R. has the longest maritime frontier in the world, almost twice that of the United States, and 15 times that of France.* Thus, considering sea borders (he does not note that most of the U.S.S.R.'s are icebound most of the time), the Soviet Union has first need for seapower.

▶ *Russians are inherently sea going people.* Therefore Peter I merely achieved a rebirth by creating "one of the strongest fleets in the world." The surge to first place today continues the trend and can produce the same large benefits.

▶ *In the homeland, the Army sorely needs a strong Navy "cooperating jointly with ground forces to achieve the goals of the war."* When Peter I did not have a powerful fleet, he failed. When he did, he won his

objectives. "The land army," Peter said, "has one arm, but the Government that possesses an army and a fleet, is a body with two arms." When Russian monarchs after Peter failed to maintain an adequate fleet, Russia either lost battles or failed to gain desired territory, especially in the Black Sea-Mediterranean area—or between wars did not attain her diplomatic objectives. Thus seapower is a main instrument of national policy.

▶ *The Army needs a fleet also for distant operations.* In the Napoleonic wars, Russia was not endangered by threat of attack from the Mediterranean. However, the conquests of Russia's Mediterranean fleet greatly furthered operations of the Army in Austria and Italy. Admiral Gorshkov calls this "strategic cooperation with the Army."

▶ *A Navy can ensure security of sea frontiers.* The U.S.S.R. wants superiority for this purpose and not for the "imperialistic designs" of the capitalistic nations. Yet this frayed mask can't hide the evidence: Peter the Great had to have a fleet to hope to expand to the Azov and Black Seas. He needed it to gain the Baltic. He and successors needed it to reach for the Mediterranean.

Taking customary communist liberty with facts, Admiral Gorshkov gives the impression that the U.S.S.R.'s present European frontiers constitute, in considerable part, the bounds of a thousand years ago. Aggrandizement since against Moslems, Persians, and others in the south, the Baltic States and Central Europe in the west, the Tartars, Mongols and Chinese in the east—all have been merely protective measures in expansion that has not ceased.

▶ *The Motherland is a Mediterranean Power, and requires free access to it.* The fleet now there "is based not only on geographical conditions (the proximity of the Black Sea to the Mediterranean theater) but also the age-old need for the Russian fleet to stay there."

▶ *When the Navy has superior strength (as against Sweden in the Baltic and Turkey in the Black Sea) then it can carry the war overseas to the enemy. Invasion and territorial gains can follow.* Illustrations of successes must whet Politburo appetites for distant shores.

Indeed, territorial expansion is a major theme of this article: expansion to the west to win the Baltic coast; expansion "toward the east for an outlet to the Pacific Ocean"; and with special emphasis, expansion to the south, which has occupied so much of Russian history, and where opportunity of critical import still awaits in the Middle East, Africa, and the Indian sub-continent.

Singularly, in recounting territorial gains, Admiral Gorshkov carefully refrains from citing the large conquests from Persia around the Caspian. He does not mention the acquisitions west of the sea grasping for the Persian Gulf and Middle East (once again, as for most of history, critical for control of civilization), where the U.S.S.R. has made significant gains in recent years. Neither does he mention the conquests to the east of the Caspian—nor the long yearning for India and the Indian Ocean, now close to fruition.

Takeover of the Crimea in one of the Turkish wars illustrates a maneuver not forgotten in Moscow. The Army with the Navy "forced the Turks to conclude a peace, according to which Russia received land between the Bug and the Dnieper, and finally established herself on the Sea of Azov and an outlet from it to the Black Sea." He adds that "The Crimea was recognized as being an independent state by Turkey and subsequently joined Russia.

Actually, of course, Catherine set up a puppet government, just as Stalin did after World War II in bordering states, employing ambitious nationals of these countries.

The Mediterranean stands out as the ultimate goal for southwest expansion (or semi-ultimate, for beyond lie the Suez Canal, Egypt, and all the vast seething continent of Africa to communize). The operations of a Russian fleet in the Mediterranean for several years in the 1760s and 1770s against Turkey evoke another statement of import. These, the Admiral writes, are "an outstanding example of autonomous operations by a large naval formation completely cut off from its home ports, which increased the international prestige of Russia and evoked warm sympathy toward Russia by all the peoples of the Mediterranean." And he adds of operations a few years later, "the Navy was the most powerful weapon of the foreign policy of Russia, who by the actions of her Navy, drew Italy, Sardinia, and even Tunisia into her own sphere of influence"—an 18th century preview of today.

The Soviet Union's predominant influence throughout the latest Arab-Israeli war, and the grave energy threat it raised for the Free World, demonstrate the correctness of Admiral Gorshkov's emphasis on the value of the Navy in international crises beyond her shores. It surely added to his stature and influence in the Politburo. Thus the Kremlin's intense drive to control the seas, and therefore civilization, will not slacken.

In condemning the U. S. employment of the 6th Fleet "as a clearly expansionary, anti-democratic, and policeman policy," Admiral Gorshkov reveals why the Russian Navy has returned to the Sea of History in force. He remembers how the Kremlin retreated in Azerbaijan, how it relaxed threats against Turkey, and how it failed to overthrow governments in Greece, Lebanon, and Jordan, to be replaced by Communist regimes.

Having shown how the Russian Navy through history has furthered conquests, the Soviet CNO concludes with a soothing note. His fleet in the Mediterranean, he avers, has only the mission "to promote the cause of stability and peace . . .

"We have no territorial pretensions whatsoever, we threaten no one and intend to attack no one."

In this connection, and as anchor to our comment, it seems appropriate to quote F. T. Jane's words of three quarters of a century ago: "Every Russian feels himself a member of the empire that will be the world empire of the future. And that empire will be a great sea-empire . . . At some future date that great struggle . . . this new Punic War . . . is . . . likely to be absolutely decisive." Since he quotes from another passage of the book where these words appear, Admiral Gorshkov must have read these words, believed them, and preached them in the Kremlin. He is obviously preparing his Navy for "that great struggle."

The Post-Napoleonic Period to Russo-Japanese War

With Commentary following the article by
Vice Admiral Edwin B. Hooper, U. S. Navy (Retired)

EDITOR'S NOTE: *This article, by the man who has commanded the Soviet Navy for the past 18 years, was cleared for publication in the Soviet Union on 31 March 1972. In this, the third of an 11-chapter series, Admiral Gorshkov stresses his countrymen's inherent love for the sea. It was this "striving for seafaring" that resulted in one of Tsarist Russia's finest hours—the circumnavigation of the globe by* Bellingshausen *in 1803. Yet, just a century later, in 1904, Tsarist plenipotentiaries had to enlist an American President's help in securing peace with Japan, a country which clearly understood what Russia's rulers obviously had forgotten, but are not likely to forget again—the importance of a Navy in the achievement of political objectives.*

At the end of the Napoleonic Wars, one of the most difficult periods in the history of the Russian Navy began, due to the economic and political backwardness of Russia, as well as underestimation by the Tsarist government of the importance of the Navy to her fate. The Navy Department was headed by Admiral Chichagov, a dull figure who considered the Navy an onerous, needless luxury for the State. His successors—the French emigrant reactionary, the Marquis de Traverse, and the German, von Muller—continued to dismantle the Navy.

President Theodore Roosevelt, friend of Captain Alfred Thayer Mahan and staunch advocate of Mahan's theories of seapower, acted as mediator between Russia's Count Serge Y. Witte and Baron Roman R. Rosen, and Japan's Count Jutaro Komura and Baron Kogoro Takahira in negotiations that ended the Russo-Japanese War.

The Decembrist [one taking part in the unsuccessful uprising against Nicholas I in December 1825–Ed.] Shteyngel' characterized the state of the Navy at that time as follows: ". . . the most splendid creation of Peter the Great which the Marquis de Traverse completely destroyed."[1] Actually, whereas 58 ships-of-the-line, 207 other sailing vessels and 439 rowed ships were built for the Baltic Fleet during the time of Peter I, in 1825 the Fleet possessed only 5 ships-of-the-line and 10 frigates capable of putting to sea. The warships almost never left port. The seamen were used for subsidiary chores. Russian admirals were replaced with foreigners. There was widespread embezzlement of public property. The distinguished admiral, V. M. Golovnin, wrote: "If rotten, poorly-equipped ships;

[1] From the letters and statements of Decembrists, edited by A. K. Borozdin. St. Petersburg, 1906, p. 61.

elderly and ailing naval commanders, without knowledge and spirit at sea; inexperienced captains and officers; and farmers, in the guise of seamen, formed into ship crews, can constitute a fleet, then we have a fleet."[2]

However, the despotic leadership of the Navy Department, while almost destroying Navy materiel, did not succeed in finally liquidating the energy of the men and their love of the sea. Only this can explain the round-the-world expeditions undertaken at the initiative of progressive naval officers, including Decembrist navymen.

Discoveries by Russian seafarers during the first half of the 19th Century, comprising an entire era in the history of geographic discoveries and making possible the charting of a large number of previously unknown islands in the Pacific, Antarctica, and islands near it, served as a basis for major advances in oceanography and publication of the most valuable scientific works and atlases. It is a well-known fact that most of the islands in the Pacific discovered by our seafarers bear the names of distinguished Russian figures: Suvorov, Kutuzov, Vermolov, Rumyantsev, Lisyanskiy, Senyavin, et al, and that not only Alaska and contiguous islands and lands of northwest America, but also part of the present state of California were first explored by Russians and belonged to Russia. The remnants of Fort Ross, built by the Russians in 1812, have been preserved to this day near San Francisco. Not everyone knows that on 21 May 1816 the king of one of the Hawaiian Islands (the island of Kauai) became a Russian citizen.[3] Moreover, he also turned the island of Oahu over to Russia. Three Russian fortresses were established on that island: Aleksandrovskaya, Yelizavetinskaya, and Barklaya (true, they had to be abandoned later due to counteraction by the Americans). It must also be noted that a significant portion of the northern shores of Europe and Asia, as well as the coast of northeast Asia and northwest America, were first described and charted by our mariners.

The Russians completed their first circumnavigation of the globe in 1803 to 1806 on the ships *Nadezhda* and *Neva,* under the command of I. F. Kruzenshtern and Yu. F. Lisyanskiy. This expedition made many astronomical determinations of the location of islands and surveys in the north Pacific, collected a wealth of scientific material, and discovered an island west of

the Hawaiian Islands and named it Lisyanskiy Island. In 1823 to 1827 the *Atlas yuzhnogo morya* (Atlas of the South Seas) was published, containing verified charts of the Pacific Ocean. The atlas received broad distribution among seafarers throughout the world.

After the *Nadezhda* and *Neva,* the second circumnavigation was made by the sloop *Diana,* under the command of V. M. Golovnin. The great difficulties and failures accompanying this voyage did not frighten the Russian seamen. M. P. Lazarev (subsequently a distinguished admiral and seafarer) on a long voyage aboard the warship *Suvorov* in 1814 discovered a group of islands in the Pacific, which was named the Suvorov Islands. In 1816–1817, the men of the warship *Ryurik* discovered several islands in the Paumotu Archipelago and in the Marshall Islands, charted the Diomedes Islands, and described the coast of Alaska. In 1820, Lieutenant Z. I. Ponafidin—aboard the warship *Borodino*—discovered two islands in the western Pacific. In 1823–1829, O. Ye. Kotsebu, aboard the sloop *Predpriyatiye,* and F. P. Litke, aboard the sloop *Senyavin,* discovered a number of islands in the Marshall and Caroline groups. A Russian Antarctic expedition aboard the sloops *Vostok* and *Mirnyy,* commanded by F. F. Bellingshausen and M. P. Lazarev, discovered 14 islands in the Pacific and called them the Rossiyan Islands. On this same voyage, the Russians were the first to reach the Antarctic Continent and to circumnavigate it, charting new islands and lands. In essence, Bellingshausen and Lazarev can be called the Columbuses of Antarctica, and world science fully recognizes their service.

In subsequent years long voyages by Russian seafarers have continued. Of particular interest are the voyages of the corvette *Vityaz'* and the clipper *Izumrud,* in connection with the exploration of New Guinea and the Indo-Malay Archipelago by N. N. Miklukho-Maklay.

Many islands and lands discovered by Russian seafarers in the Pacific were not added to Russian possessions, although as their first discoverer she was fully entitled to this right. Today they belong to the Americans, British, French, and Japanese.

Thus a love for the sea—inherent in the Russian people—and a striving for seafaring, even in the face of the waning sea power of Russia in the early 19th Century, were manifested in long and round-the-world voyages. In addition to priceless geographical discoveries, they saved the Russian Navy from total collapse and fostered the education of an entire generation of seafarers, who later brought glory to the Russian Navy. Kruzenshtern, Lisyanskiy, Kotsebu, Bellingshausen, Lazarev, Golovnin, Nevel'skoy, Litke, Ponafidin and many other names are now familiar to the whole world

[2]Z. Ye. Pavlova. Decembrist N. Bestuzhev and his *Opyt istorii Rossiyskogo flota* (Experience in the History of the Russian Fleet), in the book by N. A. Bestuzhev. *Opyt istorii Rossiyskogo flota* (Experience in the History of the Russian Fleet), Sudpromgiz, 1961, p. 9.

[3]L. S. Berg. *Ocherki po istorii russkikh geograficheskikh otkrytiy* (Sketches on the History of Russian Geographical Discoveries), 2nd Edition, revised and supplemented. Publishing House of the Academy of Sciences of the USSR, 1949, p. 161.

and symbolize the best traditions of the Homeland Fleet in the study of the World Ocean which are being honored and augmented by our Soviet seafarers.

Russian Fleet During the Industrial Revolution and the Transition From Sailing Vessels to Steam Vessels

In the middle of the 19th Century, the Industrial Revolution produced a technological revolution in naval affairs, particularly the transition from the sailing fleet to a steamer fleet.

Great Britain and France, continuing their policy of driving Russia out of the Mediterranean, sought to take over the economy and finances of Turkey, which in turn cherished the hope of restoring hegemony over the northern shores of the Black Sea. Hostilities were imminent; Great Britain and France, allied with Turkey and Sardinia, became the main belligerents, preventing by military force egress of Russia into the Mediterranean.

The Crimean War, 1853–1856. In this war, vast sea expanses separated the adversaries, and therefore navies played a significant role. However, due to the backwardness of Russia, her Navy consisted primarily of sailing vessels, whereas the primary combat power of the British and French Navies comprised steam vessels. Specifically, at the time of the war, they possessed 89 warships (54 of which were steamers) and 300 transports (many of which were likewise steam-driven). The Black Sea Fleet included 14 sailing ships-of-the-line, and 11 sailing and 11 steam frigates. It should be emphasized that with an overall 2 to 1 superiority in ships-of-the-line and frigates, the British and French had a better than 10 to 1 advantage in steamships, and screw steamers, not just paddle wheelers.

Due to the actions of Admirals P. S. Nakhimov and V. A. Kornilov, the Black Sea Fleet was at a high level of combat readiness, which ensured its success at the beginning of the war. But subsequently, due to the technological lag, the Fleet could not compete with the Anglo-French steam-driven fleet which had entered the Black Sea. The technological backwardness of the Russian Fleet engendered a defensive tendency with respect to its use, which under the circumstances was generally justified, although it contradicted the essence of the combat activity of this, most mobile, type of force designed for active operations at sea.

Combat operations commenced with the Battle of Sinope, in which a Russian squadron (six ships-of-the-line and two frigates, armed with 720 guns, including 76 bomb-throwing guns) destroyed the Turkish Fleet. Here the high leadership qualities of Admiral P. S.

Nakhimov, the squadron commander, were very much in evidence, as well as his creative approach to the execution of a difficult and dangerous mission: attacking large enemy forces (12 sailing and steam vessels, armed with 472 guns) standing in the roadstead, under the cover of heavy coastal artillery (38 guns). Nakhimov had faith in the high morale and excellent training of his subordinates, evidenced by his order to the squadron concerning the impending battle: "I am informing the senior officers that in event of an encounter with an enemy whose forces are superior to ours, I shall attack him, completely confident that each of us will perform his duty." In the order issued before the Battle of Sinope, P. S. Nakhimov stated: "Russia expects valiant deeds from the Black Sea Fleet, justification of that expectation depends on us."

The squadron commander objectively and thoroughly analyzed the enemy's capabilities and decided to totally destroy him at his base. It was a new step in the development not only of Russian naval science, but of world naval science as well.

The battle strategy was to make full use of the advantage possessed by the squadron in gunnery and in the high level of readiness of the men, in order to close with the enemy as quickly as possible within effective gunnery range and attack him with all forces. Execution of the strategy required grouping the squadron in a combat formation consisting of two columns.

The Turkish Fleet ceased to exist 3-3½ hours after the start of the battle (only one steamship escaped), and the coastal batteries were silenced.

The Battle of Sinope—one of the most brilliant pages in the chronicle of victories of the Russian Navy—was the last major clash between squadrons of sailing vessels.

The first battles involving steamships in which Russian navymen achieved significant successes occurred in this war. One of these was the capture of the Turkish armed steamship *Pervaz Bakhri* by the steam frigate *Vladimir,* commanded by Captain-Lieutenant G. I. Butakov (later admiral), creator of the tactics of the steam-powered fleet.

After the Anglo-French Fleet entered the Black Sea, our weaker Fleet was not in a position to continue the war at sea, and the command decided to disarm the warships and send their guns and personnel ashore for the immediate defense of Sevastapol.

The enemy, using his advantage in naval forces, attempted to geographically expand the war. The Anglo-French squadrons entered the Gulf of Finland, but encountered stubborn resistance from the substantially inferior Russian Fleet. The attack on St. Petersburg was disrupted.

In the Barents and White Seas, the British and

French, according to Engels, were engaged in intense attacks on the Russian and Lapp villages, and destruction of the property of poor fishermen,[4] and, of course, did not attain vital objectives. In August 1854, the Anglo-French squadron approached Petropavlovsk-Kamchatskiy, defended by a small garrison and two warships (the frigate *Avrora* and the military transport *Diana*). However, in the uneven battle the Russians, under the command of Zavoyko (later a rear admiral), displayed great tenacity and achieved victory, forcing the allied squadron to withdraw ingloriously.

Despite the heroism displayed by Russian navymen in this war, Tsarist Russia suffered defeat. The Crimean War, which cost the belligerents "incalculable losses and over a million lives,"[5] ended with the conclusion of the Treaty of Paris in 1856, in which Russia had to cede the mouth of the Danube and part of southern Bessarabia, and renounce her protectorate over the Danubian Principalities. The severest provision of the treaty—the prohibition against a Russian Fleet in the Black Sea—once again emphasized the particular importance attached to a fleet by the Western powers.

The Crimean War, waged during a period of technological revolution in military affairs, was one of the first wars in which broad use was made of steam-powered warships. This change in the technological base of the Navy also led to the most fundamental changes in the naval art.

In addition, this war demonstrated the importance of technological superiority in armed conflict, determined by the degree of economic and political development of States, as well as further expansion of the role of navies in wars. The coalition of countries possessing numerical—and above all, qualitative—superiority over the Russian Fleet, held the initiative for a considerable period, opening up new trends in armed conflict in various naval theaters. It was precisely with the aid of the Navy that the Crimean War was expanded along the entire perimeter of the maritime boundaries of Russia, although its basic missions were carried out in the Crimea, at the approaches to Sevastopol.

The significance of the Navy in this war was also determined by the extent to which its presence in a given theater could be used by diplomats of the belligerent states to support their positions at the peace talks. Russia, almost totally deprived of her Fleet in the Black Sea, was unable to oppose the fleets of the enemy States with her own naval power, and therefore had to accede to the provisions of the Treaty of Paris. Great Britain and France, having consolidated their position at sea,

acquired new possibilities for exerting pressure on Russia with the threat of attacks against her from the southwest, consolidated their control over the straits zone, and increased their influence in the Near and Middle East.

The Russo-Turkish War, 1877–1878. The Crimean War was an exceptionally important historical threshold, after which enormous changes in the socio-economic life of Russia occurred; she healed the wounds inflicted by the war, stood on the path of development of capitalism, and began modernizing her armed forces. In 1871 Russia finally achieved abrogation of the humiliating prohibition against a fleet in the Black Sea.

However, the Tsarist government did not take (indeed was unable to take) decisive measures to restore sea power in the southwest, and, when the Russo-Turkish War began in 1877, the Black Sea Fleet was very poorly prepared for it. Except for two round ironclads (so-called "*Popovki*"), the Fleet consisted only of several small obsolete warships. Necessity compelled it to arm and use, for military operations, steamships of the merchant fleet, as well as steam-powered boats and launches. Navymen under the leadership of young and energetic officers aboard such warships were able to paralyze the activity of the Turkish armorclads.

However, the British squadron entering the Sea of Marmora influenced the subsequent course of events: the Tsar prohibited the Army from marching on Constantinople and reaching the shores of the straits. The peace treaty between Russia and Turkey, signed on 3 March 1878 at San Stefano, was submitted to the international congress in Berlin for consideration, and the Tsarist government had to accede to it. At the Congress (June–July 1878), Russia had to renounce a number of provisions of the treaty and was deprived of a significant portion of the results of victory. And although her strategic position improved somewhat, the advantages which she acquired through the peace teaty were totally inconsistent with the effort expended. This occurred solely because Russia did not possess a powerful Navy.

Thus, once again, Russia had to bear the consequences of the fact that Tsarist officials continued for a long time to underestimate the importance of a Navy in international relations and in warfare. The national interests of the Balkan peoples were likewise sacrificed to Great Britain and Austria.

A major figure of the period, Russian War Minister D. A. Milyutin, commented on the results of this war in this manner: "Great Britain already effectively possesses Constantinople and the straits . . .. The British Fleet, though withdrawn from the Sea of Marmora,

[4] K. Marx and F. Engels. *Sochineniye* (Works), Vol. 11, p. 522.
[5] *Ibid,* Vol. 22, 2nd Edition. Gospolitizdat, 1962, p. 39.

can return to the straits, and even the Black Sea, at any time. Nobody can prevent it."[6]

Thus, Great Britain, and not Russia who won the war, established control in the Black Sea straits due to the power of her Fleet. Despite continuous efforts throughout the century to achieve freedom of maritime commerce with access to the Mediterranean, Russia was only able to consolidate on the northern and eastern shores of the Black Sea. She was unable to advance further, despite the victories achieved there by Russian forces.

Obviously, Peter I would not have been able to relentlessly pursue a policy of egress of Russia to the shores of the Baltic Sea without fearing the threat posed by other powers, reinforced by demonstrations of sea power, had he not created a huge army and powerful navy, satisfying the needs of the time.

The struggle for egress to the southern seas had another countenance. In the culminating moments of wars, when sea power on which policy could be based was particularly needed, the Russian Fleet was frequently too weak to compel the enemy and the powers supporting him to accept peace conditions essential to Russia. Though one of the strongest land powers, she possessed a fleet in the Black Sea sufficient only to combat with Turkey alone. Therefore, as soon as other powers, presenting primarily a naval threat, entered the war on the side of Turkey, Russia was compelled to abandon the fruits of her victories, and sometimes even suffer defeats.

Thus, tracing the role and significance of the Navy in the long struggle for outlets to the southern seas and freedom of Russian navigation on the Mediterranean, the following conclusion can be drawn. With the consolidation of Russia on the shores of the Black Sea during the period prior to the Crimean War, when the primary obstacle to the achievement of this objective was Turkey, the Russian Navy successfully executed its missions. Subsequently, when the question of a direct egress for Russia to the Mediterranean arose, affecting the interests of the major capitalist powers of Europe in their sphere of interest, the relative weakness of the Russian Navy was immediately manifested.

Navies at the Beginning of the Era of Imperialism

"Imperialism, the highest stage of capitalism in America and Europe, and later also in Asia, was completely developed by the period 1898 to 1914. The Spanish-American War (1898), Anglo-Boer War (1899–1902), the Russo-Japanese War (1904–1905), and the economic crisis in Europe in 1900 were the main historic landmarks of the new era in world history."[7]

At that time, the major capitalist powers divided among themselves almost all the territory of the world. The nations which were first to start along the path toward capitalist development and which possessed powerful navies, succeeded in grabbing the lion's share of the colonial possessions. Thus, beginning in 1583, England, making skillful use of her sea power, by various avenues and methods, was able to control, by the beginning of the 20th Century, colonies whose territory was 109 times larger than the area of the mother country, and in the process ranked first among the capitalist powers.

The center of conflict for the partition and redivision of the world shifted to the Pacific Ocean, on whose shores lay a China yet to be divided up. Squadrons with expeditionary forces from all the major imperialist powers were dispatched there in order to achieve expansionist aims. Britain was the first to pillage the Chinese people, followed by France, then the younger despoilers: the U.S.A., Germany, and Japan.

Irreconcilable differences between the colonizers gave rise to a number of armed conflicts in which navies continued to be an important means for achieving the objectives of the imperialist states, and in some of these conflicts even the main means.

The Spanish-American War. By the end of the 19th century, the U.S.A. had acquired all the characteristics of an imperialist power, and began to pursue a tough political course aimed at the seizure of colonies. Since a considerable portion of the world was already divided up, Spanish colonies in the Caribbean—as well as the Philippines—were the most appropriate for American aggression. Whereas "acquisition" of the former ensured American hegemony at the approaches to the designated area of construction of the Panama Canal, "acquisition" of the latter was an important step for subsequent expansion into China and Southeast Asia. It is quite obvious that a powerful navy could be the primary force in this struggle for overseas colonies.

At the first favorable opportunity, in 1898, the U.S.A. unleashed a war, the essence of which was stated with utmost clarity by V. I. Lenin: "They plundered Cuba and the Philippines."[8]

In the plans for seizure of the Spanish colonies, the

[6] *Onevnik D. A. Milyutina* Diary of D. A. Milyutina), Lenin State Order of Lenin Library of the USSR. Manuscript Division. Vol. III, Moscow, 1950, p. 127.

[7] V. I. Lenin. *Polnoye sobraniye sochineniy* (Complete Collected Works), Vol. 30, p. 164.

[8] V. I. Lenin. *Ibid*, Vol. 28, p. 669.

primary role was assigned to the Navy, whose forces were to be used to deliver decisive blows against the Spanish Fleet, and thereby deprive the enemy of his ability to bring reinforcements from the home country by sea. Therefore, in preparing for war (whose theaters were sure to be the Caribbean Sea and the western Pacific), the U.S.A. created a Navy substantially superior to that of economically and politically backward Spain.

The U. S. war against Spain—the first imperialist war for redivision of the world—lasted less than four months. Taking advantage of their superiority at sea, the Americans landed in Cuba. When the Spanish West Indies squadron, consisting of obsolete warships, attempted to break out to the ocean from Santiago, it was defeated by technologically more advanced American warships. The garrison at Santiago, deprived of naval support, quickly capitulated. The war in the Caribbean Sea was essentially over.

The Americans also achieved an easy victory in the Philippines: the weak Spanish Asiatic squadron was destroyed in Manila Bay, and U. S. Marines entered Manila without a struggle.

The U.S.A. won the war at the cost of insignificant personal losses, but with great losses on the part of insurgents struggling against Spanish bondage. Local insurgent armies bore the brunt of the ground war against Spain, both in Cuba and the Philippines.

According to the Peace Treaty of 1898, Puerto Rico, Guam, the Philippines—and somewhat later, Cuba—became American colonies. The U.S.A. occupied a dominant position in the Caribbean, acquired advantageous positions in the Pacific at the approaches to the Asian mainland, and then annexed the Hawaiian Islands, which are of exceptional strategic importance in the central Pacific.

After the Spanish-American War, the U.S.A. entered a prolonged period of unrestrained rearmament. The Navy and Marines advanced to first place among the U. S. Armed Forces. It was precisely in naval forces that U. S. militarism discovered the instrument of its policy. The guiding principle of American military doctrine for many years became "a Navy second to none." American military thought was essentially aimed at a resolution of the problems of naval warfare. Its ideologue was the creater of the "theory of sea power," one of the greatest apologists for American imperialism, A. T. Mahan. His theory of the decisive influence of sea power on history is reflected to this day in the policy of the U.S.A.

The Russo-Japanese War. The history of Japan after the so-called Meiji bourgeois revolution is a history of continuous wars, serving as a basis for the development of yet another young imperialist state, appearing later than the other imperialist powers in the arena of struggle for the seizure of foreign territories.

The intensive industrial development of Japan, occurring in the course of her transformation from a feudal to a bourgeois nation, and her dependence on shipping and related branches of industry, as well as the assistance and support of the major imperialist powers, enabled the island state to rapidly develop a powerful Navy. Utilizing her Navy, Japanese imperialism acquired the capability of directing her expansionist aims toward the seizure of Chinese territories.

Brief respites between aggressive wars served only for the preparation of new wars. In the process, Japanese combat operations expanded each time. In 1874 she invaded Taiwan; in 1876 she occupied the Korean island of Changjiva Do; in 1876 she forced Korea to ratify an inequitable treaty, after which she quickly occupied Korea, which was under the control of China; and in 1879 she seized the Ryukyu Islands, one of the vassal states of China.

Japan's advantageous military-geographical position vis-a-vis other powers played a significant role in the development of her expansionist policy. She was situated close to a major target of expansion—Korea—which assured Japan of military superiority in this area over the other imperialist States. Moreover, Japan, being a protege of Great Britain and the U.S.A. in their struggle against other imperialist usurpers in the Far East, received economic, financial, diplomatic, and military support from these powers. The invasion of Taiwan, for example, was prepared under the immediate direction of the U.S.A. and, encouraged by Britain, Japan seized Changjiva Do and penetrated into Korea. Both of these powers attempted to use Japan for the struggle against Russia in the Far East.

At the same time as the penetration into Korea, ruling classes in Japan demanded cultivation of the rich Chinese market, striving to achieve equal rights and privileges there with the Western powers.

All of this led to a sharp aggravation of relations between Japan and China, resulting in the Sino-Japanese War of 1894-1895. Ruling circles in Japan dared to risk this war only because they were assured of the support of Great Britain, and as soon as she confirmed this, Japanese warships attacked a Chinese squadron without declaring war.

The Japanese, transporting their forces by sea, were able to forestall the Chinese from concentrating their ground forces in Korea and invading southern Manchuria. Then the Army, landing on the shores of the Yellow Sea in the vicinity of Chinhsien and Dairen, operating jointly with the Navy, seized the Liaotung Peninsula with the naval base at Port Arthur. Then the Japanese Army, having landed east of Weihai, occupied—together with the Navy—this major Chinese naval base.

As a result of the victory, Japan imposed an inequitable treaty on China, giving her privileges far exceeding those granted to the European and American imperialists. The Chinese island of Taiwan (Formosa) and the Liaotung Peninsula with the naval base at Port Arthur were annexed by Japan. Korea was completely wrested away from China. Moreover, Japan received an enormous indemnity.

Three European powers—Russia, Germany, and France—uneasy over the Japanese conquests and expansion of her influence in Asia, demanded from Japan a change in the provisions of the Sino-Japanese peace treaty. At the time, Russia, together with France and Germany, possessed imposing naval forces in Far Eastern waters, capable of cutting the maritime communications of the Japanese Army. Forced to reckon with the real power of the opposing navies, Japan relinquished the Liaotung Peninsula.

Thus the Japanese victory gave her new possibilities for the most intensive economic development. Militarism became the essence of this development: expanding industry directed its main efforts toward equipping the Army and Navy with modern weapons.

The Sino-Japanese War demonstrated the unusually important role of navies in the achievement of political objectives of States in the struggle to divide and redivide the world. It was precisely the Navy which ensured the concentration and superiority of the Japanese Army in Korea and Manchuria, and also broad maneuvers by ground forces and the opening of new attack zones in the theater of combat operations.

A significant confirmation of the increasing role of the Navy was the seizure in 1897–1898 by the major imperialist powers of the Chinese ports of Ch'ingtao, Weihai, and Port Arthur to base their Fleets.

Thus the Sino-Japanese War not only failed to eliminate international conflicts in the Far East—on the contrary, it aggravated them. The opposition of Russia, together with that of France and Germany, to the provisions of the peace treaty concluded at the end of the Sino-Japanese War, laid the foundation for an open political struggle between Russia and Japan. With the acquisition of a lease by Russia in 1898 in Kwangtung Province and the construction of a base for the Russian Pacific Squadron at Port Arthur, the situation became even more complicated.

In connection with the so-called "Boxer Rebellion", which broke out in China in 1900, all of the major imperialist rivals in the Far East sent troops there: Great Britain, Japan, the United States of America, Germany, France, and Russia—each striving, with the sacking of China, to grab the lion's share for itself.

After the occupation of Manchuria by Russia, the primary question in the Far East policy of Great Britain, Japan, and the U.S.A. became the ouster of the Russians from the regions they had seized and annexation of these areas. Japan, incited by Great Britain and the U.S.A., openly proceeded toward the unleashing of a war with Russia and intensively prepared for it. In 1902 Japan and Great Britain ratified a treaty aimed at Russia, clearly stipulating the obligation of the allies to maintain a fleet more powerful than the Russian Fleet in Far Eastern waters. Attempting to kindle a war between Japan and Russia, the U.S.A. hoped this would weaken them both, which would enable the Americans to seize key positions in the Pacific and in China. The U. S. President warned the Governments of France and Germany that if they rendered any assistance to Russia, America would enter on the side of Japan.

The Japanese Government laid great stress on the construction of a powerful navy, to which a major portion of the national budget and the indemnity received from China was devoted. The U.S.A. and Great Britain heavily subsidized Japan and in fact served as her arsenal. Specifically, practically all of the Japanese armorclad warships, possessing the best performance data and armament at the time, were built in British shipyards. The Naval and Army officers had had war experience in China and were quite familiar with the characteristics of the theater.

The preparation of Tsarist Russia for the impending war was viewed somewhat differently. Ruling circles in the country understood that their Far Eastern aspirations could only be realized through war. However, the strategic situation in the Far East developed unfavorably for Russia. The Siberian and Chinese-Eastern railroads still had not achieved full carrying capacity for continuous and rapid concentration and supply of Russian forces in the theater.

Despite the fact that the Russian Fleet was significantly numerically superior to the Japanese (in armorclads alone, Russia had 20, whereas Japan had six), the Tsarist Government, due to shortsightedness and strategic blunders, did not deploy numerically superior forces in the Pacific at the proper time.

As is evident from Table 1, the superiority of the Japanese Fleet over the Russian Fleet in the Far East was beyond dispute. Moreover, Russian warships were deployed in various seas. Thus, there were a total of eight armorclad warships in the Yellow Sea, which was the primary naval theater. The Japanese Navy, relying on a developed system of bases, was able to concentrate its operations. And, above all, warships of the Russian Fleet were considerably less prepared than the Japanese for combat operations.

Table 1   *Number of Warships in the Fleets in the Far East*[9]

Types of warships	Russia	Japan
Battleships	7	6
Armored cruisers	4	8
Cruisers	7	12
Destroyers and torpedo boats	37	47

[9]This and succeeding tables were compiled from data in *Morskoy atlas* (Maritime Atlas), Vol. III, Part I, Sheets 33 and 34.

The construction of bases for the Russian Navy in the Pacific was not completed, and Port Arthur was not a sufficiently reliable fortress, nor was it an equipped naval base. Individual progressive officers. (S. O. Makarov, R. I. Kondratenko, et al) understood the real state of affairs, but were unable to substantially alter it.

By early 1904, without preparing for war and without having concentrated her ground and naval forces in the Far East, Russia turned out to be isolated face to face with Japan, which was the strike force of the powerful bloc of international monopoly capital.

The immediate strategic Japanese objective in the war was to gain control of the sea, which presupposed the achievement of a surprise attack on the Russian Pacific Fleet and destruction of the squadron at Port Arthur and the Russian station ships in Korea and China. The landing of armies on the continent and the capture of Port Arthur, and defeat of the main Russian forces in Southern Manchuria, with the subsequent occupation of Manchuria and the Ussuri and Amur regions were also contemplated.

Taking advantage of a favorable situation, Japan launched a surprise attack on Russian ships at Port Arthur and Chemulpo during the night of 27 January (9 February) 1904 without declaring war. This attack significantly weakened the Russian squadron, but did not result in the establishment of Japanese domination of the sea.

Was it actually a surprise attack? Was there sufficient information on the Japanese preparation for war?

Repeated reports from the Russian naval representative in Japan concerning the preparation of the Japanese Fleet provided a thorough basis for anticipation of an attack. Thus, in early January he reported that reservists had been called up in Japan; steamships capable of taking on board two divisions of troops had been chartered; long-distance steamship runs had been suspended; and the Japanese Fleet was steaming to the shores of Korea. On 18 January, our representative reported on the laying of defensive mine fields by the Japanese, and on scales of military preparations which indicated Japan's ambitious plans. On 24 January he telegraphed news of the general mobilization occurring in Japan. On 26 January Vice Admiral S. O. Makarov conveyed his views to the Naval Minister concerning the danger involved in deploying the Port Arthur squadron in the outer roadstead. But all of these warnings were ignored.

When the situation at sea became critical for the Russians, Vice Admiral S. O. Makarov was named CinC of the Pacific Fleet. He was well acquainted with the enemy and the theater of combat operations, and was a recognized authority on naval tactics. However, the Tsarist Deputy in the Far East and the new CinC Pacific Fleet differed on the role of the Fleet in war, as well as on its use in developing situations. Despite the fact that Makarov's proposals to increase the combat readiness of the Fleet encountered insuperable obstacles, he continued to energetically prepare the Fleet for battle, and achieved a certain measure of success. But on 31 March (13 April) the flagship *Petropavlovsk* was blown up by Japanese mines. With the loss of the CinC, active operations of the Port Arthur squadron were suspended.

At the end of April, the situation at Port Arthur significantly worsened: the Japanese Second Army, which landed at Chinhsien, cut the base off from the Russian Army in Manchuria, and advanced to the fortress, acquiring the capability of shelling Russian warships with siege artillery. Therefore, the command decided to have the squadron break through to Vladivostok.

The relative strength of the forces (Table 2) in the battle, with the breakthrough on 28 July 1904, afforded some basis for hope of success, but due to the lack of initiative on the part of the Russian command, the Russian squadron did not execute the mission, and returned to Port Arthur in a weakened condition. In the unsuccessful military encounter, the slow speed, poorer armor plating, and poorer quality of the Russian naval guns played a role.

The Vladivostok cruiser detachment continued its operations, but this could not significantly affect the

Table 2   *Number of Warships Possessed by the Belligerents When the Russian Squadron Attempted to Break Through From Port Arthur to Vladivostok*

Types of warships	Russia	Japan
Battleships	6	4
Armorclads	—	1
Armored cruisers	—	4
Cruisers	4	5
Torpedo boats	8	18

Table 3   *Number of Warships in the Navies in the Far East In Event of Timely Arrival of the Second Pacific Squadron*

| Types of warships | Russia | | | Japan |
	Port Arthur and Vladivostok Squadrons	2nd Pacific Squadron	Total	
Battleships	7	8	15	6
Armorclads	—	—	—	2
Armored cruisers	4	1	5	8
Armored warships, coastal defense	—	3	3	—
Total no. of armored warships	11	12	23	16
Cruisers	7	8	15	15
Auxiliary cruisers	—	1	1	24
Destroyers and torpedo boats	37	9	46	63

course of the war at sea.

Thus, six months after the beginning of the war, having lost altogether only one of seven armored ships, the Russian Pacific Fleet practically ceased to represent an organized force capable of exerting a significant influence over the future course of the war. The Japanese acquired the capability of shipping by sea without interference, replenishing their forces operating on the Liaotung Peninsula and in Southern Manchuria with men and materiel. Meanwhile, the Russian Army, although well replenished but deprived of naval support, retreated to the north under Japanese attack.

On 24 August 1904, at a meeting with the Tsar, the belated decision was made to dispatch the Second Pacific Squadron from the Baltic. A timely linkup with the Port Arthur squadron could have given the Russians a numerical superiority in naval forces (Table 3) and could have radically changed the situation throughout the theater of combat operations in favor of Russia.

The Japanese command, foreseeing this, concentrated its main efforts against Port Arthur, in order to break the resistance of its defenders and destroy the squadron before the arrival of reinforcements from the Baltic. The Japanese siege group was reinforced and led a fierce attack against the fortifications at Port Arthur.

Rejecting the use of the still rather powerful forces to engage the enemy's naval forces, when the Fleet, through its operations, could have rendered maximum assistance to the besieged Port Arthur, the inept Tsarist generals decided to remove armament and men from the warships in order to use them directly for the land defense of the fortress. On 2 January 1905 they surrendered unconquered Port Arthur, although the possibilities for defense had not been exhausted.

On 2 (15) October 1904, the Second Pacific Squadron, under the command of Rozhdestvenskiy, began the transfer from the Baltic to the Far East. The history of the Russian Navy, and indeed of the navies of other States as well, has never known such a long and protracted voyage of an enormous force, consisting of various types of warships, whose crews had had no experience in steaming in company over great distances. The majority of coastlines followed by the squadron belonged to hostile Great Britain. With increasing distance from their western bases, the danger to the Russian warships of a surprise encounter with enemy naval forces increased, which significantly complicated the passage. However, the heroism of the Russian seamen enabled them to overcome all difficulties.

While the squadron was off the shores of Madagascar, they were informed of the fall of Port Arthur and the loss of the Port Arthur squadron. But the Tsar and his entourage, recognizing in the Second Pacific Squadron the last hope for victory in the war, did not revoke their decision to dispatch it to the East.

Having completed the unparalleled seven month voyage without loss, the Russian squadron entered Korea Bay on 14 May 1905. Here it was met by a Japanese Fleet which was more sophisticated, had prepared a long time for battle, and which relied on a system of nearby bases. The opponents had numerical parity in armored warships, but the Japanese Fleet had a considerable advantage over the Russian squadron in light forces (Table 4).

Moreover, the Japanese warships had an advantage over the Russian ships in the quality of their armament, armor, and speed (Table 5). The superiority of the Japanese Fleet naturally required a high degree of skill on the part of the Russian ships in order for them to achieve success. However, the squadron commander, Rozhdestvenskiy, with no faith in his own forces, even failed to develop a plan of action and left the initiative to the enemy.

Table 4 *Numerical Strength of the Russian Squadron and Japanese Fleet in the Battle of Tsushima*

Types of ships	Russia	Japan
Battleships	8	4
Armored cruisers	1	8
Armorclads, coastal defense	3	—
Total armored warships	12	12
Cruisers	8	16
Auxiliary cruisers	1	24
Destroyers and torpedo boats	9	63

Table 5 *Performance Data of Warships of the Russian Squadron and Japanese Fleet*

Characteristics of warships	Russia	Japan
Total No. of artillery rounds/min	134	360
Total weight of metal (kg) fired per minute	8190	21,949
Armored surface, %	40	61
Maximum speed, knots	17.5	20

Using their advantage in gunnery and speed, the strategy of the Japanese was to capture the leader of the Russian squadron using their main forces, put the flagships out of action and, thereby depriving the squadron of leadership, complete its defeat with subsequent night torpedo attacks.

Despite the heroism of the men of the ships of the Second Pacific Squadron, it suffered a cruel defeat. The majority of Russian ships were lost, and a small number of them were interned in foreign ports.

Thus Japan achieved control of the sea in the Far East. V. I. Lenin wrote: "The Russian Navy was finally destroyed. The war was irrevocably lost . . . We were confronted not only with a military defeat, but also a complete military breakdown of the aristocracy."[10]

After the defeat of Russian naval forces in the Battle of Tsushima, the question of peace between Russia and Japan arose. At that time, the severe defeats in war weighed heavily on the Tsarist government, as did the rise of the revolutionary movement in the country. It was convinced that to continue the war would be senseless, since it could result in the downfall of the aristocracy.

Granted, the possibility still existed of gradually creating a superiority in ground forces in the Manchurian theater; it did not offer any promise for a victorious conclusion of the war, since without a fleet Russia could not count on the return of Port Arthur and the transfer of combat operations to the Japanese islands. The development of hostilities on the Korean Peninsula without naval support likewise promised no success. The situation with respect to the defense of

[10]V. I. Lenin, *Ibid*, Vol. 10, p. 252.

the Russian Pacific coast was even worse—it was defenseless against attacks and landings by the Japanese Navy. There was an imminent danger of a Japanese invasion of Russia.

This was the effect of the loss of the Russian Fleet on the overall strategic situation in the Far East.

It should be noted that at this point Japan had likewise exhausted her resources and had to turn to the American President for mediation.

The degradation of Tsarist Russia, her governmental, economic, political, and military backwardness and a complete lack of understanding by ruling circles of the importance of sea power (which was the basic reason for the weakness of the Navy)—all of these factors brought Tsarism to military defeat. "The connection between the military organization of the country and its entire economic and cultural structure has never been as close as it is now . . . This time, as time and time again in history, war between an advanced nation and a backward one has played a great revolutionary role."[11] The true victors in this war were the imperialists of the U.S.A., Great Britain, and Germany. Their rivals in the Far East and Pacific were significantly weakened

[11] V. I. Lenin, *Ibid,* Vol. 9, p. 156.

To most Western historians, the Battle of Santiago, facing page, and the Battle of Port Arthur, above, are a classic coincidence wherein outmanned, outgunned, entrapped squadrons tried desperately—and vainly—to survive a hurricane of fire and reach the safety of blue water. To Nikolai Lenin, the wars themselves—the Spanish-American in 1898 and the Russo-Japanese, six years later—were also similar in that they were two of the main historical landmarks of ". . . Imperialism, the highest stage of capitalism."

and mired down. Russian Tsarism became a tributary of the Anglo-French bloc.

Under the Treaty of Portsmouth, Japan was awarded a concession in Kuantung, including Port Arthur and Dairen, and privileges in Korea. She was also awarded the southern section of the Manchurian Railroad, the southern half of Sakhalin Island and all of the Kurile Islands.

As a result of the grave lessons of war, broad sectors of Russian society were beginning to understand the importance of a navy. Here a significant role was played by the so-called "youth group," which was a mouthpiece of the huge bourgeoisie, displeased with Tsarism, and, yet, at the same time, fearful of revolution. The new spirit infused by naval officers from the "youth group" fostered the interest of the general public in the Navy.

Only the Tsarist government, as demonstrated by subsequent events, failed to draw the necessary conclusions from the bitter experience of war and did not change its attitude toward the naval component of the armed forces of the country. The construction of the Navy proceeded basically from considerations of prestige, and not from the true interests of the State. Therefore, they tried to build warships similar to foreign warships, without taking into account the conditions under which they would operate, and ignoring the requirements, unique to Russia, stemming from her geographical location.

One of the most important characteristics of the employment of the Russian Navy was the need for intertheater maneuvers, governed by the absence of the necessary quantity of naval forces in individual theaters.[12] Execution of the indicated maneuver necessitated overcoming a number of difficulties (the absence of bases, fortified points, etc.). A similar situation developed in large measure as a result of the loss by Russia

of a number of islands and overseas territories first discovered by Russian seafarers (incidentally, these losses likewise occurred because ruling circles in Russia failed to understand the importance of sea power).

From the aforementioned, it is obvious that resolution of the problem of intertheater maneuvers by naval forces required the construction in Russia of warships possessing great cruising range. Exceptional strategic foresight on the part of government officials was required in order to ensure a timely concentration of forces in the required theater.

It is indisputable that had the Rozhdestvenskiy squadron arrived in the Far East at the proper time (if only before the fall of Port Arthur), the war would have broken out later or its course would have been different.

It is evident from the above that every time ruling circles in Russia failed to properly emphasize development of the Navy and its maintenance at a level necessitated by contemporary demands, the country either lost battles in wars or its peacetime policy failed to achieve designated objectives.

However, the ruling circles of Tsarist Russia, despite repeated grave lessons demonstrating the absolute need of the State for sea power, still did not understand the importance of a navy in the achievement of political objectives.

---

[12] Russia was forced to have a separate fleet on each sea, which was usually weaker than the fleets of potential opponents in the given theater.

Commentary

By Vice Admiral Edwin B. Hooper, U. S. Navy (Retired)

A 1931 graduate of the Naval Academy, Vice Admiral Hooper was retained on active duty as Director of Naval History after retirement in 1970. His service at sea included: gunnery officer of *Washington* (BB-56) in World War II; Commander Destroyer Squadron 26; Commander Amphibious Group One; and Commander Service Force, U. S. Pacific Fleet, during the Vietnam War. He earned an MS degree from MIT, and served in a variety of assignments in research and development, including: with the Atomic Energy Commission, Assistant Chief of BuOrd, and Deputy CNO (Development). A graduate of the National War College, he established the Naval Long Range Studies Project and Institute of Naval Studies. He was the Navy Member of the Joint Logistics Review Board which carried out an in-depth study of logistics in the Vietnam War era. He is the author of *Mobility, Support, Endurance*.

In his third article, Admiral of the Fleet Gorshkov summarizes selected historical events from early in the 19th century to 1905 in a fashion appropriate for convincing naval officers, the command level of the armed forces, and other Soviet leaders of the importance of a powerful, modern, and well-prepared Navy in peace and war.

Although more narrowly oriented and nowhere nearly as rigorous, the approach of this particular article is somewhat reminiscent of that of Alfred Thayer Mahan in his *The Influence of Sea Power upon History*. Admiral Gorshkov does credit Mahan as the creator of the "theory of sea power," which he concluded is "reflected to this day in the policy of the U.S.A." Rather than directly addressing such a theory, the Soviet admiral uses historical cases of sea-power's influence to derive, for his present day Soviet readers, "repeated grave lessons demonstrating the absolute need of the State [Russia] for sea power." This he accomplishes by explaining what he sees as historical consequences to Russia of the "complete lack of understanding by ruling circles of the importance of sea power;" of their alleged failure to exploit technological advances in propulsion, armament, and armor; of the lack of a system of world-wide bases; of insufficient cruising ranges of Russian warships; and of deficiencies in training and preparation for war. In contrast, he highlights the benefits to Britain, France, the United States, and Japan of superior naval power during this period of history.

Admiral Gorshkov's overall appreciation of the roles of naval power is revealed by his emphasis on the "importance of a Fleet in international relations and in war." In regretting the defensive tendency of the Russian Navy in the Crimean War which "contradicted the essence of the combat activity of this, most mobile, type of force designed for operations at sea," he recognizes the importance of offensive naval operations. He supports a strong Army but points out that successful employment of the Army was largely nullified by superior enemy seapower during the Russo-Turkish and Russo-Japanese Wars. He stresses the extent of use of the presence of a Fleet by diplomats at peace talks.

As in an earlier article, Gorshkov attempts to demonstrate that the Russians do have a naval tradition. Claiming that the Russian people have an inherent "love of the sea" and make excellent "seafarers," he draws inspiration from the memorable voyages of exploration by Russians in the early 19th century. Writing for an internal audience, he does not place these accomplishments in perspective with the voyages of discovery of other nations.

Perhaps in consideration of aspirations for naval capabilities in the present era, Admiral Gorshkov particularly stresses the importance of technological superiority for the armed forces. Concentrating on the backwardness of the Tsarist Navy, he fails to mention that, as early as the Crimean War, Russia used shell guns in ship-to-ship engagements, that they planted electrical and chemical-contact mines in this war, or that they employed self-propelled torpedoes in the Russo-Turkish War.

The senior officer of the Soviet Navy is thinking in world-wide terms. He expresses regret that Russia did not gain possession over the islands and overseas territories discovered; that positions were lost in such far-flung areas as the Pacific Northwest, Hawaii, and New Guinea; that Russia lacked suitable bases for the Russo-Japanese War; and that "nations with powerful navies grabbed the lion's share of colonial possessions." Sensitive to relative military-geographic positions of the naval powers and the separated maritime frontiers of Russia, he stresses the importance of intertheater operations. As might be expected, Admiral Gorshkov highlights the importance of control of the Turkish straits, "the struggle for egress to the southern seas," "freedom of Russian navigation on the Mediterranean," and the influence of seapower on the Near and Middle East.

The main thrust of the article is summarized by the statement that, every time Russia "failed to properly emphasize development of the Fleet and its maintenance at a level necessitated by modern-day demands, the country either lost battles in wars or its peacetime policy failed to achieve designated objectives."

Of course, readers in the West will note many distortions or downright inaccuracies in the general history of the article. Gorshkov stresses European and American expansion in the 19th century, but he does not note the remarkable eastward expansion of Russia in the same period that resulted in the seizure of the entire northern portion of the Eurasian continent and the imposition of Russian culture over numerous national groups in that area. Britain, France, Japan, and particularly, the United States are painted as imperialists, aggressors, pillagers, despoilers, and plunderers. To this reader, the future seems ominous as long as Soviet leaders continue to reiterate such inflammatory interpretations to their people.

The First World War

With Commentary following the article by
Admiral Robert B. Carney, U. S. Navy (Retired)

EDITOR'S NOTE: *In the following chapter, cleared for publication in the Soviet Union on 29 April 1972, the admiral discusses events that took place within his own lifetime. Admiral Gorshkov's birthdate, 1910, occurred almost midway between two epochal episodes of modern Russian history: the defeat at Tsushima strait in 1904, and the overthrow of the Tsarist monarchy in 1917. More-over, the Russian world Sergei Georgievich Gorshkov entered continued to be wracked, as L. T. Heath has written, by "uprisings, strikes, bomb throwings, assassinations, mass arrests, exilings, executions, and imprisonings." It is against these backgrounds, personal and national, that the admiral's words should be weighed as he recounts and assesses, selectively, the events of World War I.*

---

*P*reparation for World War I. The uneven economic and political development of the capitalist states hardened their struggle for the redivision of the world. The imperialists had been split into two hostile groups: the alliance of the Central European Powers headed by Germany, and the Triple Entente headed by England.

The Kaiser's Germany, which led Europe in industrial production, was exploiting "only" 12.5 million people in colonies, while at the same time England, who trailed her considerably in level of production, was exploiting about 400 million people. Germanic impe-

On 7 November 1917, Vladimir I. Lenin emerged from four months of hiding to lead the overthrow of the Provisional Government and seize power in Russia. That evening, in his headquarters, Lenin talked with the mustachioed editor of Pravda, Joseph Dzhugashvili, whose party name was Stalin.

rialism had set itself the goal of seizing the colonies belonging to England, and, having deprived her of her naval superiority which ensured the integrity of the British Empire, of bringing the Balkan countries under its influence, of creating its own semicolonial empire in the Near East, and of taking the Ukraine, the Polish, and Baltic areas from Russia. British imperialism, in turn, wanted to destroy the dangerous pretender to its colonial riches. Tsarist Russia, on the other hand, wanted to divide Turkey, seize Constantinople, wrest Galicia away from Austria-Hungary, and strengthen her influence on the Balkan peninsula.

These and other contradictions between the capitalist countries predetermined the character of the approaching war as an imperialist world war, i.e., a war "between two groups of plundering great powers over the distribution of colonies, over the robbing of other nations, and over advantage and privileges in the world market."[1]

The accelerated preparation of armed forces ran parallel with the political preparation for the war, which had been going on for a long time. Prior to the outbreak of war, the military-economic potential of Germany exceeded the French and Russian potentials taken together, and was approximately equal to the potential of the entire Entente.

Germany remained in the lead in the land army arms race and in their technical level. However, in the naval arms race, despite all efforts, Britain remained ahead.

In the building up of the navies in the countries of both coalitions, special attention was devoted to a thorough analysis of the Russo-Japanese War with its great naval engagements. The basic conclusion drawn by the main imperialist states was the great influence that combat actions at sea had had on the overall course of the war. Therefore, they proceeded with the accelerated build-up of naval forces. Another important conclusion was the recognition of the dominant role of heavy armored gunnery ships in warfare at sea. In accordance with this, the efforts of all of the sea powers were directed toward the creation of squadrons of major gunnery ships.

The basis of the tactics of the naval armored forces based on the experience of the battle of Tsushima, was to "envelop the head" of the enemy's squadron and concentrate all of the fire power of the guns on the leading ships. In connection with this, powerful battleship-dreadnaughts were built at an accelerated pace, armed not with four large caliber guns as in the Russo-Japanese War, but with 10 to 12 guns, and greatly surpassing the older ships in size, armor, and speed.

The torpedo, which was widely used for the first time by surface ships in the Russo-Japanese War, was acknowledged to be the next most important naval weapon after guns. In accordance with this, mass construction of destroyers and also of light cruisers having torpedo armament in addition to guns was expanded.

The remaining questions of naval construction were put off as secondary, although the level of science and technology of that day already permitted the construction of rather advanced submarines.

The Mahan theory of "control of the sea," considered indisputable, according to which only a general engagement of major line forces could lead to a victory, had a considerable effect on the one-sided trend in the development of navies. This theory did not at all take into account not only the near-future prospects, but even the notable trends in the development of naval technology.

Russia's preparation for war proceeded in a difficult situation. The results of the Russo-Japanese War had revealed the precariousness of the autocracy, and its inability to successfully decide the basic questions of state policy. Revolutionary speeches and armed uprisings, begun by the *Potemkin,* did not cease prior to the outbreak of war, and shook the Russian empire.

Russia's economic backwardness and financial difficulties also had an influence on her preparation for war. She was the main source of manpower reserves for the Entente in the forthcoming war. The large military program of the Tsarist government, undertaken in 1913 and supported by France and Great Britain, was scheduled to last three to four years, and it would sharply alter the relationship of the forces of the coalitions. That is why the Entente was interested in delaying the outbreak of war for several years, while Germany, on the other hand, was hastening to begin it. In this connection, V. I. Lenin wrote: "Is it surprising that the two robbers attacked before the three robbers managed to obtain the new knives which they had ordered?"[2]

The Tsarist government could not fail to take into account the great length and vulnerability of the maritime borders on the Baltic and Black Seas and was forced, along with the expenditures for the development of the ground forces, to devote at the same time funds for restoring the fleets which supported the stability of the strategic flanks of the entire front of the armed struggle. The fact of the matter is that after the Russo-Japanese War, the Baltic Fleet was weakened and incapable of engaging the German Fleet, and the Black Sea Fleet, although it appeared rather imposing in comparison with the Turkish Fleet, was obsolescent. In the Far East, the Russian Fleet did not represent a serious combat force, and there was no fleet whatsoever in the Northern naval theater. The Tsarist government, which was constrained by economic and financial difficulties, was slow in building up the Navy. The command was not clear on what kind of Navy Russia needed and what kind of missions it was supposed to perform in the forthcoming war. Only in 1907, after the naval arms race had already begun in the other countries, were the decisions made on these questions. Thus, the Baltic Fleet was assigned the task of preventing the landing of an enemy landing force in the eastern part of the Gulf of Finland. Getting ahead of myself, it should be recognized that it prosecuted this mission brilliantly, having adopted as a basis for the plan of military operations the idea of a defensive battle in the previously prepared Nargen-Porkkala-Udd mine and gunnery positions.

---

[1] V. I. Lenin. *Poln. sobr. soch.* (Complete Collected Works), Vol. 27, p. 1.

[2] *Ibid.* Vol. 26, p. 122.

The Black Sea Fleet received the mission to be ready to begin the struggle for free access to the Mediterranean Sea. After the strengthening of the Turkish Fleet with the German cruisers *Goeben* and *Breslau*, this mission was altered: the Fleet was supposed to destroy the enemy's naval forces in the mine and gunnery positions near Sevastopol, and then take actions connected with establishing conditions favorable for Russia in the Black Sea straits.

Having defined the missions of the fleets, Russia proceeded with their construction. The new Russian warships were constructed on the basis of advanced science and were the best warships of their type in the world at that time; however, their construction proceeded extremely slowly. In 1909, the battleships for the Baltic Fleet were laid down; in 1911, those for the Black Sea Fleet; and in 1912, the battle cruisers for the Baltic. However, they did not manage to build them before the outbreak of war, and both Fleets entered it having obsolescent major ships in their inventory.

At the same time, the Russian Navy rapidly upgraded almost all forms of the weapons and combat means, which, as a rule, surpassed analogous foreign models with respect to their performance characteristics. Many successes were also achieved in combat training.

The Conditions of the Navies at the Outbreak of War. In accordance with the views of the role of the types of naval forces, by the outbreak of the First World War the main sea powers had built vast battleship fleets. The largest of them was the British Fleet. The German Navy was growing and developing furiously, although numerically it still lagged behind the British (Table 1). The overall relative strength of the naval forces for the coalition headed by Germany became still worse after the entry into the war of Japan, the U.S.A., and Italy on the side of the Entente.

Moreover, Britain had at her disposal a widespread system of bases in the Home Country and in the colonies, and her geographical position in relation to the bases of the German Navy created favorable conditions for a naval blockade of Germany and for operations against its surface ships. Germany, on the other hand, had a system of bases suitable for defense against attacks from the sea, but they did not ensure direct access to the ocean. In addition, the basing system permitted a rapid concentration of forces in the Baltic or North Seas (but the possibility of clashes with the superior British Fleet had to be considered when exiting beyond their limits).

The French Navy (and later the Italian), by agreement with the British, deployed in the Mediterranean Sea. The developed system of bases in the central and western parts of the Mediterranean permitted the Austro-Hungarian Fleet to be shut up in the Adriatic at the outbreak of the war.

The German naval command counted on weakening the British Navy by successive destruction of its forces dispatched to blockade the German shores. It was intended to equalize the naval forces in this manner, and later to defeat the British in a general engagement. The implementation of this concept would have permitted Germany to operate freely on the seas, and then strangle England with a naval blockade (it was intended to employ cruisers widely in combatting British shipping), and to achieve the ultimate goals of the war—to divide up the world in Germany's favor and create the strongest colonial empire.

It is interesting to note that naval operations were worked out by the Germans with particular caution due to the fear of losing major combatants. In this connection, the Baltic theater initially was regarded as secondary for the German Navy. The participation of naval forces in support of ground troops was not planned at all.

The plan of the British Admiralty called for an economic blockade of Germany (by cutting off her sea

Table 1. The Relative Strengths of the Navies at the Outbreak of the War

Ship types	Entente				Central Powers		
	England	France	Russia	Total	Germany	Austria-Hungary	Total
Dreadnought-battleships & battlecruisers	29	4	—	33	19	3	22
Pre-dreadnought-battleships	40	17	9	66	22	9	31
Cruisers	82	24	12	118	44	10	54
Destroyers	225	81	62	368	144	16	160
Submarines	76	38	15	129	28	6	34

By the outbreak of World War I, the British and Germans had built impressive battleship fleets, the largest of which was the Royal Navy's, above. But Germany, whose pre-dreadnought battleships numbered barely half as many as England's, was closing fast in numbers of dreadnoughts and battlecruisers.

commerce), and was directed toward establishing control of the sea (by prosecuting the blockade of the German shores and constantly keeping, in home country bases, line forces capable of inflicting a decisive defeat on the German Navy under favorable conditions).

The German and British Fleets in the War. "The German bourgeoisie, in spreading stories of a defensive war on its part, in fact had chosen the most convenient moment for war from its point of view, using its own latest advancements in military equipment."[3]

The German plan for the war on land, which called for the lightning-like defeat of the French Army and the capture of Paris, failed. In the Western theater, both

[3] *Ibid.* Vol. 26. p. 16.

Table 2. Composition of Forces Participating in the Battle
of Jutland

Forces	England	Germany
Dreadnought-battleships and battlecruisers	37	21
Pre-dreadnought-battleships	—	6
Cruisers	34	11
Destroyers	79	31
Submarines	—	11

sides went over to protracted trench warfare. The German strategy on the main Western Front was mired down.

The operations of the raiding squadrons and individual raiders deployed by Germany against the ocean communications of the Entente also did not lead to the expected results. The friendly neutrality of the U.S.A. toward the Entente and the entry of Japan into the war on its side also aided the liquidation of the German threat to the ocean shipping of the Triple Entente. By 1914 the main raider forces of the Germans had already been destroyed and their bases in the German colonies had been captured.

The operations of the German Navy with respect to weakening the British Fleet also had no success. However, the German Naval command still hoped to decide the outcome of the war in her favor by a victory over the British in the major naval engagement which soon followed.

The Battle of Jutland (31 May–1 June 1916) was the greatest naval engagement of the First World War. The main line forces of the British and German Navies participated in it (Table 2).

In analyzing it, many observers have noted the indecisiveness displayed by the fleet commanders (especially the British), and the reluctance to risk major combatants in order to achieve complete victory. Moreover, several of them came to the conclusion that the

Battle of Jutland did not influence the course of the armed struggle.

In our view, such a conclusion is not sufficiently objective. The fact is that in this engagement Germany had the goal of defeating the British Fleet to ensure freedom of action in order to crush England by a subsequent unrestricted naval blockade, i.e., to achieve a sharp change in the course of the war to its advantage. A victory by the German forces would have permitted the Central Powers to extract themselves from a naval blockade whose severe effect was already being felt by the German economy. But the German Fleet did not achieve the established goal.

Great Britain, on the other hand, was striving through this battle to retain her existing position on the seas and to strengthen the blockade operations against Germany. She essentially achieved these goals.

Thus, the Battle of Jutland determined the immutability of the further course of the prolonged war and aided in keeping it within its former channel. This promised no success to Germany, since it meant the loss of hopes to lift the naval blockade of her shores, a further erosion of military might, and the loss of the war. In addition, the Battle of Jutland showed that it was impossible to transfer to modern conditions the experience of the Russo-Japanese War with respect to employing major battleship-type commands as the main and solitary forces for achieving victory in an engagement at sea. Therefore, it was a landmark which has been noted in the history of the naval art as the moment of recognition of the need for concerted action by different types and means of naval forces.

Unrestricted Submarine Warfare. In January 1917, V. I. Lenin wrote: "In the 29 months of the war the resources of both imperialist coalitions have been sufficiently determined, all or almost all of the possible allies . . . have been drawn into the carnage, and the forces of the armies and navies have been tested and retested, measured and remeasured."[4] "A turn has

---
[4] *Ibid.* Vol. 30, p. 340.

A desultory submarine blockade of Britain had been conducted since 1914; but when, in February 1917, Germany threw caution to the winds and began unrestricted submarine operations, two of the first to personally feel the tightening noose were these survivors of the English steamer Wathfield, *which was torpedoed early in February and sank with a loss of 18 lives.*

begun in world politics from an *imperialist war,* endowing the people with the greatest suffering, . . . to an *imperialist peace.*"[5]

The erosion of military-economic resources and the growth of the revolutionary movement in the belligerent countries forced their governments to seek avenues to hasten an end to the war.

In this connection, the economies of Great Britain and France, being supplied by sea with the resources of almost the entire world, were in a more satisfactory condition, and this made it possible for them to wage a prolonged war and count on success. Germany, on the other hand, due to the naval blockade, experienced

[5] *Ibid.* Vol. 30, pp. 339–340.

a sharp deficiency in raw materials and foodstuffs, and therefore a prolonged war promised defeat for her. Austria-Hungary held on only because of the German bayonets and was taking a line toward a separate exit from the war. In Russia, the revolutionary movement, which Tsarism was already incapable of coping with, was spreading.

Under these conditions Germany, having lost hope of rapidly ending the war through the efforts of the ground forces and not having achieved her aims in the Battle of Jutland, saw what seemed to her to be a way out in unrestricted submarine operations against the sea communications of Great Britain in order to force her to capitulate before the arrival of the American troops in Europe. In unrestricted submarine warfare the German leaders, including also the command of the ground forces, saw the only and final possibility, if not to achieve the victory, at least to conclude an honorable peace.

Germany began the submarine blockade of England soon after the outbreak of war, but she prosecuted it very indecisively due to inadequate forces and also due to the fear of straining relations with the neutral states, primarily with the U.S.A. However, in February 1917, unrestricted submarine operations were begun at the insistence of Hindenburg and Ludendorff. Of the approximately 150 units in service, about 40 operated constantly against the British communications. Submarines and mine barriers spread the mine danger to regions which until then had been considered safe in this respect. The losses of the enemy's merchant fleet rose steadily. Despite the efforts undertaken by the British, the production of merchant marine tonnage was only about 10% of the losses. As a result of the unrestricted submarine warfare, the lack of the necessary spare parts began to be felt on the ground front, and Great Britain herself seemed to be on the verge of economic catastrophe, nearly forced to her knees.

Vast ASW forces of the Entente, including a large number of ships, airplanes, and dirigibles, were thrown into the battle against the submarines. A strict convoy system was introduced, an ASW defense for the bases and their approaches was set up, minefields off the coast of Germany were strengthened, and they began to lay a minefield between the Orkney Islands and Norway, which was supposed to close off the submarines' access to the ocean from the North Sea. However, despite this, the merchant marine losses continued to be high.

Only in the latter part of the war did the effectiveness of the submarines drop, primarily due to the fact that the German command, after having assigned the prosecution of the main effort to them, failed to divert other naval forces to support their operations (which was particularly necessary in connection with the growth of the ASW forces of the Entente countries.) In response to the sharp increase in the British ASW defense forces and means, the Germans merely put new submarines into service. However, their introduction turned out to be too little too late (due to the absence of support of their operations). In the final analysis, Germany turned out to be incapable of executing the mission of a submarine blockade against England. As for the members of the Entente, having received considerable support and aid from the U.S.A., they continued to increase their efforts in the battle against the submarines. In 1918, about 5,000 ships of various types, 2,000 aircraft, and a large number of dirigibles and barrage balloons were already being used for this purpose. More than 700,000 men participated in ASW operations.[6] The decrease in the effectiveness of the blockade also fostered an increase in the replacement of merchant marine tonnage (in 1918, replacement tonnage exceeded losses).

Yet despite this, the submarine blockade of Great Britain had a considerable effect on the overall course of the war. The German submarine forces paralyzed the enemy's shipping for a prolonged period. The allies'

[6] V. Belli. *Deystviya flotov na severnom, sredizemnomorskom i okeanskikh teatrakh* (Naval Operations in the Northern, Mediterranean, and Oceanic Theaters), Vol. 2, Voyenizdat, p. 188.

losses from the merchant marine required vast expenditures for the expansion of new ship construction and the building up of ASW forces and means.

German submarines achieved many successes in the battle against British surface combatants. And, although the latter did not lose the ability to execute the missions assigned to them, the operation of the British surface ships was at least significantly hindered.

All of this permitted Germany to continue the war.

At the same time we must point out a great miscalculation of the German command: it did not employ submarines to sever military sea shipping, which was widely used by the Entente countries.

The Russian Navy in the War. Combat operations in the Baltic theater had a considerable effect on the overall course of the war on the Russo-German front. The success of the groupings of troops in the strategic maritime sectors to a great degree depended on the situation at sea, which in turn could not fail but to have an effect on the state of the entire front.

The operations of the Baltic Fleet against the sea communications of the enemy had special significance, both under conditions of the blockade of the German coast in the North Sea and within the overall plan for damaging the German economy. The Baltic Fleet successfully prosecuted this mission. The blockade operations in the southern part of the sea, where in the fall of 1914 and in the course of 1915 mine laying operations were conducted secretly and on a wide scale, paralyzing the enemy's warships and transports, should be considered one of the brightest pages in the Fleet's history. The Germans were forced to reduce sea transport operations (particularly of Swedish iron ore which they needed), and for a long time to refrain from active operations against the Russians in the Baltic.

In order to produce a favorable situation at the beginning of the war, a defensive system was built up in the Baltic theater including the central mine and gunnery position, which, together with the fortifications of Revel and Sveaborg, was the main center of defense. In the course of the war, the system was strengthened by forward fortified positions in the Moon Sound and Åbo-Åland Islands. In the rear of the defensive system was the fortified Kronstadt region. The defense of the Gulf of Finland safely ensured the security of the capital from enemy attacks from the sea. Its strength was so evident that the Germans, having lost the cruiser *Mardeburg* (August 1914) and seven of their newest destroyers (November 1916) in attempts to break through, no longer risked overcoming it. The position covering the entrance to the Gulf of Riga was tested twice by major German naval forces, but showed itself to be sufficiently strong. This was especially vividly displayed in the Moon Sound operation in support of the right flank of the front which extended to the coast on the Gulf of Riga.

The Moon Sound operation (12 to 20 October 1917), in which the entire main body of the German Fleet (Table 3) participated, had the far-reaching goal of uniting the Central Powers, Britain, the U.S.A., and France in the struggle against the Russian Revolution. In analyzing this event, V. I. Lenin wrote: "Does not the complete inaction of the British Fleet in general, and also of the British submarines in the German seizure of Ezel prove . . . that a plot had been hatched between the Russian and British imperialists and between Kerensky and the Anglo-French capitalists to turn over St. Petersburg to the Germans and to smother the Russian Revolution by this route? I think that this proves it."[7]

Despite the limited personnel strength of the naval force dispatched to defend the Moon Sound, they did their duty to the end. A vivid example of this was the actions of the personnel of the pre-dreadnought-battleship *Slava*, the gunboat *Khabryy*, and the destroyer *Grom*. The Baltic Fleet foiled the plan to stifle the Russian Revolution, and the Germans, in suffering costly losses (Table 4), succeeded only in capturing the Moon Sound Islands. The German command acknowledged that this "victory" did not permit the achievement of the intended goal.

By its actions in the southern strategic area, the Black Sea Fleet had a considerable effect on the course of the military campaigns on the Caucasian (and later also on the Rumanian) front. Initially, the Turkish Fleet was inferior to the Russian and did not undertake active operations. However, after the introduction into its composition of the German battlecruiser *Goeben* and the cruiser *Breslau*, which were faster than the old Russian warships, the relative strength of forces in the Black Sea changed significantly. Availing themselves of this, the German command on 29 and 30 October 1914 organized a raiding operation against Odessa, Sevastopol, Feodosiya, Kerch, and Novorossiysk which was the act by which Turkey entered the war. Due to the confusion of the Black Sea Fleet command, the enemy carried off the raid with impunity.

After this, the Russian Fleet, beefed up by new battleships of the *Imperatritsa Mariya* class, was able to blockade the surface ships of the German-Turkish Fleet in the straits, to go over to systematic operations off the enemy coast, and render direct aid to the maritime flanks of the ground fronts with gunfire support, the landing of landing parties, and transporting troops and supplies. Moreover, by mass mine-laying and oper-

ations against ports and ships at sea, the Black Sea Fleet hindered the sea communications of the enemy and forced him to change over to shipping exclusively with small ships, which had a negative effect on troops, logistics, and the economy of the main areas of Turkey (by cutting off the supply of coal, oil, and other forms of supplies).

Throughout the entire war, the Black Sea Fleet ac-

Table 3.   Forces in the Moon Sound Operation

Forces	Germany	Russia
NAVAL		
Battleships & battlecruisers	11	2
Cruisers	9	3
Gunboats	—	3
Destroyers	68	33
Escort ships	5	9
Submarines	6	3 (Eng)
Minelayers	1	2
Netlayers	3	3
Minesweepers & patrol boat-sweepers	95	17
Transports	40	15
Auxiliaries	about 70	9
GROUND FORCES		
Infantry	about 25,000 men (marine corps)	about 10,000 men (island garrison)
Cavalry	—	about 2,000 men
AVIATION		
Airplanes	94	30
Dirigibles	6	—

Table 4.   Losses in the Moon Sound Operation

Type of loss	Germany	Russia
Sunk	13 destroyers 6 sweepers	1 battleship (scuttled by crew)
Damaged	3 battleships 14 destroyers 3 sweepers 1 sweeper tender	1 battleship 1 cruiser 3 destroyers 2 gunboats

[7] V. I. Lenin. *op. cit.* Vol. 34, p. 347.

tively prepared for the execution of one of the main missions in the South—the landing of a major landing force to capture the Bosphorus. However, this operation was never carried out even though the ships repeatedly approached the Bosphorus and fired at targets on its shores.

The experience gained by the Baltic and Black Sea Fleets in the First World War had a great effect on the further development of the naval art of the Motherland.

Some Conclusions on the Influence of the Navies on the Course of the War. The fate of the First World War was sealed on the ground fronts. The main masses of troops and military equipment were concentrated precisely here, and precisely here the belligerents suffered their main losses. The conduct of combat operations on land consumed the greater part of the economic resources of the coalitions. Although the war was positional in character, the insignificant movement of troops into the depth of the enemy's territory did not once create a critical situation fraught with the sudden capture or withdrawal from the war of one country or another in the coalitions. The German Army, for example, immediately upon the outbreak of war penetrated into French territory, and all subsequent operations were conducted there. However, this in no way brought France toward defeat.

The Eastern Front played the greatest role in disrupting the German plans: at the beginning of the war the offensive of the Russian troops in Galicia and

The Russian pre-dreadnought battleship Slava, *having sustained a half-dozen severe hits from two German battleships on 17 October 1917, limped back with her squadron toward the northern Moon Sound but, afire and unable to enter the Moon Sound canal, she was scuttled in order to block the canal's entrance.*

Eastern Prussia diverted considerable German forces from the Western Front (therefore, to a certain degree the Russians were the creators of the "miracle on the Marne"). The activity of the Russian Army in 1915 permitted the allies to fortify the trench front in the West. The Brusilov offensive in 1916 saved Italy from defeat and aided the emergence of Rumania on the side of the Entente. However, these successes in the war by Russia as well as the further seizures by Germany on the Eastern Front did not fundamentally change the situation in the land theaters of military operations.

The struggle in the oceanic and sea theaters in the First World War did not play such a decisive role as in the earlier wars. However, the decisive character of naval actions in individual strategic sectors in several cases produced the severest crisis situations influencing the overall course of the armed struggle (for example, as was indicated above, the German submarine blockade of 1917 put Britain on the threshold of catastrophe).

The dependence of the British economy on imported raw materials, and also on the fact that without a supply of food products the British population would have been threatened with starvation, made her especially sensitive to a naval blockade. And the German submarine forces delivered an attack of staggering force in this direction. During the war they sunk more than 11 million tons making up 65% of the British merchant marine, which was the largest merchant marine of the prewar era.

Great Britain managed to avoid catastrophe·only owing to errors by the German command, which committed a strategic blunder and did not provide for a timely increase in the necessary size of its submarine forces and for widescale measures with all the power of its own fleet in support of their operations against the ocean communications.

The increase in Britain's ASW forces and the entry of the U.S.A. into the war with its strong Navy, in the final analysis, led to Germany losing the battle for control of ocean communications.

The armed struggle at sea had a serious effect (of a strategic nature) on the course of operations and campaigns in the ground theaters of military operations. This was displayed both in the German submarine blockade of Britain and in the long British blockade of the German coast. It was precisely as a result of the blockade operations of the British Fleet that Germany was cut off from her colonies, and lost markets and sources of raw materials overseas.

For Germany, the most important condition for achieving victory was the shortness of the war, and the transformation of it into a protracted war was equivalent to defeat. The navies of the Entente members played a great role in converting the *Blitzkreig* into a prolonged armed struggle. Therefore Schlieffen's plan for a "lightning-like war" lost its meaning at the very onset because, even if the Germans had taken Paris, France would have been able to continue the struggle, being supported by the resources of her colonies with the aid of the Navy and the aid of the British Empire, and subsequently also of the U.S.A.

The desire of the allies to stifle the German economy found expression in a whole system of methods of warfare, the main one being the blockade carried out by the Navy according to schedule. It had an effect not only on the armed forces of the Germans, but also on their wellspring, the economy, thereby in the final analysis depriving Germany of her advantage in technical equipment of the Army and Navy and shutting up her merchant marine in her own ports. It is true that Germany retained trade through the neutral countries contiguous to her borders (Denmark, Holland, and Switzerland), but she was not able to localize the effects of the systematic naval blockade.

The blockade also had an exceptional effect on the political condition and morale of the population.

The victory of the Great October Revolution in Russia and her revolutionary withdrawal from the war activated the masses in Germany. As a result, a revolutionary explosion also occurred there in which the Navy played the role of the fuse: the uprising in it was the beginning of the revolution in Germany. On 28 October 1918, the sailors aboard the battleship *Markgraf* refused to obey the officers. They were joined by the crews of other ships who on 5 November seized the main base at Kiel.[8] The revolutionary movement rapidly spread to the troops and throughout the country. Under these conditions the impossibility of continuing the imperialistic war became evident, and this forced the German government in spite of the difficult conditions to ask the enemies for the immediate conclusion of an armistice.

On 11 November 1918, the First World War was concluded with the signing of the conditions of the armistice in the forest of Compiegne. The conference which convened in Paris worked out the peace treaty which was signed on 28 June 1919 at Versailles. Peace treaties with Germany's allies were concluded in the following year. All of them together made up the postwar Versailles system reflecting the relative strength of the forces of the imperialists at the termination of the war. However, this ratio could not remain constant because the unevenness of the development of the imperialist powers exceeded the short life of the peace. The fragility of the Versailles system was exacerbated by its anti-Soviet trend, and by the fact that it was in contradiction to the basic interests of the masses. Thus, the Versailles Peace Agreement not only did not eliminate the contradictions between imperialist countries, it, quite to the contrary, gave birth to new ones. It was not able to and did not put an end to war, but only to a degree regulated the conditions under which the preparation for new wars was begun, again threatening the entire world.

In this regard, V. I. Lenin wrote: "This entire international system, order, which is being maintained by the Versailles Peace Agreement, is resting on a volcano . . ."[9]

In analyzing the role of navies in the era of imperialism, it is easy to note that just as at the dawning of its development—in the period of the seizing of colonies and the division of the world—navies played

---

[8]Dates given by Ye. Tarle, *Sochineniye* (Works), Vol. V, p. 436.

[9]V. I. Lenin, *op. cit.* Vol. 41, p. 353.

a significant role both in the wars which were abundant in this era, and as a weapon of state policy in the periods between armed conflicts. Therefore, after every major war, the trends in naval development and construction were defined with ever greater care in order, while still at peace, to ensure one's own superiority over the enemy fleet not only in numbers, but also in the fire-power of the main types of combatants. A country possessing this kind of superiority strived to employ its own naval forces as an important political instrument to create definite prestige in the international arena and in mutual relations with other states.

It was precisely for these reasons that Germany was deprived of her rights to have a Navy and to build submarines (for herself or anybody else). Her main surface forces and all of her submarines were turned over to the Entente countries. In addition, the victors received all of the merchant ships greater than 1,500 tons and half of the smaller ships. The equipment of all of the shipyards was turned over to England as compensation for the German warships sunk by German crews in defiance of the Treaty. The severe fate which befell the German Navy attested to the importance which the imperialist powers attached to it.

After the First World War stimulated the sharp growth of the U. S. naval forces, the British Navy lost its leading position and Britain was forced to renounce its "two-power standard"[10] which had been firmly adhered to up to the war. Now she maintained her Navy with difficulty at the level of the strongest—the American Navy.

In analyzing the course of the armed conflicts in the naval theaters in the First World War, one must not fail to note that the trend in the struggle of the navies for control of the sea continued: it was regarded as an important factor ensuring the achievement of strategic and operational goals in the oceanic and sea theaters of military operations.

The supporting of the movement of large bodies of troops across the sea and oceans was a typical mission of the navies in this war.

In addition, it is essential to note the almost complete repudiation of such a form of joint naval and army operations as amphibious operations: actually only one attempt was made to carry out a major landing operation in the area of the Dardanelles. However, the allied operation did not achieve its goal, and this circumstance for a long time held back the development of the theory and practice of such operations in foreign navies.

It should be noted that the retrospective method

[10] According to this "standard" the British Navy was supposed to be equal in power to the two strongest fleets of the other states.

prevailing among the naval powers for determining the character and form of employment of navies in a future war without taking into account imminent changes in the development of science, technology, and production, and also the appearance of new forms of weaponry often did not permit the bourgeois theoreticians to foresee the development of naval forces. And only another military clash revealed the utter falseness of this method.

Thus, the course of the military actions at sea showed that the transfer of the experience from the Russo-Japanese War to the First World War was not justified. In this connection, the belligerents were forced to alter the trend in the construction of their own naval forces significantly right in course of the armed conflict. In particular, it became clear in the First World War that submarines, and not major gunnery ships as in the Russo-Japanese War, represented the main threat both for the navies and for the economies of the belligerents. It was precisely the growth of submarines and the means for combatting them which turned out to be the most furiously developed in the course of the war in comparison with the other forms of naval forces.

The retrospective method was essentially the only method for determining the trend in the development of navies under feudalism and at the start of premonopolistic capitalism, when science and technology were developing relatively slowly. However, in the era of imperialism when the rates of development have increased considerably, it no longer can be the solitary and main method for determining the trend in construction of naval forces, much less to determine the methods for their employment in combat. The constantly growing complexity of the designs of ships and their equipment to an ever greater degree has hindered the correction of the errors in the naval construction trends adopted in the prewar years. Whereas Peter I was able to build an entire fleet during the war with Sweden, in the 20th century it is impossible to carry out such a task even with the greatest efforts by all of the state's resources.

In constructing a modern Navy it is essential that it be based on scientific prediction of the development of science and technology and on the forecasting of the probable conditions of combat employment of naval forces. Moreover, it must be taken into account that the construction of a ship takes years.

The First World War clearly showed that the concerted action of various types of naval forces and means had become an indispensable condition of armed combat at sea and that the construction of balanced navies had become the most important trend in their construction. An analysis of combat experience leads to the conclusion for the need to give preference to the development of new, highly promising types of forces whose employment will to the greatest degree correspond to the conditions of future armed combat.

However, the adherence to already outmoded methods of determining the prospects for naval development which have taken root over the centuries did not permit the mapping out of the correct paths for their postwar construction. In particular, there was still an overestimation of the importance of major gunnery ships, a clear underrating of the capabilities of aviation, and completely insufficient attention was given to the construction of powerful submarine forces. The retribution for these errors followed in the very first months of the Second World War. For Britain and the U.S.A., this resulted in great losses of major surface ships from enemy air strikes, while Fascist Germany, who had gained the greatest experience in the employment of submarine forces, but did not take it into account when rebuilding her Navy, was forced to make a cardinal change in the trend of its construction in the course

of World War II.

In conclusion it should be noted that as the First World War once more showed, in the era of imperialism, the navies play a significant role in the armed conflicts of states, and, in the periods between the wars, "the political force at sea," as F. Engels[11] called navies, continue to have a most important significance as a political weapon of the great powers.

Recognizing the essential role of navies in war and in peace, the imperialist powers repeatedly attempted in the period after the First World War to regulate the growth of naval arms in special conferences (it is interesting that other forms of armed forces were not subjected to this). However, as is well known, all of these attempts did not lead to a reduction of the navies of the powers, and from the mid-1930s a new unrestrained, and in no way regulated, naval arms race began.

[11] F. Engels. *Izbrannyye voyennyye proizvedeniya* (Selected Military Works), Voyenizdat, 1957, p. 18.

Commentary

By Admiral Robert B. Carney, U. S. Navy (Retired)

A graduate of the U. S. Naval Academy with the Class of 1916, Admiral Carney was Gunnery and Torpedo officer of the USS *Fanning* when she sank the German U-58 in November 1917. His World War II service included convoy/ASW operations (1941 to 1942), command of the cruiser *Denver* (1942 to 1943), and Chief of Staff to Admiral William F. Halsey, Jr., first with the South Pacific Force and later with the Third Fleet (1943 to 1945). He was Deputy Chief of Naval Operations (Logistics) from 1946 to 1950. Following command of the Second Fleet, he commanded concurrently Allied Forces Southern Europe (NATO) and U. S. Forces, Eastern Atlantic and Mediterranean. He served as Chief of Naval Operations and as a member of the newly designated Joint Chiefs of Staff from 1953 until his retirement in 1955.

Comprehensive analyses of the series of Gorshkov articles by the Center for Naval Analyses are valuable as reference documentation, but they are not needed to convince experienced professionals that Russia has well and truly digested, and put into practice, the fundamentals of Sea Power.

It is necessary to keep that point in mind in reviewing the individual articles, for it is from that platform of today's conclusions and policies that Admiral Gorshkov must have conducted his own reviews.

Basically, his appraisal of the moves, and the effects of those moves, in World War I is sound. He shrewdly differentiates between tactical results and the broader strategic implications of tactical confrontations. His critique of the Battle of Jutland is a good example; he clearly sees that strategic advantage remained with the British after the battle, regardless of debatable material factors and tactical command decisions.

Parenthetically, after World War I, there was such U. S. naval preoccupation with the tactics of the Battle of Jutland that broader contemplation of *campaign* realities of sustained combat effort, attrition, and logistics suffered considerably.

Admiral Gorshkov indulges in a certain amount of Communist rhetoric which Free World readers have learned to distrust, and one might be tempted to brush aside his credits to World War I Russian naval performance. However, careful scrutiny of his observations reveals a realistic view of government policy shortcomings, offsetting possibly biased slants toward uniformed performance. For example, he might be expected to downgrade Tsarist thinking, but obviously the Tsarist regime was not ready for World War I as it unfolded.

U. S. naval thinking has given little attention to the Baltic naval operations of World War I, but Gorshkov is correct in his view that they did siphon off some German naval effort from the Western Front strategic struggle. But, pass over Admiral Gorshkov's obvious pride in Russian naval performance in the Baltic sub-theater; in the context of the situation in 1973 there are other parts of his review of the First World War more in need of attention.

When he looks at submarine warfare in World War I, one must read between the lines because, inevitably, he is considering the submarine aspects of today's military, and therefore diplomatic, developments. As he speaks of submarine effectiveness in World War I, my own thoughts turn back to visions of the sea littered with the debris of sunken ships as we approached Queenstown, Ireland, in the late Spring of 1917. At that time, merchant ships were steaming singly, escorting was haphazard, and hydrophones and big depth charges were only anxiously-awaited counter-measures.

By the Fall of 1917 the convoy system was in effect and the submarine's job was tougher, as illustrated by the fact that my gallant little destroyer sank the U-58 and captured her crew. Fast troop ships proceeded independently for the most part, and, with few exceptions, went unscathed.

Admiral Gorshkov correctly concludes that the German unrestricted submarine campaign very nearly brought Britain to her knees, but he also makes another important observation. The ships, air surveillance, men, and material mobilized to counter the threat posed by a handful of submarines was staggering. I think it is obvious that the Admiral is mulling over in his mind the requirements of ASW vis-a-vis nuclear-powered submarines, including the SSBN.

Although he is impressed by the necessary massive, all-out, sapping ASW drain, and certainly ponders the implications of a comparable effort in terms of modern technology, it seems clear that he concludes that substantial broad effort is called for in support of the spectrum of modern submarine operations.

He faults the German High Command for failing to provide more and better support, surface and air, for submarine operations. Here, however, the Admiral is on shaky ground; German submarines could only accomplish their strangulation mission by operating along the approach lanes to Britain—in the open Atlantic. Germany did not have properly located or adequately equipped bases to render any sustained effective support to submarines in that great area. As a matter of fact, given the situation and technology of the times, operational support was scarcely possible. German intelligence did, however, do good work in uncovering approach routes and sailing schedules.

We can dismiss ocean raiding with the admission that it tied up some Allied forces, but had little effect on the ultimate outcome of the war.

Admiral Gorshkov's thinking with respect to modern naval roles and missions is a topic reserved for review of later installments. Here it need only be said that in his examination of The First World War he was seeking principles of universal application, as well as considering the general progress of hostilities. He saw the error of blindly extrapolating such confrontations of the past as the Russo-Japanese War; he correctly assessed the values and dangers of prolonged struggle; he clearly saw the importance of residual military power as a prime factor in post-hostilities determinations.

Having sorted out what he believes to be the enduring principles, we may be sure that he applies them to his thinking concerning modern fleet composition and employment. Of importance to current U. S. naval planning and execution is a correct evaluation of Russian naval capabilities and intentions, with emphasis on tactical, strategic, and diplomatic aspects of submarine warfare and ASW concepts. It is to be hoped that later reviewers will give these matters careful attention, for Admiral Gorshkov's writings undoubtedly furnish some valid clues to current Russian maritime thinking.

Propaganda and any obvious pro-Russian slant aside, this is sound analysis which qualifies Admiral Gorshkov as an author to be taken very seriously. He may, or may not, be an authorized spokesman for overall Soviet naval policy, but the composition, characteristics, quality, and global projection of the modern Soviet Navy, in conjunction with Admiral Gorshkov's analyses, pose disturbing questions that challenge top-level U. S. government scrutiny.

The Soviet Navy in the Revolution

With Commentary following the article by
Rear Admiral Robert J. Hanks, U. S. Navy

EDITOR'S NOTE: *In this article, cleared for publication in the Soviet Union on 29 May 1972, Admiral Gorshkov recalls the birth of "the first workers' and peasants' state in the world." While, to most Westerners, the image of the October Revolution is conveyed in the figures of two soldiers, pausing at the foot of a staircase in the Winter Palace, the author recalls that Lenin "personally sent detachments of sailors to the most crucial sectors. Thus navymen played an important role in the overthrow of the autocracy and in supporting the victory of the Great October Socialist Revolution . . . They were a true bulwark of the Communist Party and a reliable conductor of its policies."*

In the era of imperialism the contradictions in the capitalist system were aggravated to the maximum degree. A powerful wave of the revolutionary movement arose with Russia at its center. In October 1917 a new era in world history began: as a result of the Great October Revolution, the first workers' and peasants' state in the world was born.

Our navymen took an active part in the struggle to establish Soviet rule and to defend it against the encroachments of international reaction and internal counterrevolution. The social make up, which was closely tied to the working class, the efficient organization, glorious revolutionary and combat traditions, and a devotion to the proletarian cause made the Russian navymen, in V. I. Lenin's estimation, the leading detachment of the Revolution.[1]

[1] V. I. Lenin. *Poln. Sobr. soch.* (Complete Collected Works) Vol. 35, p. 114.

The Navy in the October Revolution. The revolutionary movement in the Navy headed by the Bolshevik Party was an integral part of the class struggle of the Russian proletariat against the rule of the exploiters. The traditions of the heroic actions of the crews of the battleship *Potemkin,* the cruiser *Pamyat' Azova,* and the garrisons of Kronstadt and Sveaborg, which were born in the period of the first Russian revolution, were expanded and strengthened among the navymen.

During the decisive battles of the classes, the navymen fulfilled with honor the role of one of the shock forces of the Revolution assigned to them by the proletarian leader.

By the fall of 1917, the Russian Navy had more than 1,100 combatants, auxiliaries, and merchant ships and numbered more than 180,000 men. The main part of the Navy, being situated in the Baltic, was based in Helsingfors, Revel, Kronstadt, and Petrograd, and represented a great force in the proletarian Revolution. The Baltic Fleet was given one of the chief roles in the plan for the armed uprising. V. I. Lenin wrote that "The Fleet, Kronstadt, Vyborg, and Revel can and must move against Petrograd, defeat the Kornilov regiments, stir up both capitals, promote mass agitation for a government which would turn over the land to the peasants immediately and propose peace at once, overthrow the Kerensky government, and create such a government."[2]

According to Lenin's plan for the armed uprising in Petrograd, the Baltic Fleet was not only supposed to prevent the German Fleet from attacking the capital from the sea, but also participate directly in the revolutionary activities in the city and on the approaches to it. The first task was successfully carried out in the Moon Sound battle. To carry out the second task, warships entered the Neva, large detachments of navymen landed on the shore and, in cooperation with the Red Guardsmen and the revolutionary soldiers of the garrison, cut the rail lines leading to Petrograd. A composite naval detachment (about 4,500 navymen from Helsingfors and more than 10,000 from Kronstadt) arrived to take part in the seizure of the post office, the telephone and telegraph stations, bridges, railroad stations, power stations, the main headquarters, and the Winter Palace.

At 2140 hours on 7 November 1917 the historic shot of the *Avrora* thundered out. The storming of the Winter Palace had begun, which ended at 0150 hours on 8 November. The armed uprising had triumphed. The bourgeois government, convoyed by sailors, was led to the Petropavlovsk Fortress. The workers and peasants of Russia led by the Party of Bolsheviks had taken the governmental reins in their own hands.

After the victory of the October armed uprising in Petrograd, navymen actively participated in the struggle for the overall consolidation of Soviet rule and in the defeat of counterrevolutionary revolts. In addition to the men of the Baltic Fleet, revolutionary navymen of the Black Sea Fleet, and the Arctic Ocean, Caspian, Amur, Siberian, Saimaa, Amu Darya, and Chudskoye flotillas took part in the struggle.

V. I. Lenin personally sent detachments of sailors to the most crucial sectors. For example, Baltic Fleet men, together with the Red Guards, participated in the crushing of the counterrevolution in Moscow, in the liquidation of the main seat of it on the front—the General Headquarters in Mogilev—and also in other places.

Thus, navymen played an important role in the over-throw of the autocracy and in supporting the victory of the Great October Socialist Revolution. They were a true bulwark of the Communist Party and a reliable conductor of its policies.

The Navy—an Indispensable Integral Part of the Armed Forces of the First Socialist State in the World. V. I. Lenin pointed out that: "Any revolution can stand only so long as it is able to defend itself."[3]

Therefore, after the Great October Socialist Revolution, the historical need immediately arose for our Party to defend the young Soviet Republic militarily from the encroachments of its enemies. V. I. Lenin was the first of the Marxists to develop the principles of the building up and organizing the armed forces of the proletarian state and to define the military tasks of the country and the avenues to implement them. In a short time in the course of the armed struggles with the enemies of the Soviet Republic, armed forces of a new type were created—the regular Worker-Peasant Red Army and the Red Navy.

The military policy of our Party is directed toward ensuring the external security of the country. It is based on the invincibility of the Soviet Armed Forces, the foundation of which is the Army. This proposition was confirmed in the very first year of the existence of our state by the decree for the creation of the Workers' and Peasants' Red Army.

Moreover, the Central Committee and the Council of Peoples' Commissars, headed by V. I. Lenin, taking all factors concerning the protection of the state into account, including the length of its maritime borders and the threat on the part of the great imperialist powers in whose aggressive plans powerful naval forces had been given an important role, devoted a great deal of attention to the defense of its maritime borders from the very first days of the formation of the Soviet Republic. A clear expression of this was the decree on the creation of the Workers' and Peasants' Red Navy. This important political act, which laid the foundation for the planned construction of the Soviet Navy, opened a new stage in its development, since the Navy was actually defined as the second basic branch of the Armed Forces, an indispensable integral part of them.

Since the Workers' and Peasants' Red Army and Navy were parts of the peoples' Armed Forces, they represented the instrument of the just policy of the Socialist state. Consequently, the Workers' and Peasants' Red Navy, like the Red Army, by its mission, character, and socio-political essence, differed radically from the navies of the capitalist powers, since it was an instrument to protect the independence of the So-

---

[2] *Ibid,* Vol. 34, p. 390.

[3] *Ibid.* Vol. 37, p. 122.

cialist state and the interests of the workers, and was imbued with the spirit of proletarian internationalism, and friendship and brotherhood among peoples.

The Leninist Principles of Soviet Military Science. Marxist-Leninist teaching on war and the Army serves as the scientific and ideological-theoretical basis for the construction of the Armed Forces of our state. V. I. Lenin said that in any area of Soviet construction, it is essential to take into account the objective laws and patterns, and the dependence of practical actions on political and economic conditions. This also applies to the Armed Forces. Therefore the creation of armed forces of a new type also required the creation of our own Soviet military science, for, as V. I. Lenin pointed out, one cannot build a modern army without science.

The fighting men of an army and navy must possess the requisite knowledge to successfully combat a strong enemy. In this connection, V. I. Lenin required that "military knowledge be acquired, and military affairs be studied in the proper manner." That is why this problem was given the greatest attention in all of the Communist Party congresses and Central Committee plenums in the period of the Civil War. V. I. Lenin tirelessly occupied himself with the development of Soviet military science. He made a scientific analysis of the laws of modern warfare and the characteristics of the methods of waging it. In contrast to many authorities of the past who limited the content of military science only to the sphere of the art of war, Vladimir Ilich regarded the theory and practice of military affairs as an inseparable part of the social activity of people living in a class society. As early as 1905 in the article "The Attack on Port Arthur," he showed the effect of the objective laws of modern warfare, the decisive role of the masses of the people in it, the importance of moral and economic factors, and drew the conclusion that the outcome of an armed struggle depends not only on the army, but also on the entire people, i.e., on the rear (in the broadest sense of the word).

In defining the volume of military knowledge needed by the workers, V. I. Lenin noted that this knowledge includes both questions of tactics and also questions of organization, waging armed combat according to a plan, mastering new, complex military equipment, and modern methods of waging war. The workers need not only a code of military affairs, he said, but also knowledge of the laws, principles, and rules of the art of war.[4]

In analyzing military forces, V. I. Lenin pointed to the need to take into account the numerical strength and level of training of the personnel of the Army and Navy and also the quantity and quality of the weaponry and military equipment. He sharply criticized a scornful attitude toward evaluating the forces and capabilities of the enemy, and always demanded a study of the enemy and his strong and weak points. "Everyone agrees that the conduct of an army which does not train itself to master all forms of weaponry, and all means and devices of combat which an adversary has or could have is foolish or even criminal.[5] On a theoretical plane, this position, which is of real import even today, determined the justification for the extent of borrowing in military science taking the form of our use of the individual elements and achievements of the bourgeois art of war.

V. I. Lenin pointed out to the Party the fact that "In every war, in the final analysis, victory is due to the state of the morale of those masses who shed their blood on the battlefield. A conviction in the justness of the war and an awareness of the need to sacrifice one's life for the good of one's brothers raises the morale of the soldiers and induces them to bear unbearable burdens."[6] In the era of imperialism, when wars are being waged by the people, this thesis is taking on special significance. Just wars give birth to patriotism, high morale among the people and Army, and, on the other hand, unjust wars are not able to lift their morale because they are conducted in the interests of a handful of exploiters.

"The supremacy of the policy of the Communist Party must be openly acknowledged" in the actions of all of the organs of the Soviet state including also the military organs.[7]

The leadership by the Communist Party of the Armed Forces and the Party-political work in the Army and Navy have been and remain one of the main sources of their might. V. I. Lenin believed that it is essential to strengthen moral steadfastness and to skillfully support with all your strength the ideological influence of the Party on the masses through the organizing role of the party organizations, political organizers, and command personnel. He repeatedly said that where the Party-political work is handled best, there discipline is better, the order and spirit of the troops is better, and there are more victories.[8]

The Leninist theses played a great role in the development of the principles of Soviet military theory and are fully retaining their every growing importance in the age of the technological revolution, of the creation

[4] *Ibid,* Vol. 10, p. 340.

[5] *Ibid,* Vol. 41, p. 81.
[6] *Ibid,* Vol. 41, p. 121.
[7] *Ibid,* Vol. 41, p. 402.
[8] *V. I. Lenin o voyne, armii i voyennoy nauke* (V. I. Lenin on War, the Army and Military Science), Vol. II, Voyenizdat, 1957, p. 421.

of armed forces which are new in principle, and the age of our building of an ocean-going Navy. They are the methodological basis of Soviet military doctrine, the foundation of our military and naval sciences, and today comprise the basis of the military policy of the Party which orients the people toward the need to maintain the defensive capability of the Soviet state at the highest level.

Vladimir Ilich devoted a great deal of attention to the art of war, and above all to strategy, which is inseparably linked to state policy. The vitality of this art lies primarily in its creative and scientific character, in the strict consideration of the laws of armed combat, in the ability to determine the main direction of the war, to select the time, place, and method of delivering the decisive blow, and also to utilize the vast revolutionary energy, initiative, and enthusiasm of the people.

Flexibility in choosing the form of combat and an amazing ability to determine the moment to go over to decisive actions are typical of Lenin as a strategist. The most important principles of achieving victory in practice were implemented under his leadership: be stronger than the enemy at the decisive moment at the decisive point; master all forms and means of armed combat; and intelligently combine defense and offense, depending on the actual situation. The leader of the proletariat was a proponent of all-out offensive operations (right up to the complete rout of the enemy), and considered one of the factors ensuring victory to be surprise attacks, and seizing and maintaining of the initiative. It is essential to try to catch the enemy unawares, he wrote, to seize the moment when his troops are scattered. At the same time it is essential that military vigilance be carried to the highest limits. "To slip up or lose your head, is to lose everything."[9]

Like a red thread the idea runs through all of Lenin's directives, letters, and orders concerning the need for firmness and purposefulness in carrying out intended plans, and of the falseness of any kind of wavering and indecisiveness at the crucial moments of the struggle.

V. I. Lenin included the particularly thorough preparation of planned operations as one of the characteristic special features of the art of military leadership. Every battle, he pointed out, includes the abstract possibility of defeat, and there is no other means of reducing this possibility than to organize the preparation of the battle.[10]

The principles of the strategy developed in the years of the Civil War—the study of the strong and weak points of the enemy, predicting his intentions, activeness and daring, purposefulness and flexibility in plans,

the creation of a superiority of forces and means in the main sectors, the correct determination of the most dangerous groupings at a given moment, and decisiveness of action—received further development in the years of the Great Patriotic War and in the postwar period.

Many theses presented by Lenin in his works, directives, and orders pertain to operational art (for example, determining the intent of an operation, the employment of forces and means, the selection of the methods and forms of operations on the front, fleet, army or flotilla scale). The need to always achieve a unity of intent and actions of the forces in an operation and to establish rigid control over the implementation of orders, directives, and dispositions is of vast importance for us even today.

He considered the principle of one-man leadership, centralism, and a unity of wills from top to bottom to be the basis of correct and goal-oriented leadership.

V. I. Lenin was not only the founding theoretician of Soviet military science, but also a great practitioner—the military commander of the army of the triumphant proletariat. His work in commanding the fronts in the years of the Civil War is an incomparable example of the ability to foresee the course of events and to mobilize and direct the efforts of the entire country and its armed forces toward a triumphant victory over the enemy. All of the most important operations of the Red Army and Navy in this period were worked out under the leadership of Vladimir Ilich.

The vivifying ideas of Vladimir Ilich and the tireless organizational work of the Communist Party in bringing them to life found full support among the navymen and served as a guiding star for them in the struggle with the enemies of the Soviet state.

Navymen in the Civil War. Upon the call of the Communist Party immediately after the victory of October, navymen were in the front ranks of the defenders of Soviet rule. They actively battled against the troops of Kerensky and Krasnov at Petrograd, Kaledin's band at Rostov-on-the-Don, the Central Rada in the Ukraine, the anti-Communist Poles in Belorussia, and the Ataman Dutov at Orenburg.

The victory of the Revolution in Russia evoked sharp resistance from all the forces of the old world. In 1918, the imperialists of Germany, Britain, France, Japan, the U.S.A., and their satellites came out against the young Soviet Republic with the goal of destroying the first workers' and peasants' state in the world. The governments of these countries undertook to support Kolchak, Denikin, Yudenich, Wrangel, and Pilsudski. On 18 February 1918, the German troops went over

---

[9] *Op. cit.,* Vol. 39, p. 55.
[10] *Ibid,* Vol. 6, pp. 136–137.

The Soviet Baltic Fleet at Kronstadt in August 1919 just before eight British coastal motor boats entered the harbor (arrow) in the early morning darkness of 18 August, and, under diversionary bombing attacks from the cruiser-carrier Vindictive, *torpedoed and sank two battleships and a depot ship at their moorings. Most of the large ships in this photograph are cruisers.*

to the offensive on all lines of the front, while the ships of the Kaiser's Navy entered the Gulf of Finland in order to deliver a blow against the heart of the Revolution—Petrograd. The German armies rapidly moved forward and soon reached Revel, Pskov, and Narva. A terrible threat hung over the Soviet country. The Red Guards and the temporarily formed detachments were unable to carry out the task of defending the Revolution and protecting the country. The Party took measures to create the Workers' and Peasants' Red Army and Red Navy which were formed during the course of the savage struggle.

On 21 February, V. I. Lenin made an appeal to the people: "The Socialist Motherland Is In Danger." Work on an unprecedented scale was initiated to create Armed Forces capable of defending the Revolution. Petrograd's workers and navymen became their backbone and cementing force.

Having been met by a serious repulse by the young Red Army and Navy, the German command agreed to renew peace talks. On 3 March 1918, the Brest Peace Treaty was signed. However, the position of the Baltic and Black Sea Fleets turned out to be exceptionally difficult. The fact of the matter was that the Baltic Fleet, which was based in Helsingfors and Revel, under the conditions of the Brest Treaty were supposed to sail immediately for Russian ports or disarm themselves. The Germans counted on seizing our ships, since they believed that these would be unable to break through the ice of the Gulf of Finland. However, upon a direct order from V. I. Lenin, the Baltic Fleet made a heroic ice cruise, and arrived in Kronstadt and Petrograd. The rescued Fleet gave stability to the defense of the capital, which strengthened the overall position of the Soviet Republic.

In the summer of 1918 the imperialists, having set

themselves the goal of breaking through to Petrograd from the sea, concentrated considerable naval forces in the Gulf of Finland. On 9 August, Lenin gave the order to immediately mine the approaches to Kronstadt. The 1,435 mines laid on 14 August, which were covered by warships, barred the enemy's way to Petrograd from the sea. The coastal artillery of Kronstadt and the forts created a powerful defensive semicircle of fire covering the citadel of the Revolution. Moreover, the Kronstadt fortress was the artillery reserve of the ground troops: field batteries and mobile batteries of heavy guns were formed in it.

As is seen, the Baltic Fleet deserves a great deal of credit for the fact that the interventionists and White Guards did not succeed in capturing Petrograd.

During the Civil War, the Red Banner Baltic Fleet became not only the forge of personnel for the young Soviet naval forces, but also their materiel base as well: ships, aircraft, and armament were dispatched from its inventory to form numerous flotillas and sea detachments.

In the south of the country, due to the treachery of the Central Rada, the Germans continued to forge ahead and soon occupied the entire Ukraine. In connection with this, the Black Sea Fleet had to vacate Sevastopol for Novorossiysk. On 1 May 1918, the Germans captured Sevastopol and demanded the return of the ships there and their surrender. Since Novorossiysk was also threatened by occupation, in order to avoid their capture by the enemy, at Lenin's order the ships of the Black Sea Fleet were scuttled in Tsemesskaya Bay and the personnel were sent to the river flotillas and the ground fronts. Thus, the men of the Black Sea Fleet remained in service as warriors for the Revolution.

The November 1918 revolution in Germany relieved our Homeland from the one-sided provisions of the Brest Pact. However, even before this, British and French squadrons had entered the Gulf of Finland and the Black Sea. In March 1918 foreign troops landed in Murmansk, in Vladivostok in April, and later also in the Black Sea ports. The intervention had begun.

It should be noted that the interventionists landed where the Soviet Republic had no naval forces at its disposal. In the Baltic, however, where a sufficiently powerful fleet had been retained, the interventionists decided not to make an invasion from the sea.

The main events of the Civil War took place on land. Nevertheless, the leading proletarian leaders saw in the Navy a force capable of having a considerable influence on the course of the armed struggle. Here, in particular, is a statement on this question by CinC of the Armed Forces and member of the Revolutionary Council of the Soviet Republic S. S. Kamenev: "With respect to his combat qualities, the enemy, in view of his large number of trained command personnel and greater wealth of equipment, was stronger than the Red Army. Another no less characteristic earmark of the overall situation was the support given the enemy's rear via the sea. The enemy had a constant connection with the Entente via the sea, hence the constant support given the enemy's weakest forces and means by the Entente. *Without this support, probably, the enemy would have been forced to give up after the very first battles which were unsuccessful for him.*"[11]

In other words the navies of the imperialist countries during the Civil War and the intervention served as an important weapon of their policy, which was being used to liquidate the gains of the Great October Revolution by force of arms.

The Soviet Red Navy considerably trailed the interventionist fleets with respect to number of combatants and armament, which complicated the conditions of the armed struggle on all fronts of the Civil War. The Red Army was forced to engage the armies of the enemy after he, having seized a beachhead and set up supply bases ashore, had occupied the combat positions which he needed. The young Soviet Armed Forces, not having the necessary fleet at their disposal, were unable to oppose the enemy during his sea transit where greater results could have been achieved with less effort. They also were unable to oppose the landing of the enemy's troops in the coastal areas chosen by him, since our ground troops were less maneuverable than the forces of the enemy fleet. Therefore, each time, the Red Army was put in the position of the defending side, which had to marshal its forces and make a prolonged preparation in order to drive the enemy into the sea and oust him beyond the borders of our Motherland through a decisive counterattack.

The Communist Party and the Soviet government correctly understood the importance of naval forces in the Civil War, and took active measures to strengthen and employ them for the country's defense. In particular, a great deal of attention was devoted to the river and lake flotillas, which, under the conditions requiring maneuverability in the war, and owing to the poorly developed rail networks in the areas of military operations, played an important role. The flotillas were built up and a wide range of military missions was executed owing to the enthusiasm and military mastery of the navymen under the most difficult devastating conditions. In addition to the surviving older warships, more than 2,000 different river and lake ships which were

---

[11]S. S. Kamenev. *Zapiski o grazhdanskoy voyne i voyennom stroitel'-stve* (Notes on the Civil War and military construction), selected articles. Voyenizdat, 1963, p. 58.

re-outfitted as warships operated within the Navy at that time.

In the spring of 1919, the imperialists organized a new offensive against the Soviet Republic. The main battles developed on the Eastern front against the troops of Kolchak. The Volga Flotilla, which operated on the Kama, Vyatka, Belaya, and Ufa Rivers, played an important role in the defeat of the White Guards.

At the same time, the troops of Yudenich, together with the anti-Communist Finns, began an attack on Petrograd. The Petrograd Defense Committee, led by Zinovyev, developed a plan. Instead of strengthening the defenses of the city of the revolution he envisioned scuttling the ships of the Baltic Fleet and evacuating the main factories, which in essence would have undermined the defensive capability of Petrograd and liquidated our main Fleet. Having learned of this treacherous plan, V. I. Lenin immediately countermanded it by telegraph. Subsequently the Baltic Fleet and the Onega Flotilla actively participated in the defeat of the enemy troops and rendered great aid to the Seventh Army defending Petrograd.

In trying to occupy revolutionary Petrograd, the British massed more than 100 warships in the Gulf of Finland. Upon V. I. Lenin's order, the men of the Baltic Fleet deployed in active combat operations against them, as a result of which 34 enemy ships were sunk and 24 damaged. The interventionist fleet was forced to quit the Gulf of Finland without having executed their missions.[12]

Denikin attacked in the South. Lenin's letter "Everyone to the Struggle Against Denikin," published on 9 June 1919, said that the most critical moment of the Socialist Revolution had arrived. A fierce battle broke out on the southern and southeastern fronts, and the forces of the Red Navy aided the Red Army units in every way. Thus, the Dnepr and Volga-Caspian Flotillas operated successfully on the flanks of the fronts anchored on the Dnepr and Volga Rivers. The Eleventh Army and the Volga-Caspian Flotilla, under the leadership of S. M. Kirov, steadfastly defended the lower Volga and prevented the White Guards of Kolchak and Denikin from linking up.

In the spring of 1920, the imperialists prepared for a new strike against the Soviet Republic with the forces of the bourgeois landlords of Poland and Wrangel's army. The Western Dvina and Dnepr Naval Flotillas jointly with the Red Army conducted combat operations against these enemies.

In June 1920, Wrangel's army went over to the attack from the Crimea. Simultaneously, in order to unite the counterrevolutionary forces of the Don and Kuban, the enemy undertook an attempt to land a landing force in the rear of our troops on the coast of the Sea of Azov. The landing parties were defeated by the coordinated operations of the Red Army and Azov Flotilla.

Naval flotillas took an active part in the struggle with the counterrevolution in Transcaucasia and Central Asia, and in battles to free Siberia and the Far East.

About 75,000 navymen fought on the Civil War fronts. The names of A. Zheleznyakov, B. Lyubimov, N. Markin, M. Martynov, A. Mokrousov, P. Khokhryakov, and many other navymen who displayed wonderful courage and heroism in battles with the enemies of the Soviet Republic were widely known among the people.

As we have seen, the main burden of the struggle with the interventionists and White Guards was carried by the Red Army and detachments of revolutionary workers. However, the Fleets and also the numerous naval flotillas created in the course of the war and which imparted a scale to the combat operations on the rivers and lakes unprecedented in history, also played a great role in this struggle. In joint operations the navymen rendered the ground troops fire support, landed landing parties for them, battled the sea and river forces of the enemy, supported the crossings of our troops of water obstacles, handled military shipping, and took an active part in the battles on land as part of units of the Red Army.

Yet, whereas by making use of his advantage with respect to forces in the sea theaters, the enemy had the possibility of taking the initiative in selecting the direction of the attacks and began the military operations, it was another matter in the river and lake theaters. In an overwhelming majority of the cases our Armed Forces skillfully made use of the advantage over the enemy on the rivers and lakes to deliver surprise attacks, swiftly maneuver forces in the process of attacking along the rivers, and to pressure them without pause. Where the river and lake flotillas operated, the enemy was unable to use the water as a natural defense line for a prolonged period. The presence of the naval flotillas fostered the employment of maneuvering fighting methods which were most characteristic of the strategy and tactics of the Red Army during the Civil War.

In this difficult struggle the Navy fully justified the trust of the Party, the government, and the people, and was an important factor in gaining the victory on the numerous fronts of the Civil War and in the struggles with the interventionists. The events of those years once more confirmed the need for our country to have a powerful, comprehensively developed Navy.

---

[12] *Boevoy put' Sovetskogo Voyenno-Morskogo Flota* (The Combat Path of the Soviet Navy), Voyenizdat, 1967, p. 127.

Above: Vladivostok, 10 March 1918. HMS Suffolk *and USS* Brooklyn, *two elderly armored cruisers moored stern to in the ice to help safeguard American-produced stores and ammunition at this Far Eastern port. Facing Page: Novorossiysk, March 1920. A White Russian destroyer tows a lighter full of Cossack soldiers, presumably en route to the Crimea. White ship at left is the Italian cruiser* Etna, *six-funneled ship is the French armored cruiser* Waldeck Rousseau, *and ship in the middle is a French destroyer. Right: Leon Trotsky, chief of the Soviet delegation to the Brest-Litovsk peace conference (white muffler) and party are greeted by German officers in January 1918.*

The Development of the Soviet Navy in the Period From the End of the Civil War to the Outbreak of the Great Patriotic War. This period can be divided into two stages: 1921–1928, the reconstruction; and 1929–1941, construction based on the industrialization of the country.

The Reconstruction of the Navy (1921–1928). Having defeated the interventionists and the White Guards, our people began peaceful Socialist construction. The situation was extremely grave: destruction ruled in the country, the imperialist states were conducting a policy directed at destroying the Soviet government, and the struggle with the unbeaten vestiges of the counterrevolution continued.

At this time, the naval forces consisted only of the Baltic Fleet and several river flotillas. Some ships had been deemed unsuitable for further service and they had to be scrapped, and the remaining ships were in serious need of overhauling. The total tonnage of the Soviet Navy was only one-fourth of the 1920 level and

its personnel strength had decreased to almost one-sixth of the 1920 level. A large part of the command personnel consisted of officers of the old Fleet and the rest needed theoretical and practical training.

In evaluating the condition of the Navy of that time, M. V. Frunze wrote: "It was the lot of the Navy to sustain particularly severe blows in the overall course of the Revolution and in the events of the Civil War. As a result of them we lost the largest and best part of its materiel, lost a vast number of experienced and knowledgeable officers who played an even greater role in the life and work of the Navy than all of the other forms of weapons, we lost a whole series of naval bases, and finally, we lost the main nucleus of the other ranks of Red Navy personnel. In short, all this meant that we had no Navy."[13]

In contrast to the ruling circles of Tsarist Russia who did not understand the role of the Navy in the military might of the country, the Communist Party and the Soviet government attached great importance to it. This predetermined the success of the country's efforts in the restoration and the subsequent furious development of the Soviet Navy.

V. I. Lenin constantly devoted a great deal of attention to the Navy. In 1920 he personally signed the resolution, confirmed by the Council of Labor and Defense, which marked the birth of the Navy. The most important landmark of the building of Socialism in our country was the 10th Party Congress, which took measures to solidify Soviet rule, improve the economy and culture, and further strengthen the defense of the Motherland. Its decisions served as the basis for developing widespread and planned work on the creation of the needed Navy. However, due to the economic destruction and the decay of industry, at first it had to be limited only to the restoration of the naval forces, to some modernization of their combat units,

and also to the scientific development of new models of warships and their armament.

The decisions of the 10th Party Congress said: "The Congress considers it essential in accordance with the general condition and the material resources of the Soviet Republic to take measures toward the revival and strengthening of the Red Navy."[14] The Congress also singled out concrete measures for carrying out these decisions. The 12th Party Congress confirmed that "The Party as a whole must as before devote all-round attention to the material and cultural needs of the Red Army and Red Fleets."[15]

Of special significance for the restoration and construction of the Navy were the decisions of the 14th Congress directed toward the industrialization of the country and the creation of heavy industry—the foundations for strengthening the defensive capability of the state and, in particular, of its Navy.

The Leninist Komsomol, which at the Fifth Congress of the Russian Young Communist League became the patron of the Navy, made a great contribution to the building of the Soviet Navy. In two years about 8,000 youths came to the Navy under the sponsorship of Komsomol and about 1,000 were sent to naval training institutions.

The repeated holding in the country of "Red Navy Weeks," which rendered it significant material aid, displayed the concern of all the people for the Navy.

In 1921 the restoration of the ports and shipbuilding industry was begun, and in 1922 they proceeded with the overhaul of combatants and auxiliaries and the formation of forces, which, although small, had a combat capability. As a result, by 1924 the Baltic Fleet had two battleships, one cruiser, eight destroyers, nine sub-

[13]M. V. Frunze. *O molodezhi* (About Young People), Izd-vo "Molodaya Guardiya," 1937, p. 81.

[14]*KPSS v rezolyutsiyakh i resheniyakh s" yezdov, konferentsiy i plenumov TsK* (The CPSU in the Resolutions and Decisions of the Congresses, Conferences and the Central Committee Plena), Vol. 2, 1917–1924. 8th Edition, Politizdat, 1970, p. 265.

[15]*Ibid,* Vol. 2, p. 409.

marines, and other warships. In the Black Sea Fleet, which was created anew, one cruiser, two destroyers, two submarines, and 12 other warships went into service. Flotillas were born on the Caspian Sea and the Amur River.

An indicator of the rates of restoration of the Navy is the growth of its total tonnage (in thousands of tons): 1923–82; 1924–90; 1925–116; 1926–139.

In 1926 the Council of Labor and Defense approved the first (six-year) naval shipbuilding program under which it was intended to construct 12 submarines, 18 escort ships, and 36 torpedo boats. At the same time the Navy was also recruiting personnel. A large number of young men were required to learn a naval specialty in a short time. The Navy was actually transformed into a vast training detachment. From 1921 to 1924 they succeeded in training about 20,000 qualified specialists. The naval training institutions in the period 1923–1928 graduated about 1,200 naval officers.

At the same time, creative military theoretical work was being done. The low strength of the ship inventory demanded that ways be sought to carry out the tasks of defending our maritime borders by forces of a "small" Navy in concert with ground troops. In the process of these quests a "small war" theory was born which, proceeding from the actual conditions, singled out rational methods and forms of combatting a stronger maritime enemy. Its essence was the delivery of short attacks against the main enemy objective without being cut off from one's own bases, and the secret marshaling of different kinds of forces from different directions acting in concert. The concentrated (combined) attack of surface ships, torpedo boats, submarines, aircraft, and coastal artillery organized in mine-artillery positions was proposed as the basic form of joint effort. This method of employing our naval forces at that time most approximated their actual combat qualities, and corresponded to the pressing defensive tasks and the economic capabilities of the Soviet state.

Thus, in the first stage of development of the Soviet Navy, ships were restored and built, new personnel were trained, the organizational foundations of the Navy were laid, and methods and forms of conducting combat operations at sea were developed. The Navy was revived as a combat force of our state. The Armed Forces received the capability of increasing the maritime might of the Socialist Motherland and of strengthening her combat capability.

The Soviet Union, having revived the Navy, acquired a real means of defending her maritime borders which are over 40,000 kilometers in length. And although her forces were not yet large, and were unable to independently carry out missions on a strategic scale, the young Soviet Navy became an important political factor. And the enemies of our country were forced to reckon with this.

Commentary

By Rear Admiral Robert J. Hanks, U. S. Navy

A graduate of the U. S. Naval Academy with the Class of 1946, Rear Admiral Hanks served in the USS *St. Paul* (CA-73) from August 1945 to January 1949. He was assigned to AirASRon 892 in 1951–1952 and to the NROTC Unit at Oregon State University from 1952 to 1954. He was operations officer of the USS Arnold J. Isbell (DD-869) from 1954 to 1956, and for ComDesRon Eleven in 1956–57. After serving as executive officer of the USS *Floyd B. Parks* (DD-884) from 1960–1961, he commanded the USS *Boyd* (DD-544) from 1961 to 1963. Following two years on the staff of ComCruDesPac, he attended the Naval War College and then served first as Assistant for NATO Affairs, and later as Deputy Director for Nuclear Planning Affairs in the Office of the Assistant Secretary of Defense (International Security Affairs). While serving as ComDesRon Thirteen he won the 1970 Prize Essay Contest. He is now Commander, Middle East Force.

In this, the fifth installment of his treatise, Admiral Gorshkov undertakes the task of "founding" the Soviet Navy. If one ignores—only for the moment—the fulsome praise devoted to Vladimir Lenin's alleged military brilliance and strategic acumen, Gorshkov seems to be broadcasting a two-fold message. First, he seeks to root the traditions of today's Red Navy in the Bolshevik Revolution and, second, to extol the "leading" part played therein by revolutionary sailors from the Tsarist fleets. This latter thrust serves the purpose of proving the value of the Navy to the Communist Party of the Soviet Union.

Tradition, of course, provides the main frames—if not the keel—of any sound naval organization. Gorshkov clearly recognizes this vital factor and dwells on it at considerable length. He has, however, a basic problem. The Soviet Navy was born of the Red Revolution. Moreover, that Navy began its existence with mass mutiny, a word Gorshkov carefully avoids, and an act not exactly revered by the world's other navies. Since in the Soviet Union loyalty to the regime is a tradition transcending all others, however, the mutiny was not at all a bad thing in Communist eyes. Moreover, despite periodic flashes of efficiency and professionalism in the past, the performance of Russian fleets, especially in recent history—the Russo-Japanese War and World War I—has been something less than inspiring. It certainly isn't the sort of record which sires motivating tradition.

Thus, Gorshkov's initial objective is to turn a normally abominable act into a virtue. By concentrating on the efforts of the "revolutionary sailors" in the abortive uprising in 1905, the overthrow of the Tsarist and Kerenski governments, and in the subsequent defense of the revolution, he ties primary loyalty directly to the Communist Party of the Soviet Union. All in all, a quite understandable and predictable approach.

Of greater significance is his description of those revolutionary sailors' exploits during the fighting. Their endeavors encompassed service ashore as infantry, widespread scuttling to prevent ship captures, and a heavy shift to riverine and lake operations. As an aside, one might note the striking similarity to Confederate naval operations during our own Civil War—another inferior power with extensive sea-coasts, confronted by seapower in the broad sense.

But the significance of this portion of Admiral Gorshkov's article lies not in what the sailors did during these first years, but how their experience ultimately affected the fledgling Soviet Navy. For it seems clear that the role of that Navy over its first three decades of existence—essentially limitation to defense of the seaward flanks of the Red Army—stemmed directly from the Bolshevik experiences during and immediately after the October Revolution.

During this period, the Russian Navy—its leadership in particular—was decimated by the stresses and strains of revolution. That which remained was incapable of functioning as a normal, national navy. Therefore, the Bolshevik-led sailors, along with the ships and operable equipment left to them, were necessarily put to whatever useful purpose they could serve. Of the severely emasculated Navy's many deficiencies, Gorshkov describes the most significant as its inability to defend against seaborne incursions mounted by those Western nations which intervened during the doomed White counter-revolution. The

flanks of the Red Army were literally in the water and defenseless.

Once the revolution was relatively secure, of course, the Bolsheviks turned their attention to the building and development of permanent, regular armed forces. First priority went quite naturally to the Army, the main instrument for ensuring internal security—the most pressing order of business—and defense against further military threats from abroad.

As for the Navy, the experience of the recent fighting and the prostrate, backward state of Russian industry combined to severely limit the kind of fleet which could be fashioned. What resources could be transformed into naval weapons were fitted to the one naval role the Bolsheviks perceived: an adjunct of the Army, charged with protection of its salt-water flanks. Given the constraints which bound the Soviets, this, too, is an altogether understandable approach.

But why this particular albatross, represented by such strategic thinking, should hang around the neck of the Soviet sailor for two long decades *after* the U.S.S.R. had become a heavy-industry state, and thereby capable of building a modern, seakeeping fleet, is a question which has always puzzled Western naval experts. Gorshkov neither admits to this failure, nor offers an explanation. One can speculate that it is directly attributable to short-sightedness on the part of the Soviet leadership and the complete inability of that leadership to comprehend the role or even the meaning of seapower.

If this be so, it would appear to follow that the internal battle to produce a Soviet blue-water Navy has been long and difficult. In this light, the space Gorshkov devotes to adulation of Lenin's military acuity—indeed, the entire article—could be viewed as a continuation of that campaign. Certainly, one can argue that the present size of the Soviet fleet, the modernity and technological sophistication of its units, and the world-wide pattern of its operations, prove that the internal struggle over Soviet seapower has been won by the pro-Navy advocates. On the other hand, the extensive invoking of an oracular Lenin suggests that Gorshkov has as yet unfulfilled plans for further quantitative and qualitative expansion of the Red Fleet, plans which he is still battling to implement.

The future will most surely reveal the truth or falsity of the latter thesis. In the meantime, it would seem wise for us to study Gorshkov's words and to bounce them against events as they develop. We may thus divine that truth before it suddenly confronts and confounds us in the form of unpalatable, accomplished fact.

The Soviet Navy Rebuilds, 1928–41

With Commentary following the article by
Vice Admiral J. F. Calvert, U. S. Navy (Retired)

EDITOR'S NOTE: *This article by the man who has commanded the Soviet Navy for the past 18 years, was cleared for publication in the Soviet Union on 11 August 1972. In this, the sixth of an 11-chapter series, Admiral Gorshkov recalls the late 1920s and 1930s when, while most of the great powers were caught in the grip of the Depression, Russia was building a navy which, at the outbreak of the 1941-to-1945 "Great Patriotic War," would rank about sixth or seventh in the world. It was a navy short in ASW ships, minesweepers, and landing craft; none of its four fleets had Marines; its air defenses were negligible and its store of mines was small. Yet, it entered the war against Germany with a submarine fleet that was—as it is today—the largest in the world.*

The First World War did not resolve the contradictions which had been engendered. Even during the course of the war, while having economic superiority over their rivals, the U. S. monopolists were laying plans to gain world domination. In this connection, the ruling circles of that day felt that the avenue to world supremacy lay in the strengthening of their naval might.

The struggle for superiority at sea has always occupied a significant place in the aggressive acts of U. S. foreign policy. However, this was displayed with particular force in the initial postwar years, when American imperialism, having done its bloody business during the war, sharply expanded its activities in the countries of Latin America, Africa, and Asia. In striving to eliminate the opposition of its traditional competitors on the paths of imperialist expansion, the American leaders set themselves the primary goal of weakening the sea power of England. "Anglo-American 'cooperation' has turned into a clear Anglo-American rivalry, expanding the prospects for a gigantic clash of forces," the Sixth Commintern Congress stated.[1]

The war of the diplomats for supremacy at sea was waged between all the imperialist powers at the Washington Conference of 1921–1922, the 1927 Geneva

The Soviet submarine Komsomolka, *left, together with her sister* Komsomoletz, *both built in 1933, were unusual among the Soviet Union's large prewar submarine fleet in that they were built by subscription from members of the Komsomol, the Communist Youth Movement.*

[1] *Kommunisticheskiy internatsional v dokumentakh, 1919–1923* (The Communist International in Documents, 1919–1923). Partizdat, 1933, p. 772).

Naval Conference, and the London Conferences of 1930 and 1936. As a result of the prolonged struggle, the U.S.A. achieved international recognition of the "parity" of its naval forces with the British forces, which meant that the U.S.A. and England emerged with equal rights in this area. However, Japan, Italy, and later also Germany, not having achieved the armament relationships which they desired and favorable positions for themselves in the world markets by the diplomatic route, continued to feverishly prepare for war. The regrouping of the forces of the imperialist powers had begun, and the contradictions between them continued to grow.

In the late 1920s and early 1930s a most severe economic crisis broke out in the capitalist countries, and the U.S.A., England, France, Japan, and Germany were hardest hit.

As a result of the crisis, the conflicts became even sharper between the imperialist countries, between the states which were the winners and losers in the First World War, and between the home countries and their colonies. At the same time the crisis evoked a new upsurge in the class struggle. The revolutionary movement became particularly widespread in Germany, which was economically drained by the war, by the indemnities to England and France, and by the crisis which had begun. In order to preserve their power and prevent a further growth of the revolutionary movement, the German bourgeoisie with the support of the bourgeoisie of other countries brought Hitler's Fascist Party to power.

The German Fascists marked their assumption of power, as we know, with the savage suppression of the working revolutionary movement, with the complete annihilation of bourgeois democratic freedoms, and with the unbridled militarization of the country and its economy. The foreign policy also took on a clearly anti-democratic aggressive character: Germany withdrew from the League of Nations, demanded a review of the borders of the European states for her own advantage, and overtly prepared for this redivision by means of arms.

One of the points of the military program of Hitler Germany was the rapid restoration of a powerful Navy, which was rather successfully carried out according to the principle of "cruisers instead of butter." Thus, in March 1935, the Germans began the construction of battleships, cruisers, and submarines. At the same time, Hitler's diplomats initiated talks in London to lift the restrictions on naval armaments which had been laid down by the Treaty of Versailles. In the summer of the same year an Anglo-German treaty was signed under which Germany was permitted to have a naval fleet with a total tonnage of up to 35% of the tonnage

of the British Navy; in this case the submarine tonnage was limited to 45% of the tonnage of the British submarine fleet; however, under "special circumstances," it could be equal to it (the preparation by Germany for a war against the Soviet Union implied "special circumstances.") In connection with this, the English press wrote that "Great Britain, having herself experienced this terrible naval weapon in the war period, is agreeing that the very same weapon will again appear in European waters right under her nose."[2]

Such an unceremonious breach of the Versailles Treaty was the consequence of the blind hate of imperialism toward the U.S.S.R. and the belief in the fact that Fascist Germany with a weapon thrust into her hands would use it only to destroy the first and only Socialist state on earth at that time.

The conclusion of the Anglo-German naval agreement marked the beginning of the Munich Policy of the Western powers in Europe, aided the Hitler leadership to finally cancel all of the other restrictions of the Versailles Treaty, and was the stimulus for an open-ended naval armaments race.

In 1937 a new economic crisis broke out, hitting primarily the U.S.A., England, and France (it touched Germany, Italy, and Japan only slightly because their economies were supported by military orders). The battle for commodity markets, sources of raw materials, and spheres of capital investment heated up with new force among the imperialist powers. The threat of an armed attack by international imperialism on the Soviet Union also increased. The policy of the Western powers attested to this. Thus, the ruling circles of France assumed that Hitler's aggressive operations in the East would weaken Germany, and this would facilitate the establishment of French supremacy in Europe. The U. S. imperialists, stimulating the aggressive intentions of Germany, believed that this would aid their policy of asserting world supremacy. Thus, the American "isolationists" and the European "peacemakers" essentially conducted the very same policy—a policy of [encouraging] the aggressive drive of Hitler Germany against the U.S.S.R.

This is also attested to by the agreement in November 1937 of the British government's representative, Halifax, with Hitler concerning the creation of an Anglo-German-French alliance, and also the conducting of a secret conference on the capturing of the commodity markets in the U.S.S.R. and China, called at the same time by the financial circles of Germany and the U.S.A.

In conducting planned preparation for war, Fascist Germany strengthened her military might on land, at

---

[2] *The Times*, June 19, 1935.

sea, and in the air. She not only re-established her main bases on the Baltic and the North Seas, but also built new ones. Ship construction was accelerated. Thus, in 1936, two 35,000-ton battleships, a 19,250-ton aircraft carrier, six 1,811-ton destroyers, and eight submarines were laid down, and in 1937 warships of an equal total tonnage were laid down. It was assumed that at those rates of construction Germany would fully restore her Fleet by 1939. In 1938, Hitler demanded parity for his submarine fleet with that of the British. In 1939, the Navy of Fascist Germany numbered four battleships, 11 cruisers, 37 destroyers, and 57 submarines; and two battleships, two aircraft carriers, four cruisers, 16 destroyers, and eight submarines were under construction. The tonnage of Germany's merchant marine, which was the reserve of the Navy, was about 4.5 million tons at that time.

Thus, the center for the outbreak of a new world war was formed in the West, in the center of Europe.

A second center for the outbreak of a new world war was formed in the East. The imperialists of Japan, seeing that the European powers and the U.S.A. were busy with their own domestic affairs, brought on by the economic crisis, decided to better their position by the armed seizure of Northern China, and later of the Soviet Far East. In order to ensure herself freedom of action, imperialist Japan, like Fascist Germany, withdrew from the League of Nations.

In preparing for aggressive operations Japan strengthened and expanded her system of naval bases at which the naval fleet, which was under intensive construction, was scheduled to be based. By 1939 it had ten battleships, ten aircraft carriers, 35 cruisers, 106 destroyers, and 58 submarines. In addition, one carrier, two cruisers, eight destroyers, and eight submarines were under construction. The merchant fleet tonnage (counting ships larger than 1,000 tons) was about five million tons.

Quite naturally our Party and government could not overlook these facts, and, while continuing to consistently follow a policy of peace, they took measures to strengthen the defensive capability of the Soviet Union.

In order to protect herself from the aggression of such powerful capitalist powers as Germany and Japan, who were putting their entire economies, science, and technology at the service of their militaristic aims, the Soviet Union needed powerful armed forces equipped with the latest weaponry and combat equipment. And the Soviet people did everything possible to have such Armed Forces. In this period aviation was furiously developed, armored forces were created, and the mobility of the infantry and their firepower were increased.

Since Japan was a major naval power, Germany was devoting particular attention to the restoration of a strong fleet, and England, the U.S.A., France, and Italy, possessing large naval forces, had not dropped the thought of destroying the Soviet state, to protect its maritime borders, the U.S.S.R. needed a fully modern powerful Navy having a sufficient amount of all types of naval forces and all ship types in its inventory.

However, at the end of the 1920s our Navy consisted of combatants, batteries, and bases restored after the First World War and the Civil War, and reconditioned in the postwar period.

Significant in the history of the Navy were the decisions of the expanded meetings of the U.S.S.R. Revolutionary Military Council in May 1928, which defined the missions and the overall trend of development of the naval forces and which served as the basis for developing a naval ship construction program in the First Five Year Plan. The decisions said: "In developing the Navy, we shall strive to combine surface and submarine fleets, coastal and mine positional defenses, and naval aviation appropriate to the character of the combat operations to be conducted in our naval theaters in the situation of a probable war."[3] In other words, in those years the principle of creating a Navy consisting of harmoniously developed diverse forces had already been affirmed.

The very same, but even more vividly expressed, trend in the development of the Navy was also retained in the naval shipbuilding plan for the Second Five Year Plan. As the basis of the new plan, the requirement was levied for construction mainly of a submarine fleet and heavy aircraft possessing strong maneuvering capabilities on a priority basis.[4]

The character of naval construction in that period was determined by the missions confronting the Navy, views of the methods of its combat employment, the capabilities of industry, and the achievements of science and technology both at home and abroad. In this connection, the experience of past wars and also the trend in the development of naval forces of foreign states were taken into account.

On the basis of the developing international situation and the need to defend the country under the actual historical conditions, the Eighth Party Congress made a wise decision with respect to the need of the Soviet Union to have a mighty sea and oceanic Navy, corresponding to its interests. The naval forces existing at that time did not correspond to those needs. It was essential to create such a Navy in a short time. And the country proceeded with its creation.

The industrialization of the country, the collectivization of agriculture, the liquidation of the exploiter

[3] Central State Archives of the Navy, Photo 1483, List 1, File 80, pp. 23–24.
[4] *Ibid,* Photo 1483, List 1, File 201, pp. 1–2.

classes, and the cultural revolution implemented by the Soviet people in the years of the initial five-year plans under the Party's leadership permitted a sharp increase in the economic might of the Soviet Union. It was precisely in this period that the automotive, aviation, electrical engineering, and defense industries were created, and new shipbuilding yards were redesigned and built, thereby providing the material base for the construction of a new Fleet.

As early as 5 March 1927, the first *Dekabrist*-class Soviet submarines were laid down in the enterprises of the shipbuilding industry. From 1930 to 1934 the *Leninets*-class minelaying submarine, the *Shchuka*- and *S*-class medium submarines, and the small *Malyutka*-class submarines were turned out for the first time by industry. Soon construction was begun on the *K*-class ocean-going submarines. By 1 September 1939 the Soviet Navy had 165 submarines. The Soviet submarines were intended to operate in coastal areas as well as on the high seas, and were distinguished by their high performance characteristics. Thus, our Navy by the outbreak of the Great Patriotic War had become the possessor of the most powerful submarine forces in the world.

The creation of the naval surface forces was begun with the completion of cruisers which had been laid down as early as the First World War years. At the end of the 1920s and in the early 1930s the Black Sea Fleet was expanded with the cruisers *Chervona Ukraina* and *Krasnyy Kavkaz*. Later, construction of new surface ships of various types was expanded. Initially stress was put on torpedo boats, escort ships, and destroyers, and later on light cruisers. In the first two five-year plans the shipbuilders gave the Fleet 106 surface ships: four cruisers, seven destroyer leaders, 30 destroyers, 18 escort ships, 38 minesweepers, one minelayer, and eight river monitors.

In 1938, with the adoption of a resolution on the construction of a large sea and oceanic Fleet, major surface ships were acknowledged to be its nucleus, although the interaction of different types of naval forces remained the main condition for the successful execution of missions. The shipbuilding program developed in accordance with this was weighted toward battleships and heavy cruisers, which were superior in quality to similar foreign ships. The change in views on the role of major surface ships took place under the influence of the fact that all the sea powers con-

Performance Data of Soviet and U. S. Ships Laid Down Before the War

PERFORMANCE DATA	BATTLESHIPS		HEAVY CRUISERS		LIGHT CRUISERS	
	Soviet Union 1938	Iowa 1940	Kronstadt 1938	Alaska 1940	Kirov 1935	Brooklyn 1936
Displacement, tons						
full	65 150	59 000	38 360	32 000	11 500	11 580
standard	59 150	45 000	35 240	27 500	9 000	9 700
Propulsion power, hp	231 000	200 000	231 000	150 000	110 000	100 000
Max. speed, kn	28	30	33	30	35	32.5
Guns, mm	9—406	9—406	9—305	9—305	9—180	15—152
	12—152	20—127	8—152	12—127	6—100	8—127
	8—100	80—40	8—100	—40	16—37	4—40
	32—37	48—20	24—37	—20		
	8—12.7		8—12.7			
Torpedoes	—	—	—	—	2×3—533	—
Mines	—	—	—	—		
Aircraft	1 catapult, 4 aircraft	2 catapults, 4 aircraft	1 catapult, 4 aircraft	2 catapults, 2 aircraft	1 catapult, 2 aircraft	2 catapults, 4 aircraft

tinued to feverishly build them, considering them to be the foundation of the fleet.

From 1938 to 1940 the laying down of the first of the *Sovetskiy Soyuz* [Soviet Union]-class Soviet battleships, the *Kronstadt*-class heavy cruisers, and the *Chapayev*-class cruisers took place. By the outbreak of war, there were 219 ships in various stages of construction in the yards, including three battleships, two heavy cruisers, ten cruisers, 45 destroyers, and 91 submarines.

Naval aviation was also expanded. However, it did not have special naval aircraft, and therefore was equipped with aircraft designed for the other branches of the Armed Forces. While effective for operations against land targets, they were poorly suited for carrying out combat missions at sea. Thus, due to the low speeds, short flight range, and small load capacity, the naval attack aircraft were unable to employ torpedoes with adequate success against warships at sea which had been detected at long ranges from the airfields. It is true that when the Navy received the DB-3 (IL-4) aircraft that this deficiency of naval attack aircraft was partially eliminated. Due to the short operating range, weak armament, and short endurance, naval fighter aircraft were not in condition to reliably cover forces at sea even at relatively short distances from shore. This considerably limited the employment of major fleet surface forces in zones within range of hostile aircraft.

The power of our coastal defense increased considerably: its equipment was upgraded, and areas of combat employment were expanded. In 1940 alone, the number of coastal artillery batteries grew by almost 45%, and the number of AA batteries doubled.

In the years of the prewar five-year plans, naval scientific and technical thought made a great contribution to the creation of new, and the upgrading of existing, models of mine, torpedo, and especially gunnery armament. In these same years the first radar sets were created in our Navy, models of infrared equipment made their appearance, subunits of remote-controlled torpedo boats were formed, the first types of air-cushion patrol boats were tested, and the employment of fighter-carrying mother aircraft was developed, which operated successfully at the outbreak of the Great Patriotic War. All of this considerably increased the capabilities of the Navy.

Thus, in line with the development of the Socialist economy, the defensive might of our state was strengthened and the power of the Soviet Navy as an integral part of the country's Armed Forces grew.

The development of a Navy—a most difficult process in which outmoded weapons systems are replaced by new ones corresponding in the fullest measure to the latest level of development of equipment and to the requirements of naval warfare—is the final result of vast scientific work determining optimal variants for decisions of the most major strategic, strategic-tactical, and technical problems. The solution of these problems permits, through the most intricate combining in each ship of technical devices, systems, and complexes made up of the peak in engineering thought based on the very latest achievements in science, technology, and production, to concentrate the maximal combat capabilities with the most economical "expenditure" of weights, dimensions, and displacements.

However, the construction of a Navy is not just the building of combatants and batteries and the creation of new models of naval equipment. The construction of a Navy is also great organizational measures adhering to certain principles, the further development of the naval art, and the training of cadres of specialists.

The great importance attached to the Navy in the armed defense of the country was expressed organizationally in the formation in December 1937 of the People's Commissariat of the Navy.

The formation of the People's Commissariat of the Navy permitted concentrating the leadership of all of the measures connected with the construction of a large

DESTROYERS		ESCORT SHIPS	
Ognevoy 1940	*Fletcher* 1940	*Yastreb* 1940	*Tacoma* 1940
2 950	2 750	1 059	1 100
2 240	2 050	900	
54 000	60 000		5 500
37.1	34	31	18
4—130	5—127	3—85	3—76
2—76.2	4—40	4—37	—40
3—37	4—20	3—12.7	—20
4—12.7			
2×3—533	1×5—533	1×3—450	—
Depth charge projectors, 96 mines	Depth charge projectors	—	Depth charge projectors
—	—	—	—
—	—	—	—

ocean-going Fleet in a few hands.

One of the organizational measures was the creation in 1932 of the Pacific Fleet and the creation in 1933 of the Northern Fleet. After the entry in 1940 of Estonia, Latvia, Lithuania, and Bessarabia into the U.S.S.R., the Baltic and Black Sea Fleets considerably expanded their basing areas: the former emerged from the eastern part of the Gulf of Finland into the expanses of the Baltic Sea, and the latter toward the mouth of the Danube, where the Danube Flotilla was created. Major formations of forces, e.g., brigades and squadrons, made their appearance in all of the Fleets.

As the warship construction and the organizational measures were proceeding, a scientific quest was being made for more effective methods of combat employment of naval forces and of their weaponry in battle with a powerful enemy. In other words, the development of the naval art took place in accordance with the actual materiel-technical base of the Fleet.

The international situation and the overall missions of the Armed Forces stemming from it determined the Navy missions: cooperation with the Red Army, repulsing enemy operations against our coast from the direction of the sea, the creation of favorable conditions for operations by our own forces in a naval theater (not just in the littoral area, but throughout the entire depth of the operation,) and action against the enemy's economy by severing his sea and ocean communications.

Taking into account the state of the Soviet and foreign navies and the immediate prospects for their development, our naval science came to the conclusion that the outcome of the war would be decided on land, and therefore the Navy would have to carry out missions in the war stemming from the missions of the ground forces. In addition, our naval thought did not rule out the fact that in some stages of the war the Navy could also carry out the main mission in one theater or another.

Questions concerning theory in the naval art were worked out in accordance with the new missions of the Navy in the academies and scientific research institutes. This creative process took place amid a situation of a sharp clash of opinions between proponents of offensive and defensive views on the role and employment of naval forces in the forthcoming war. The

former were still under the influence of the "small war" theory, which was correct in its day, while the latter, believing that our Navy had already become capable of conducting combat operations beyond the limits of our own coastal waters, held to the "control of the sea" theory. However, the interpretation of the term "control of the sea" was somewhat different than that held in the West. Thus, in a Naval Academy course of lectures of that period it was stated: "To achieve superiority of forces over the enemy in the main sector and to pin him down in the secondary sectors at the time of the operation means to achieve *control of the sea* in a theater or a sector of a theater, i.e., to create such a situation that the enemy will be paralyzed or constrained in his operations, or weakened and thereby hampered from interfering with our execution of a given operation or in our execution of his own operational mission."[5] It was precisely this interpretation of sea control which was the basis of the employment of naval forces in naval warfare.

Naval combat training in the prewar years was directed toward the development of the tactics of a naval battle primarily in our own areas which had been previously equipped. The main attention was focussed on the organization of a joint concentrated attack of surface ships, torpedo boats, aircraft, and submarines against groupings of hostile surface ships in the coastal zone of a sea and against our mine and gunnery positions being built in the narrows and at the approaches to the naval bases. In addition, a great deal of attention was also attached to so called hit-and-run operations (in the form of strikes against ports, naval bases, and groups of ships in enemy coastal waters) carried out by surface forces independently or in concert with the aircraft.

A great achievement of Soviet naval science was the development in the 1930s of a new chapter in naval art—the theory of the operational employment of naval forces. It correctly analyzed the role of various types of naval forces in armed combat and, in particular, pointed out that in actual operations the role and significance of one type of naval force or another or

[5]Captain 2nd Rank V. A. Belli. *Teoreticheskiye osnovy vedeniya operatsiy. Konspekty-tezisy.* (Theoretical Principles of Conducting Operations. Synopses-Theses.) Naval Academy, 1938.

In 1939, two modern Type VII destroyers and one of Russia's three battleships, the October Revolution, *maneuvered in the Baltic. After 28 Type II destroyers were built with Italian cooperation between 1935 and 1941—18 of which were assigned to the Baltic—the Soviet Navy improved on the Italian design with the Type VII-U, of which 26 were built.*

ship type depends on the missions being executed, the relative strength of the forces, and the military geographical conditions of the theater.

In contrast to bourgeois naval science, Soviet naval science correctly determined the role of aviation in naval warfare. And although in the official documents governing the employment of the Navy (including also those published in 1940) aviation was relegated to the role of one of the main means of reconnaissance and support, it was clearly stressed in the speeches of the Navy leadership, in the pages of the press, and in the courses for the students at the Navy Academy, that no naval operation is conceivable without air forces.

On the basis of Soviet experience in landing landing forces, Soviet naval art in the 1930s developed the very first theory of amphibious landing operations which was checked in the course of combat training.

It should be noted that in its zeal to somehow justify the shameful failure of the Dardanelles operation of 1915 by objective reasons and to save the faltering prestige of the "Mistress of the Seas," the British Admiralty went so far that it not only convinced others, but also itself, of the impossibility of landing amphibious forces. As a result, as one of the most important conclusions from the experience of the First World War, naval theoreticians of the Western countries acknowledged the complete lack of a future for joint operations of fleets with ground forces, and especially one of such diversity as the landing of a landing force. This conclusion was contrary to the combat experience of the Russian Fleet, which successfully landed a landing force at Lazistan [Rize, Turkey] and also with the wealth of experience of Soviet naval forces in the struggle with the White Guards and interventionists on the Civil War fronts. It was precisely due to the ignoring of this experience and due to the inability to discover trends in the development of the form and nature of armed combat that at the outbreak of the War not one of the navies of the Western powers had a developed theory for amphibious operations and not one had specially constructed landing ships and troop units trained for these operations.

From what has been said it is evident that Soviet naval art in the prewar years took a giant step forward and surpassed bourgeois naval art with respect to a series of issues. Prior to the outbreak of the Great Patriotic War it represented a structured and completely modern (for that day) system of scientific views of the strategic and tactical employment of naval forces for the execution of the missions facing them. In this connection, in our naval art of those years the point of view predominated of employing naval forces for defensive purposes, although the missions and strategic and tactical plans were carried out strictly by offensive

methods. The employment, however, of submarines, including also raiding submarines having a very long operational range, was limited by the framework of the tactical missions executed by them which were primarily in nearby areas of the theaters. It was precisely because of this that the question of conducting combat operations in the ocean was not even raised, although the capability for this already was there.

Unfortunately this was not the only minus in the prewar construction of our Navy. Thus, the well developed theory for conducting amphibious operations did not receive the needed material or organizational implementation for several reasons (mainly of an economic nature): by the outbreak of the war not one of our Fleets had a single specially constructed landing ship. The Fleets also did not have the required number of surface gunnery ships to support the landing of a landing force because it was believed that this would be done by gunboats, cruisers, and destroyers. However, the cruisers and destroyers were trained mainly to combat enemy surface ships, and firing at shore targets was a secondary mission, while many slow-running gunboats, armed with one to three medium-caliber guns, were obsolete. All of this limited the Navy's capabilities to carry out missions in concert with ground troops and made it difficult to conduct landing operations in far-off areas of a theater.

Unfortunately, questions of joint operations between the branches of the Armed Forces were also not given the requisite attention. One can see in this one display the underestimation by some leaders of the Armed Forces of the role of the Navy in the forthcoming war. However, precisely because of this reason, no unity of views was achieved on the principal questions of joint operations of naval forces and ground troops in coastal areas. Thus, as a result, the tactical cooperation of ships and army units was worked out only within general frameworks, and the amphibious training of the ground troops was relegated to a secondary position.

New guiding documents—regulations, directives, rules, and methodologies—were developed and introduced in the prewar years in accordance with the new missions of the Navy, methods of executing them, and the materiel base. They were all imbued with a spirit of attack in any situation. The requirement for maintaining a high level of combat readiness for active offensive operations at sea, in the air, in coastal waters, off of enemy bases, and against sea communications was important in these documents. The documents recommended executing missions with concerted action by diverse forces, marshalling of forces for attacks, and a fuller utilization of firepower and mobility by the groupings participating in the battle.

The increase in the naval ship inventory and the

number of naval units required training a large contingent of naval specialists and, above all, command cadres. In connection with this, in the late 1930s the network of naval training institutions was considerably expanded, and the schools training command personnel for the Navy were the first in the Armed Forces to be converted to higher training institutions. Thanks to this, the Navy was expanded by remarkable officers having sound general and special training prior to the Great Patriotic War.

By the outbreak of the Great Patriotic War, our Navy had four major force formations: the Northern, Baltic, Black Sea, and Pacific Fleets, and also the Danube, Caspian, Pinsk, and Amur Flotillas. The inventory of the Navy included three battleships, seven light cruisers, 66 destroyers and destroyer leaders, 22 escort ships, 80 minesweepers, 269 torpedo boats, 218 submarines, 2,529 aircraft of all types, and 260 coastal artillery batteries, which permitted carrying out the tasks of coastal defense and of supporting the Red Army. Although distributed throughout the individual theaters, the Navy as a whole still represented a considerable force. With respect to ship inventory and total displacement, it was about sixth or seventh in the world.

However, the insufficient number of ASW ships, minesweepers, and auxiliaries, and the absence of specially built landing craft considerably reduced Fleet capabilities with respect to maintaining favorable conditions in the theaters and made the execution of certain missions difficult. It cannot be considered normal that not one of the Fleets had naval infantry, that the air defense forces and equipment were weak, and that the stores of influence mines and sweeps turned out to be small.

Yet despite the series of deficiencies in construction and preparation, the Navy as a whole on the eve of the war possessed a high degree of combat readiness. This was one of the most important results of the work of our Party, which directed Navy personnel to maintain every ship and unit in constant combat readiness. The Navymen, educated by the Communist Party and Komsomol, were distinguished by exceptionally high morale and combat qualities. Their fleet friendship, faithfulness to their military duty and to their remarkable revolutionary and combat traditions, and their fidelity to the Motherland ensured a constant high state of combat readiness and the combat capability of all of our Fleets.

This to a great degree fostered the introduction of a new system of combat training which permitted the working out of Fleet force and unit training missions the year round and a reduction in the length of preparation for large all-Fleet exercises. (Whereas earlier such exercises were normally conducted in the fall, in 1941 the Black Sea and Northern Fleets were able to complete them in the summer before the outbreak of war.)

An important moment was the new organization of the transfer of our Fleets to a higher state of combat readiness, which was worked out and checked even before the outbreak of the Great Patriotic War. It was precisely owing to this system that the Fleets were brought to full combat readiness in time, successfully repulsed the first surprise attacks of Fascist Germany against our bases on the night of 22 June 1941, and avoided many severe consequences.

It follows from what has been said that the constant concern of the Party and government for the security of the maritime borders of the Motherland permitted the creation in a short time of an essentially new, fully modern Navy capable of executing the missions with which it was charged.

By the outbreak of the Great Patriotic War of 1941 to 1945 the Soviet Navy represented an imposing force which our enemies were forced to take into account. It was completely prepared to defend the state interests of the U.S.S.R. in the contiguous naval theaters, to repulse the attacks of enemy fleets, and was able to operate in concert with major ground force groupings in the littoral areas and reliably cover their flanks and rear. Moreover, our Navy was capable of undertaking active operations against the enemy's sea communications and against coastal groupings of his ground forces.

The fact of the creation of a rather strong Navy in our country did not go unnoticed by the naval powers, as evidenced by Britain's invitation to the Soviet Union in 1936 to take part in the work of the London naval arms limitation conference. The Soviet government, true to its peace-loving policy, entered into negotiations with Great Britain in order to check the naval arms race to some degree. However, Moscow laid down the condition at London that Germany also be obliged to limit armaments. Great Britain was forced to sign such an agreement with Germany. However, the accelerating preparation of the imperialist powers for a new world war made such an agreement unrealistic. The London naval arms limitation talks showed only the final alignment of the imperialist powers prior to the outbreak of the Second World War and showed that the imperialist powers were grouping themselves not for the purpose of limiting naval armaments, but to wage the forthcoming war and to seek allies for themselves for a future war.

The creation of the Soviet Navy attested to the readiness of the Soviet Union to protect her freedom and independence from encroachments by aggressors in all of the maritime theaters contiguous to it.

Commentary

By Vice Admiral J. F. Calvert, U. S. Navy (Retired)

A graduate of the U. S. Naval Academy with the class of 1943, Admiral Calvert was a submariner during World War II. He commanded the USS *Skate* (SSN-578) when, in 1958, she became the first submarine to surface at the North Pole. He was Commander of Cruiser-Destroyer Flotilla Eight prior to becoming the 46th Superintendent of the U. S. Naval Academy in July 1968. He assumed command of the U. S. First Fleet in 1972 and retired from active duty in 1973.

It appears from reading Admiral Gorshkov's 50,000 word polemic on Soviet seapower that there is by no means clear agreement within the U.S.S.R. on either the size or the basic mission of its Navy. He has apparently written these articles in an attempt to justify his policy which has shaped the Soviet Navy for so many years. Almost surely, that policy is once again under internal attack.

His articles are Gorshkov's own version of the influence of seapower on history. He attempts to defend his Navy by establishing the importance of all seapower, but Soviet seapower in particular, through the recitation of its history. It is anything but objective. Reading it brings to mind the book by Admiral Moorer's old friend entitled "An Unbiased History of the War Between the States From the Southern Point of View."

Underneath all the puffery, however, lies the shadow of two great factors in naval theory which Gorshkov is unable to master—nuclear war at sea and the ballistic missile submarine. Despite the fact that these eleven articles have apparently been written for a specific internal political purpose, Gorshkov is honest enough to reveal that the dilemma posed by these two factors in the structuring of his Navy has given him deep pause. As he attempts to come to grips with the nuclear exchange and the ballistic missile submarine, he talks increasingly about "presence." For all its importance, "presence" can never be a major purpose of a Navy. It can be a convenient auxiliary use but, almost by definition, never a central one.

This is not meant to derogate Gorshkov or imply that any Western theoreticians have done better. It is only to ask that all of us try to learn from the experience of watching Russia's leading seapower advocate stumble over the same questions that have plagued all of us for the last two decades.

This particular article deals with the rebuilding of the Soviet Navy from 1928 until the outbreak of World War II. The year 1928 is chosen because it saw the meeting of the Revolutionary Military Council which set forth the missions and development plan behind the naval construction program in Stalin's first Five Year Plan. (It is an interesting commentary on Soviet political thought that Gorshkov never mentions Josef Stalin despite the fact that he dominated Soviet history throughout this period as few men have ever dominated a society.)

The plan set forth by the Revolutionary Military Council was a modest one which clearly reflected the dominance of the Soviet Army at the time. The Army and, more importantly, Stalin, saw the Navy as a coastal defense organization in a supporting role for the land forces. Two important characteristics of today's Soviet Navy had their origins in this period—the emphasis on submarines and the use of landbased rather than seabased air. Both were probably extensions of Stalin's view of naval forces; neither was developed very effectively.

Gorshkov recites a long, glowing list of conceptual achievements by the Soviet naval profession during this period: the "correct" determination of the role of aviation in naval warfare, the "very first theory" of amphibious landing operations, and a "structured and completely modern" system for the strategic and tactical employment of naval forces, to name only a few. To be fair, Gorshkov does admit to a few shortcomings, mainly because of economic and material problems.

At no time, however, does he come close to the heart of the matter—the fact that the period between the World Wars was critical to the development of an effective Soviet Navy for World War II and, in that regard, the Soviet naval profession of the 1920s and 1930s failed. It failed to develop three of its most fundamental needs in the struggle with Germany: an anti-submarine capability, a means of supplying logistic support at sea, and a means of effectively projecting naval airpower over the sea. As a result, during the Murmansk resupply efforts, the task of protecting allied convoys had to be left entirely to the British and the Americans. In addition, the effectiveness of the Soviet Navy against the German surface Navy and merchant convoys was hampered by weaknesses in logistics and naval air.

In honesty, it must be admitted that the Soviet naval profession had serious handicaps in the 1930s. It was operating in a totalitarian society heavily dominated by a dictator who was certainly no naval theoretician. Indeed, there is no evidence that Stalin put much value on seapower as an instrument of national policy. Further, according to an oft-repeated, but unconfirmable story, Stalin's great purges of the late 1930s took a heavy toll of Soviet naval leadership, particularly those who had a background in submarines.

Whatever the truth of the story, something, clearly, was wrong with Soviet submarine leadership in World War II. At the outbreak of the conflict the Russians call the Great Patriotic War, the Soviet Navy had 218 submarines with more building—the largest submarine force in the history of the world

to that time. It was more than twice as large as either the German or the American submarine forces of the time. And yet the Russians could make it count for only a very little in the struggle of 1941 to 1945.

These criticisms of what the Soviet naval profession was able to accomplish in the 1930s, however, only serve to highlight what the author himself has been able to accomplish in the nearly two decades that he has headed the Soviet Navy.

Gone, now, is the preoccupation with coastal defense and support of the Army. Gorshkov's Navy is blue water, its communications and logistics can and do support distant operations, it has a respectable amphibious capability, and its submarine force shows many signs of the sophistication it once lacked.

Rarely in the history of navies has one man been able to remain in control of a navy for so long. In most totalitarian countries, the politics of the high military are too treacherous for such longevity and, in the Western nations, the custom of taking turns with the Fleet precludes any more than a passing touch by one personality. Gorshkov, however, has prevailed through it all. Through Stalin, Krushchev, and Brezhnev, the nimble admiral has remained at the helm. And it cannot be denied that he has created a formidable weapon of seapower. Perhaps most important of all, he has rarely forgotten what is so easy to forget—that the purpose of a navy is to fight at sea.

Whether or not he will prevail against his present critics remains to be seen. The very fact that he has been forced to defend himself with these articles is proof of his success. The Soviet Navy now looms so large in the Kremlin's budget that the inevitable cries of disarm, withdraw, and scrap are being heard. As always.

But whether he succeeds or fails in his present internal skirmishes, those two larger shadows referred to earlier—the nuclear war at sea and the ballistic missile submarine—threaten his policy as they do that of every large Navy. These are the two great riddles of our profession today.

Do they mean that naval power is now the only truly relevant power—or do they mean that no naval power can ever again influence the course of international affairs as in the past? Either conclusion can be reached by the use of today's theory and both cannot be correct. How long will it be before someone can articulate the answers?

The Second World War

With Commentary following the article by
Admiral George W. Anderson, Jr., U. S. Navy (Retired)

EDITOR'S NOTE: *In the following chapter, cleared for publication in the Soviet Union on 7 September 1972, the admiral continues to draw on the lessons of history to make a case for seapower in general—and Soviet seapower in particular. Yet, as he assays World War II, the lessons he sees are in almost total disagreement with those of Western historians who, he argues, are more interested in pleasing "their imperialistic masters" than in an impartial treatment of history, and who are now striving to distort history in every possible way. They are wrong, he asserts, in exalting allied naval success; for it was the land battle at Stalingrad that made defeat inevitable for Germany and Japan.*

---

*P*reparation for War. After the division of the world into two systems as a result of the October Revolution in Russia, the policy of the imperialist powers was determined to a considerable degree by their constant desire to destroy the Soviet Union. Therefore, the U.S.A., Great Britain, and France, intending to use Germany as a tool to implement their plans, aided her with liberal subsidies to recover from the consequences of the military damage of the First World War in a short time, to rapidly restore her military and economic

There was reason for dancing in the snow-covered streets of Stalingrad. The six-month-long battle was over; Germany's crack, 250,000-man 6th Army was destroyed. V–J Day was more than two years away but, says the author, this was the pivotal point since Japanese military leaders now became convinced of the hopelessness of their offensive strategy.

potential, and to revitalize her powerful armed forces. The imperialists were fully confident that the military might of Germany would be directed against the U.S.S.R. Moreover, weakened by the war, Germany seemed incapable of opposing the main imperialist groupings.

International monopolistic capital aided the German Fascists to come to power in order to implement this concept. Hitler's government threw off the restrictions of the Versailles Treaty which prohibited the armament of Germany and returned to preparations for war: it reorganized industry, put the development of the entire economy on the military track, and began a corresponding ideological manipulation of wide circles of the German people. In 1935, an Anglo-German naval agreement was concluded. It abolished the restrictions of the article of the Versailles Treaty concerning naval armaments and freed the hands of Hitler Germany to build a powerful navy. By the end of 1939, the German Army and Air Force surpassed the armies and air forces of any of the capitalist countries. By having such armed forces, Germany, in Hitler's opinion, was able to establish supremacy in Europe. However, this was not the final goal of the aspirations of Hitler Germany, but was considered only a prerequisite for gaining further world supremacy which, according to the concept of the Fascist ringleaders, would be achieved in two stages: first, the establishment of supremacy in Europe and the destruction of the Soviet Union, and second, the seizure of the overseas colonial possessions of the European states.

This policy predetermined the special attention given by the leaders of Hitler Germany to the creation of primarily ground and air forces. However, since the achievement of world supremacy was connected with the seizure of overseas colonies, Fascist Germany also considered it essential to create a powerful Navy capable of ensuring the achievement of her set aims. According to "Plan Z," worked out as early as 1938 and scheduled [to last] nine to ten years, by 1948 Germany's Navy was supposed to have in its inventory 13 battleships, four aircraft carriers, 33 cruisers, 267 submarines, and a large number of destroyers and other combatants.[1]

The failure of the 1936 London Conference, which tried to find ways of further regulating naval armaments, served as a signal for an unlimited arms race by the imperialist powers. The very fact that there were repeated attempts to regulate naval armaments by international agreements, especially after the First World War, attests to the important significance the major imperialist countries attached to naval forces.

Yet despite this, by the outbreak of war, the German Navy was not as powerful as the navies of England and France, although this was somewhat compensated for by the presence of Germany's allies in the aggression—Fascist Italy in Europe and Japan in the Pacific Ocean had major fleets at their disposal (Table 1). However, the trends in the development of the navies were significantly different due to the concepts of employment adopted by their leaders.

The disruption of the enemy's shipping by attacking his merchantmen and combatants with all available forces was considered the chief mission of the German Navy.

The British plan for naval warfare operations was

based on the fact that the conditions for the employment of the Navy would not be essentially different from the situation in which it operated in the First World War, and called for a long-range naval blockade of Germany and the protection of her own sea communications. The military geographical situation made it easier for the British to organize a naval blockade of Germany, although under the conditions which were arising, it could no longer be as effective a means as in World War I.

The French Navy and part of the forces of the British Navy, supported by a developed system of bases, were supposed to ensure supremacy in the Mediterranean Sea.

Thus, the naval doctrines of both the opposing coalitions were oriented toward achieving definite goals by active methods of employing their own naval forces, but the doctrines differed in content. Thus, whereas the German command intended to distribute their naval operations practically throughout the entire Atlantic Ocean, the English and French commands strove to concentrate their main efforts in comparatively limited areas of the seas contiguous to German territory. The concentration of larger forces in limited areas of the theater in direct proximity to the system of bases of the German Fascist Navy stood in contrast to the dispersal of the efforts of a Navy with a smaller strength over vast ocean expanses.

The Role of Navies in the Second World War and Their Effect on the Course and Outcome of the War. The Second World War began as an imperialist war for the division of the world, which Germany, Japan, and Italy demanded.

After Hitler Germany seized Austria, Poland, and Czechoslovakia, the ruling circles of England and France still hoped to direct the Fascist aggression against the Soviet Union, and for a long time they essentially conducted no military operations on the ground fronts. Hitler and the Wehrmacht generals, considering the defeat of the neighboring bourgeois states and the establishment of supremacy in Western Europe to be a necessary prerequisite for an attack on the U.S.S.R. had the opportunity to concentrate troops on their borders under tranquil conditions. In this period military operations were conducted only in the naval theater.

In order to protect its transoceanic shipping and consequently to counter the naval forces of Fascist Germany, the British Fleet had to disperse its forces throughout the entire Atlantic theater, which produced great difficulties in the employment of an insufficient number of antisubmarine, antimine, and escort ships and did not yield the desired effect. As a result, in the first ten months of the war the Germans destroyed 701

[1]Belli, V. A., V. P. Bogolepov, L. M. Yeremeyev, Ye. N. Lebedev, B. A. Pochikovskiy, and A. P. Shergin. *Blokada i kontrblokada. Bor'ba na okeanskihk soobshcheniyakh vo vtoroy mirovoy voyne.* (Blockade and Counterblockade. The Struggle for Ocean Communications in the Second World War). Izd-vo Nauka, 1967, p. 81.

Table 1.   *Composition of the Navies of the Main Imperialist Countries at the Outbreak of World War II.*

Ship types	England	France	U.S.A.	Total	Germany	Italy	Japan*	Total	Relative strength
Battleships and battle cruisers	15	7	15	37	2	4	10	16	2.3 : 1
Aircraft carriers & aircraft transports	8	2	6	16	—	—	10	10	1.6 : 1
Cruisers (heavy, light, & air defense)	66	19	37	122	11	22	35	68	1.8 : 1
Destroyers	119	70	181	370	42	128	111	281	1.3 : 1
Submarines	69	77	99	245	57	115	63	235	1.05 : 1

*Data on Japanese Fleet as of 1 December 1941.
Table compiled from book by L. M. Yeremeyev and A. P. Shergin "Submarines of foreign navies in World War II,"
Voyenizdat, 1962, pp. 21, 227, 273, 285, 323, 375.

merchant ships of Great Britain and her allies with a total tonnage of more than 2,335,000 tons, of which 300 ships with a total tonnage of 1,137,000 tons were sunk by submarines.[2] The total tonnage of ships sunk per submarine in the inventory of the German Fleet reached 22,000 tons, whereas in 1918 it was only 15,000 tons. As is evident, the effectiveness of the operations of the German submarine forces was higher than in the last ten months of the First World War. However, in that period Germany lost 23 submarines (i.e., 40% of all the submarines which she had at the outbreak of the war) which attests to the rather intense warfare at sea.

Concurrently with the submarines, German major combatants—two "pocket" battleships and five auxiliary cruiser raiders—were also operating against Britain's sea communications. In addition, German cruisers, destroyers, and surface minelayers made nine cruises to the shores of England where 1,700 mines were planted by the beginning of February 1940.[3]

In addition to merchant ships, England lost a battleship and an aircraft carrier, while two battleships, two cruisers, ten destroyers, an air defense ship, and two submarines were put out of action.[4]

The course of the battle for communications had a serious effect on the military-economic potential of England: her economy began to feel the stress as early as the summer of 1940. In particular, the British were forced to live to a considerable degree on stores accumulated in the home country even before the war.

Thus, the so-called "phony war" on land, having the political goal of directing the aggression of the

Hitlerites toward the East, did not extend to the sea: on the contrary, only the active combat activity of the British at sea was able to aid the achievement of the cited goal. However, the dispersal of British naval forces throughout the entire Atlantic theater created a favorable situation for German naval operations in the coastal waters of Northern Europe. In April 1940, with the support of superior air forces, the German Fleet made a surprise landing in Norway and took it in a short time (the British attempt to land a landing party in Narvik was unsuccesful.) This naval operation of the German Navy had a serious effect on the further course of the war since it permitted the Germans to improve the strategic position of the Navy's northern flank, to expand the opportunity for combat operations by her Navy (especially for submarines), and to support the delivery to Germany of Scandinavian iron ore through covered coastal sea routes.

On 10 May 1940, the "phony war" ended: taking advantage of the lack of action of the Anglo-French armies, the Hitler command, having concentrated overwhelming forces on the Western front, began to invade France. The Germans knifed through the Anglo-French armies and headed for the Channel, pinning nine English and 18 French divisions to the sea in the area of Dunkirk. Only with the aid of the Navy (more than 860 different combatants and auxiliaries), which suffered great losses, did they succeed in evacuating 338,000 men to England, leaving all of the heavy equipment to the enemy. Such were the initial fruits of the Munich policy and the prolonged inactivity of the military command of England and France, the results of urging Fascist Germany on to march eastward. In the final analysis, all of this led to the capitulation of France and the development of a direct threat of an invasion of the British Isles by German

[2] *Ibid,* pp. 146–147.
[3] *Ibid,* p. 130.
[4] *Ibid,* p. 149.

troops. The German airfields were considerably closer to England, and the submarine bases were extended out to the ocean shore directly off the main British sea shipping lanes.

It seemed as though the plan of Hitler Germany to gain supremacy in Western Europe by the efforts of the ground forces and the air force alone was close to successful completion. However, England remained unbeaten, and it was impossible to force her to surrender without sufficient naval forces. The German military command (just as in World War I) tried to find a way out of this situation by strangling England with a naval blockade. In November 1941, at a meeting with Hitler an expansion of the submarine construction program was adopted (in defiance of the earlier naval development plans) in order to permit them to carry out this task which, in point of fact, meant dropping the implementation of the original plans for invading the British Isles. This was due mainly to the relative strength of the naval forces which was unfavorable for Germany.

As is seen from the above, in the first stage of the war naval forces had a very considerable effect on its course: Hitler's invasion of England was put off due to the might of the British Fleet; however, with the aid of the Navy the Germans occupied Norway and were able in the first months of the war to inflict great losses on shipping and England's economy as a whole.

The treacherous attack of Fascist Germany on the U.S.S.R., in which an overwhelming part of the armed forces of Germany and her satellites participated, determined the beginning of a new stage in the course of the world war, drastically changing the entire situation in the theaters of military operations.

Eastern Europe, where the fate of the entire Second World War was decided, became the main theater. It was precisely there where Germany and her satellites concentrated their main forces. All other theaters of military operations were transformed into secondary theaters. That is why the role of the navies in the war and their effect on its overall course cannot be regarded separately from the events on the Soviet-German front.

The attack of the Hitlerites on the Soviet Union and the transfer of all of their military efforts to the East had an immediate effect on the course of the armed struggle in the other European theaters. In particular, the air attacks against England and her sea communications were reduced. Again, just as in World War I, on the whole, only submarines operated against British shipping, and now they did not have the requisite combat support on the part of the other naval forces, which permitted the British without any particular difficulty to strengthen the defense of her sea communications.

In considering the Soviet-German front to be the main one, the Hitler command sent not only the main army and air forces against the Soviet Union, but also a considerable part of the Navy. Thus, major surface ships and many submarines were transferred to bases in Northern Norway for operations against the communications linking our northern ports with the ports of the allies. Therefore, the "Battle for the Atlantic" was shifted to a battle with the German submarines, which had already become commonplace for the British and Americans. However, even under these conditions, despite the furious development of ASW forces, the Anglo-Americans were able only to reduce losses from German submarine operations, but were unable to force them to refrain from active operations against communications.

The entire course of the war showed that the deciding role in the defeat of Hitler Germany and her allies belonged to the Soviet Union, and the events on the main, Soviet-German front had a vast effect on the character of the armed struggle in all other theaters of military operations. The success of the main major amphibious operations of the allies in Africa and Europe became possible only owing to the heroic efforts of the Soviet Army and Navy, who prevented Hitler from taking troops from the East which were needed to repulse or destroy the Anglo-American landing forces.

The statements of state and military leaders of the countries of both groups attest to the effect of the events of the Soviet-German front on the course of military operations on the other fronts. Thus, in a letter to Mussolini on 21 June 1941 Hitler reported: "An attack on Egypt before fall is ruled out," when, in his opinion, military operations against the U.S.S.R. would be concluded.[5] The well known Hitler general Guderian indicated that "after the failure of the CITADEL plan (the battle for Kursk), the Eastern front took away all forces from France."[6]

In a report to the War Cabinet on 20 January 1943, British Prime Minister W. Churchill noted that "All of our military operations taken together are on a very insignificant scale in comparison . . . with the gigantic efforts of Russia."[7] He is also credited with such widely known statements as "The Russian resistance broke the backbone of the German armies"[8] and "It was precisely the Russian Army which took the life

[5] *Les lettres secrètes echangées par Hitler et Mussolini.* Paris, 1946, p. 126.
[6] Cited by L. M. Yeremeyev. *Glazami druzey i vragov. O roli Sovetskogo Soyuza v rasgrome fashistskoy Germanii* (Through the Eyes of Friends and Enemies. The Role of the Soviet Union in the Defeat of Fascist Germany). Izd-vo Nauka, 1966, p. 150.
[7] W. Churchill. *Op. cit.* Vol. III, p. 613.
[8] *Ibid,* Vol. II, p. 352.

out of the German war machine and at the present moment is holding by far the largest part of the enemy's forces on its front."[9]

U. S. Secretary of the Interior Ickes wrote in 1944: "The greatest gift that the Russians gave the United Nations was time, without which England would not have even been able to recover from the wounds received at Dunkirk and the United States would not have been able to expand military production and create armies and fleets. . . ."[10]

And a major U. S. figure, Stettinius, said in 1949: "The American people should not forget that they were not far from catastrophe. If the Soviet Union had not been able to hold its front, the Germans would have been able to take Great Britain. They would have been able also to seize Africa and, in this event, they would have succeeded in making a beachhead in Latin America."[11]

On 2 December 1944 General de Gaulle said: "The French know what Soviet Russia did for them, and know that it was precisely Soviet Russia who played the main role in liberating them."[12]

Many prominent Soviet military figures point to the direct effect of the events on the Soviet-German front on the course of combat on the other fronts. Thus, Marshal of the Soviet Union A. A. Grechko stresses that "The victory at Stalingrad, Kursk, on the Don, and in the Caucasus considerably strengthened the positions of our allies in the Near East and in the Mediterranean Basin and made it easier to gain a victory in North Africa over the armies of General Rommel."[13]

The victories of our armed forces in 1943 foiled the plans of the Hitlerites to stabilize the situation on the Soviet-German front and to shift troops to the West to repulse the expected allied invasion of Europe to open a second front.

The landing of allied troops at Normandy in June 1944 was the largest amphibious operation in history. Preparations for it were carried out over a 30-month period in a relatively calm situation. Vast allied naval, ground, and air forces participated in the operation: more than 2,800,000 troops, about 6,000 combatant and landing ships, about 11,000 combat aircraft, and up to 2,000 transport aircraft.[14]

With the opening of the second front in the summer of 1944 the U.S.A. and England made their greatest (albeit tardy) contribution to the cause of victory over Fascist Germany. However, the consciously delayed opening of the second front was not the turning point in the course of the war as Western falsifiers of history depict, for by that time there was already no doubt of the fact that the Soviet Union was in condition to defeat Fascist Germany and to wind up the war without the aid of the allies. As early as 1943, U. S. President F. Roosevelt stated: ". . . If things continue as they are now in Russia, then it is possible that by next spring the second front will not even be needed."[15] Clearly the importance of the second front at that time was no longer decisive. And it was not the opening of it which aided the Soviet armed forces in the struggle with Hitler Germany, but, on the contrary, the victories of our troops not only permitted the allies to marshal vast forces and achieve a 12-fold superiority over the Hitlerites in naval forces and a 22-fold superiority in the air, but also created favorable conditions for the allied invasion of western Europe.

As for the war at sea, the navies of the belligerent countries carried out major missions which had a great effect on the overall course of the war. Thus, the successes of the allies in the Mediterranean theater, first in North Africa and later in Italy, to a certain degree were determined by naval operations supporting the landing of major landing forces in Northwest Africa, on the island of Sicily, and in Italy. The allied fleets disrupted the sea logistics of the Fascist troops of Rommel. These successes on a secondary front of the struggle played their own positive role in the course of the war, although they diverted relatively small German forces.

A different type of situation was created in the armed conflict in the Pacific Ocean, where the navies were of greater import than in the European theaters. However, the general strategic situation, created on the main, Soviet-German front, also unquestionably had an effect on the course of military operations here. The selection by the Japanese of a Southern option for the initiation of their aggression, the refraining from a further continuation of the offensive, and the transition to a strategic defense were the consequence of the disruption of the Blitzkrieg and the series of defeats inflicted on the Hitlerites by the Soviet armed forces.

In the Pacific Ocean the amphibious landing operations by both sides and the disruption of Japanese

[9] (Perepiska Predsedatelya Soveta Ministrov SSSR s Prezidentom SShA i Prem'yer-Ministrom Velikobritanii vo vremya Velikoy Otechestvennoy Voyny 1941–1945 gg. (Correspondence of the Chairman of the USSR Council of Ministers with the U. S. President and the Prime Minister of Great Britain during the Great Patriotic War 1941–1945.) Vol. I, 1957, p. 260.

[10] Krasnyy Flot, (Red Fleet), 27 June 1944.

[11] E. Stettinius. Roosevelt and the Yalta Conference. London, 1950, p. 16.

[12] Sovetsko-frantsuzskiye otnosheniya (Soviet-French Relations), 1959, p. 340.

[13] A. A. Grechko. Bitva za Kavkaz (The Battle For the Caucasus), Voyenizdat, 1971, p. 546.

[14] Vtoraya mirovaya voyna 1939–1945 gg. (The Second World War, 1939–1945). Voyenizdat, 1958, p. 641.

[15] E. Roosevelt. Ego glazami (Through His Eyes), Moscow, 1947, p. 161.

Table 2.   *Composition of Naval Forces in the Pacific Ocean on 7 December 1941.*

Ship types	U.S.A.	Great Britain	Holland	Total	Japan	Relative strength
Battleships & battle cruisers	9	2	—	11	10	1:0.9
Aircraft carriers	3	—	—	3	10	1:3.3
Cruisers	24	8	3	35	36	0.97:1
Destroyers	80	13	7	100	113	1:1.1
Submarines	73	—	15	88	63	1.4:1

Data compiled from the *Morskoy Atlas* (Naval Atlas) Vol. III, Part 2, line 30.

shipping by the blockading operations of the American Navy became the basic types of combat operations. All other combat operations were essentially only in support of landing or antilanding operations.

The war here began on 7 December 1941 with relatively equal forces on both sides (Table 2) with a surprise attack by the Japanese on Pearl Harbor, the main base of the American Pacific Fleet. As a result of the attack, Japanese carrier aircraft sunk or damaged all eight battleships in the harbor and one cruiser, and destroyed about 200 landbased American aircraft.[16] Within three days the Japanese had succeeded in sinking an English squadron in the Gulf of Siam, and in February 1942 [they sank] a hurriedly assembled Anglo-Dutch-American squadron in the Java Sea. Japan had gained control of the sea, which permitted her to carry out several amphibious operations in the first stage of the war. In two months the Japanese occupied the Philippine Islands, the Malacca Peninsula with the major British base of Singapore, Indonesia, Burma, and many islands in the Pacific Ocean. Japan seized the vast economic resources of Southeast Asia. However, as a result of the victories achieved on the Soviet-German front, particularly in the Battle of Stalingrad, which determined the turning point in the course of the entire war and which was consolidated by subsequent victories of the Soviet Army, by 1943 the Japanese were already refraining from further offensive operations and had gone over to a strategic defense.

Western historians assert that the turning point in the course of the war in the Pacific Ocean came before Stalingrad when, on 3 to 6 June 1942, four Japanese aircraft carriers and only one American carrier were sunk in a successful American engagement off the island of Midway. However, the relative strengths of the naval forces after this battle contradict such assertions, since even after it Japan retained supremacy at sea in forces: eight aircraft carriers (counting also those

newly commissioned)[17] against four American carriers.[18] The Japanese also had superiority in battleships and cruisers. Indeed, the nature of the combat operations following the Battle of Midway Island also attests to the fact that it was in no way the turning point in the course of the war. Actually the Japanese continued to land landing forces, to conduct an offensive on New Guinea, and in the Solomon Islands, and to create a difficult situation for the Americans which was aggravated by the loss of two more of their aircraft carriers, the *Wasp* and the *Hornet*.

W. Churchill wrote that in the fall of 1942 the Americans turned to England with a request to aid them with aircraft carriers. ". . . We understood that a serious crisis had arisen in the Solomon Islands."[19] By that time the U.S.A. had only two carriers left there, the *Saratoga* and the *Enterprise* (and those were damaged). The real threat of a Japanese invasion of Australia arose. How can one speak of a turning point in the war in the Pacific after Midway?

Also unfounded is the attempt by Western historians to represent as a turning point of the course of the war in the Pacific the landing in August of 1942 by one (!) Marine Division on the island of Guadalcanal, which conducted protracted battles with the Japanese forces with varying success. By the way, the President of the United States, F. Roosevelt, in a report to Congress on 7 January 1943 indicated that the actions at Midway and Guadalcanal islands "were essentially defensive. They were a part of the strategy of containment which characterized this phase of the war."[20]

Yet suddenly, in a situation which was so difficult for the allies, the Japanese Imperial Staff on 31 Decem-

[16] *Morskoy atlas* (Naval atlas), Vol. III, Part 2, line 30.

[17] Kodzima Noboru. The War in the Pacific Ocean. Tokyo, Vol. I, pp. 249–250.
[18] F. S. Sherman. American Carriers in the War in the Pacific. Voyenizdat, 1956, p. 104.
[19] W. Churchill. The Second World War. Vol. V, 1955, p. 28.
[20] The President's War Addresses to the People and to the Congress of the U.S.A., Washington, 1945, p. 61.

ber 1942 decided to drop the offensive strategy and go over to the defensive. It is quite evident that the most important reason for this was the victory of the Soviet troops at Stalingrad, when for the first time the faith of the Japanese military leaders in the power of the German Army was really shaken. The Japanese leaders recognized that "if Germany . . . weakens, in a short time Japan would face a world-wide coalition."[21] The Japanese understood that "the victory of the Soviet Army at Stalingrad was a blow not only to Germany but also to Japan."[22]

Thus, the actual course of the armed conflict quite clearly shows that the victory of the Soviet armed forces at Stalingrad was the beginning of the pivotal events in the course of the entire Second World War.

Yet, nevertheless, Western historians, speaking out as defenders of their imperialist masters, not interested in an objective treatment of history, are now striving to distort history in every possible way. Thus, in the "History of the 20th Century" published in England by the firm "Purnell," they again return to the attempt to reduce the importance of the Battle of Stalingrad. In enumerating the most important events of the war which hurt Germany, they speak of the battle of Midway, of "The Battle for the Atlantic," and of the battles at El Alamein, and only after this do they refer to the battle of Stalingrad, attributing limited significance to it (and by that only a significance pertaining to the war in Eastern Europe) although five enemy armies were defeated and taken prisoner in it, which shocked

Admiral Gorshkov asserts that neither the battles of Midway nor Guadalcanal, above, can be considered as turning points of the war in the Pacific. After Midway, he argues, Japan still retained supremacy at sea. Equally unfounded is the attempt by Western "falsifiers of history" to exalt the efforts of "one (!) Marine Division" whose actions on Guadalcanal "were essentially defensive."

[21] *Nyurnbergskiy protsess. Sbornik materialov.* (The Nuremburg Trial. Collection of Materials), Vol. I, Gosyurizdat, 1952, p. 402.
[22] *Istoriya voyny na Tikhom okeane* (History of the War in the Pacific Ocean), Vol. IV, Foreign Literature Pub. House, 1955, p. 16.

the entire military machine of Fascist Germany and her allies.

Enough has already been said above concerning the battle of Midway Island. The struggle of the navies for communications in the Atlantic Ocean in 1942 also did not lead to any sort of decisive results which could have served as the beginning of Germany's defeat. And the battle near El Alamein in which two small armies with a total strength on both sides of about 250,000 men participated (about 2% of the number of troops fighting on the Soviet-German front!), of course could not be the turning point in the course of the war.

The course of the war in the Pacific theater once more confirmed that the political goals, which were supposed to be implemented by military means, were directly dependent on the capabilities of the economy and of the armed forces. It is precisely this which explains why Japan so attentively followed the course of the struggle on the Soviet-German front and the position of her main partner, and changed her plans depending on this.

On 1 February 1943, Japanese troops began to evacuate the island of Guadalcanal, and by fall, a new, shorter defense line had been established. In the summer of 1943 the Japanese tightened their defensive belt even further, withdrawing it to the Caroline and Mariana Islands, and the main forces were brought back to rear bases. By the fall of 1943 the economic advantages of the U.S.A. were felt, and control of the sea irrevocably went over to the Americans, which permitted them to initiate offensive operations.

With the shift to the defensive, troop shipments by sea between the home country and the defense lines and also the delivery of materials to Japan from occupied territories took on greater significance for the Japanese. However, these shipments were more vunerable in the Japanese defense system. And when the initiative was shifted to the Americans, and they began offensive operations, then the Japanese turned out to be incapable of either maneuvering forces on the defensive lines or of delivering strategic materials to Japan. The battle for sea communications took on a one-sided character. Japanese submarines operated only against major enemy surface ships and were not used against his communications lanes. Therefore, American shipping remained essentially unopposed. The Americans, on the other hand, from the very outbreak of war, attacked enemy shipping (mainly with submarines). Beginning in 1944 American aircraft and surface ships were also involved in these operations. In this connection, due to the weakness of the defense of the Japanese communications their attacks were delivered under the most simple, almost training-range conditions.

Moreover, taking the defeats of the Hitlerites on the Soviet-German front into account, the Japanese avoided the risk of employing their main naval forces to defend the occupied islands, relegating the execution of this task to small garrisons who had no naval or air support.

As a result of the operations of the American forces against the sea communications, by 1945 the economic potential of Japan was undermined, and she was unable to replenish the losses in warships and aircraft, while at the same time the U.S.A. continued to accent the construction of ships and aircraft (as the figures in Table 3 attest). This permitted the U.S.A. to create a decisive superiority in forces in the chosen areas and to control the conduct of operations in the area. At the same time, in order to disrupt Japan's economy, the U.S.A. began to make systematic air attacks on industrial targets.

The offensive operations of the American Navy began in late 1943 when favorable conditions emerged for this as a result of the victory of the Soviet armed forces over the troops of the main partner of the Fascist bloc—Hitler Germany. In this connection, the operations of the Americans were first directed not against the main military forces of the enemy, but rather against peripheral garrisons located on the islands occupied by them. Having the advantage in naval forces, the Americans were able to select the direction of the attacks which confused the Japanese, and they were late in giving support to their garrisons.

The Americans, having broken through the outer defensive line of the Japanese and having consolidated themselves by landing landing forces behind them, went over to operations against the inner line of defense in the fall of 1944. The Japanese employed their main naval forces to oppose the landing of the Ameri-

Table 3. *Composition of the U. S. Navy*

Ship types	Year	
	1941	1944
Carriers (heavy, light, escort)	7	125
Battleships	16	23
Cruisers	36	67
Destroyers and escorts	180	879
Subchasers	—	up to 900
Submarines	112	351
Landing craft, ships, and auxiliaries	—	75,000 +

*Data from book by L. M. Yeremeyev and A. P. Shergin "Submarines of Foreign Navies in World War II," (p. 375) and "Handbook of the Ships of the Navies of the World. 1944" (Voyenizdat, 1945, p. 295).

cans in the Philippine Islands. Here in the waters of the Philippine archipelago the largest naval engagement of its time also took place in which significant forces on both sides participated (Table 4). As a result of the battle, the Japanese Fleet suffered heavy losses: four aircraft carriers, three battleships, ten cruisers, 11 destroyers, and two submarines.[23] This battle had a considerable effect on the further course of military operations in the Pacific theater, predetermining the success of the American capture of the Philippines and the subsequent shift of their amphibious operations toward Japan itself.

The last American amphibious operation was the landing on Okinawa in 1945. The struggle for this island lasted three months despite the six-fold superiority of the landing forces over the enemy garrison and the complete American control of the sea and air.

The attacks by American aircraft on the cities and ports of Japan were continually expanded, but even in 1945 Japan's Army had suffered very insignificant losses on the Pacific islands. The most powerful and combat-capable grouping of Japanese ground forces, the Kwantung Army in Manchuria, not only was unweakened by military operations, but continued to be strengthened, being supported by the military/economic base of Japanese imperialism, the industry of Manchuria and Korea.

In August 1945 Japan still had major armed forces at her disposal: five million men, 10,000 aircraft, and about 600 warships.[24] This permitted her to continue the war despite the capitulation of Germany and the loss of Japanese occupied territories. The Americans, not relying on their own capability of forcing Japan to surrender quickly, developed plans for landing operations against Japan itself according to which the landing of troops on the island of Kyushu was scheduled for late 1945 and in the Tokyo area, in 1946 or even later. The plans called for a prolonged struggle with the employment of major ground forces which the Americans did not have. However, the Americans had insufficient superiority in naval forces to achieve success. That is why they needed the U.S.S.R. to enter the war against Japan. This was precisely the reason for so many appeals by Churchill and Truman to Stalin to begin military operations with the Soviet Army in the Far East.

In fulfilling its obligations as an ally, the Soviet Army and Navy crushed the Kwantung Army with powerful blows which also forced Japan to surrender.

In examining the events which took place in the Pacific and Far Eastern Theaters of military operations

Table 4. *Composition of the U. S. and Japanese Naval Forces in the Battle of the Philippines*

Ship type	U.S.A.	Japan
Aircraft carriers	34	4
Battleships	12	9
Cruisers	23	20
Destroyers	113	32
Submarines	29	17

Data taken from Naval Atlas, Vol. III, Part 2, line 48.

in the years of the Second World War, we cannot fail to emphasize that the struggle between Japan and the U.S.A. was waged for a long time primarily by naval forces. Thus, the Japanese were guided by strategic concepts stemming from their military doctrine which stressed the seizure of vast territories (not commensurate with the actual capabilities of exploiting and retaining them), and greatly oriented toward the success of her ally in the aggression, Fascist Germany. The Americans, however, conducted their operations in the peripheral regions of the Japanese defense zone in accordance with a "palm-tree to palm-tree" strategy which permitted only a methodical step-by-step advance of military operations toward the homeland of the enemy. These operations had little effect on the Japanese ground forces, whose main forces practically did not even participate in the war against their main enemy in the Pacific Ocean—the U.S.A. The Americans also did not attack either the Kwantung Army or the sea communications linking them with Japan. The military industrial base in Korea and Manchuria also did not suffer any opposition, although it was also located in a zone accessible to the American attack forces (especially carrier aircraft). The Americans extended their operations to this zone only after the Soviet Union had entered the war with Japan, had smashed the Kwantung Army, and was preparing the final blow. American operations in this period were expressed mainly in the active laying of mines in the paths of the Soviet naval forces driving toward the coast of Korea and the Liaotung peninsula. These operations had the goal not so much of weakening the Japanese Army as hindering the decisive movement of Soviet naval forces in support of Soviet troops, i.e., hindering their own ally in doing just what the American command had studiously avoided throughout the entire war—direct opposition to the enemy forces making up the basis of his military might.

With such a strategy, clearly the war in the Pacific theater would not have been concluded even by 1946 without the participation of the Soviet Union despite

[23] *Op. cit.* Naval Atlas, Vol. III, Part 2, line 48-b.
[24] *Op. cit.* The Second World War 1939–1945. p. 789.

the fact that the U.S.A. employed nuclear weaponry in it. Only the crushing of the Kwantung Army by the Soviet armed forces sharply reduced the military potential of Japan and her capability to continue military operations. Also an analysis of the operations of the American Fleet which were based mainly on an overwhelming superiority of forces also serves as a basis for such an assertion. While having large numbers of submarines at their disposal, the Americans, however, employed only a small part of them for operations against Japan's communications. An average of no more than 15 submarines were at sea at one time (Fascist Germany operated this number of submarines at sea when she had only about one-third as many as the Americans).

In the course of the war the lack of preparedness of the Japanese Navy to protect sea communications was revealed with ever greater clarity, which prevented her from using the resources of the occupied territories to build up her power. Nevertheless, despite the exceptionally favorable conditions, American operations against Japanese communications were not distinguished by activity.

As was already indicated above, the reasons for the Japanese shift to a strategic defense were not at all due to the actions of the American Navy or to the fact that after the Pearl Harbor catastrophe the U.S.A. expanded construction of aircraft carriers, as Western historians assert. These reasons lie in the defeat of the German Fascist army at Stalingrad, which convinced the Japanese military leaders of the hopelessness of the offensive strategy which they had adopted and of the blind devotion to her ally in the anti-Communist aggressive bloc.

Consequently, such prolonged military operations in the Pacific Ocean, in which the forces of the Japanese, American, and British fleets took part, in themselves could not have brought a rapid close to the war without the decisive intervention of the powerful forces of the Soviet land Army which brilliantly carried out its assigned missions, forcing Japan to capitulate, thereby victoriously concluding the Second World War.

Commentary

By Admiral George W. Anderson, Jr. U. S. Navy (Retired)

Admiral Anderson graduated from the U. S. Naval Academy in 1927. A naval aviator from 1930, he served in various squadrons of the Fleet, on the carrier *Yorktown* and in the flight test division at NAS, Norfolk. Prior to and during World War II, he was assigned to BuAer, as navigator of the USS *Yorktown,* and successively on the staffs of ComAirPac, CinCPac, CinC U. S. Fleet and on the Joint War Plans Committee. After the war he commanded two aircraft carriers, USS *Mindoro* and USS *Franklin D. Roosevelt,* served with Sixth Fleet and SACEur staffs, and was assistant to the Chairman of the JCS. After attending the National War College in 1949–1950 he was assigned to command the Taiwan Patrol Force, as Chief of Staff to CinCPac, as ComCarDiv Six, and commanded the Sixth Fleet in the Mediterranean. He served as CNO from 1961 until 1963. In 1963 he was appointed U. S. Ambassador to Portugal and remained in that post until he retired from Government service in July 1966.

Since then Admiral Anderson has been in private business, and served as a member of the Board of Directors of several corporations. In March 1969 he was appointed to the President's Foreign Intelligence Advisory Board and designated chairman of that Board as of 1 May 1970.

Admiral Gorshkov's article on World War II revealed to his officers, and now to us, the thoughts, views and beliefs of the Admiral of the Soviet Fleet, who also is a full member of the CPSU Central Committee and a Soviet historian. This combination elevates the value and meaning of each article in this series and enables us to study one of the most prominent Soviet leaders, and the one individual who is most responsible for the development of the Soviet Navy as it is today.

At the beginning of World War II, Admiral Gorshkov was a newly selected flag officer responsible for the defense of an area threatened by German occupation. His positions and personal contributions to the Soviet cause during this war were extremely significant, as evidenced by his writings. A brief glance at his career during this time-frame may help explain some of his views.

In 1941, Admiral Gorshkov became the youngest admiral in Soviet history and was assigned as commander of the Azov Flotilla, then a component of the Black Sea Fleet. He was responsible for protecting the maritime flanks of the Red Army during the 1941–42 retreat to the Caucasus, and for amphibious actions on German rear forces. He was personally involved in the outcome of the battle at Stalingrad, having lost his command when the Azov Sea fell into enemy hands early in 1942. Following the Soviet victory at Stalingrad in 1943, Gorshkov was personally rewarded by his reassignment as Commander of the reactivated Azov Flotilla and he successfully took part in the liberation of the Crimea. Shortly thereafter, in 1944, he assumed command of the newly formed Danube Flotilla, into which the Azov Flotilla was incorporated. As a Vice Admiral, he distinguished himself in the landing on Kerch Peninsula and supported others in the liberation of the Ukraine, Rumania, Bulgaria, and Hungary.

Although heavy personal emphasis is placed on the importance of the battle of Stalingrad as related to the war in the Pacific, the Admiral's views do not significantly depart from those previously published by numerous Soviet historians. The accounts and opinions expressed by the author largely parallel those published in the Soviet Government approved six-volume "History of the Great Patriotic War of the Soviet Union." However, it must be remembered that the Admiral is a firm member of the Communist party hierarchy and by doctrine, Communists do not hesitate to interpret—if not outrightly distort—history to further the ideology and their objectives.

Gorshkov wrote this article while in a position of naval leadership and political authority. It reemphasizes the somewhat older views held by the Soviet Government. Of the numerous differences between his views and those held by "Western historians," two are considered of primary interest:

▶ That the battle of Stalingrad was not only the turning point for the war in Europe but was the primary cause for the turn of the war in the Pacific. He states, "The reasons for the Japanese shift to a strategic defense were not at all due to the actions of the American Fleet . . ."

▶ That the primary reason for the capitulation of Japan was the "decisive" intervention of the Soviet Army and Navy and not the introduction of the atomic bomb.

It is doubtful that western historians and the author will ever agree on these controversial points. However, the author's explanation of his views by the use of innocuous quotations, and reliance upon "heroic" cliches, further weakens his effort to establish these differences in only one article. The specific points will not be argued in this commentary but a close study of his views should be made, keeping in mind the author's personal involvement in the battle of Stalingrad and the obvious omission of any discussion relating to the successful implementation of atomic weaponry.

Gorshkov is not considered a prolific military writer. It will be necessary to study the entire series in order to adequately evaluate his concepts. Selectively, however, one can see signs of military and strategic concepts in this month's article. The concept during his discussion of World War II is centered around the Soviet military and political forces which, in the Admiral's opinion, were the primary causes for the allied success in both Europe and the Pacific.

Numerous strategic areas are mentioned by the author in his historical coverage that appeared to reveal his primary areas of interest. Whenever the opportunity presents itself, he refers to the Navy as an integral and indispensable component of the Soviet Armed Forces. His stress of submarines and antisubmarine warfare confirms his extreme interest in that area and reveals his views on the importance of maintaining an open sea line of communication during periods of peace and war. His opinion that the American Fleet had little to do with the outcome of the war in the Pacific is unjustified. He weakens his own position by discussing the importance of the aircraft carrier to both the United States and Japan.

Admiral Gorshkov's writings continually reenforce actions taken by the Soviets since 1956 in the expansion of its seapower. Under his leadership, the Soviet Navy has been elevated to an equal component of the Armed Forces and most probably will soon be considered the premier service among the branches of the Soviet Armed Forces. As its architect, he has placed accent on sophisticated nuclear missile armed strategic submarines, cruise missiles, attack submarines, new large surface ships and sophisticated aircraft. In addition, he has introduced carrier aviation.

Admiral Gorshkov has changed Soviet naval strategy to emphasize five primary missions: strategic attack, strategic ASW, defense against aircraft carriers, distant operations, and interdiction. In short, the author of this article has produced the emphasis on the Navy's strategic offensive capabilities and changed the pre-1963 home-based, day-running, fair-weather outlook to the global philosophy we now see.

It will be remembered that in 1968, Admiral Gorshkov stated "The United States will have to understand that it no longer has mastery of the seas." This should be taken in a most serious manner by all who have responsibility for the conduct of American foreign policy and the assurance of American security.

The Soviet Navy in the Great Patriotic War

With Commentary following the article by Arleigh Burke

EDITOR'S NOTE: *In the following chapter, cleared for publication in the Soviet Union on 6 October 1972, the admiral describes the operational and strategic support given to the Soviet Army by the Soviet Navy in the "main theater" of the war—the Soviet-German front—"where the outcome of World War II was decided."*

On 22 June 1941, the perfidious attack by Hitler Germany interrupted the peaceful labor of the Soviet people. A savage armed struggle, unprecedented in scale, had begun between the most reactionary Fascist state and the first Socialist country.

The war did not catch our fleets unawares, despite the fact that in the very first hours of it many naval bases were subjected to attacks by the enemy air force. The Soviet Navy did not lose a single warship or aircraft from the enemy's initial blow. The Hitlerites also did not succeed in achieving another aim—the planting of influence mines in the areas of our bases to prevent combatants from putting to sea.

During World War II, the Soviet Navy sent more than 400,000 nonrated and rated men and officers to the ground fronts, including this detachment of Baltic Fleet sailors seen on their way to participate in the defense of Leningrad.

From the very first day of the war the Soviet Navy engaged in lone combat with the enemy naval forces which were supported by three air forces and which had considerable strategic advantages. In particular, they were able to maneuver forces from theater to theater and create a numerical superiority in areas where the more important missions were being carried out. For example, in the period of the most intense battles around Leningrad, the German command marshalled a major grouping of surface ships in the Baltic Sea to destroy our fleet. A similar grouping was subsequently also created in the North in order to cut our external sea communications. In the period of the battle for Odessa and Sevastopol, the Hitlerites transferred powerful groupings of bomber and torpedo aircraft from the Mediterranean to the Black Sea. In addition, surface ships, submarines, and aircraft of Germany and also naval forces of her satellites were constantly active in all of our theaters.

On the other hand, our Navy's capabilities for inter-theater maneuver were very limited. Thus, the Northern Sea Route permitted the transfer of units of naval forces from the Pacific Ocean to the North and back again, but first, this could only be done once a year, and second, it required about two to three months. Soon after the outbreak of war, intertheater movement using the inland waterways had to be curtailed due to the fact that the main canals turned out to be in the zone of the ground fronts. Even the transport of patrol boats and small submarines by railroad did not satisfy requirements.

The withdrawal of the Soviet Army toward the East made the conditions for basing our fleets worse. Thus, by the autumn of 1941, the Red Banner Baltic Fleet already was unable to base itself at points in the Leningrad—Kronstadt—Lavensaari region which were in range of enemy guns. The Black Sea Fleet had to move its bases to ports on the Caucasian coast, which were not equipped for this. Nevertheless, from the first to the last day of the war, all our fleets conducted active combat operations. Submarines put to sea to seek out and destroy enemy warships and transports. Aircraft and surface ships also continually sought out the enemy and destroyed him on the open seas, and in coastal waters and bases, and attacked shore objectives and airfields in enemy territory. The activity and the constant desire to seek the enemy out and attack him everywhere which was displayed at all command levels in all of our fleets—this is the best recommendation for the command personnel of the Soviet Navy and for their training and educational system.

The battle against sea communications required tremendous efforts. Throughout the entire war, submarines, aircraft, torpedo boats, destroyers, and coastal artillery destroyed enemy ships with troops and cargoes. These operations were conducted systematically, and, very likely, there was not a single day which did not bring success in the accomplishment of this mission. Even when in order to put to sea the Baltic Fleet submarines had to pass through the Gulf of Finland, which was literally saturated with mines and covered by several antisubmarine positions, the enemy constantly felt the force of attacks by our Navy. The Northern Fleet retained control over the solitary sea route by which the German troops in Norway and in Northern Finland were reinforced and by which nickel was exported from Petsamo. The men of the Black Sea Fleet also inflicted great losses against enemy sea communications.

The opposition to sea shipments considerably aided Soviet Army units on the ground fronts, since it hindered the enemy's capability to significantly reinforce his groupings with manpower, or with fuel, ammu-nition, and foodstuffs which he needed. During the war Soviet navymen destroyed some 1,300 transports with a total displacement of 3,000,000 tons on the enemy sea routes and sunk more than 1,200 combatants and auxiliaries. It is quite natural that this had a great effect on the course of the armed struggle on the Soviet-German ground front, where the outcome of the war was decided.

According to incomplete data from the headquarters of the 17th German Army, during the evacuation of Fascist troops from the Crimea in the period from 3 to 13 May 1944 alone, the men of the Black Sea Fleet destroyed more than 42,000 officers and men.[1] This was a considerable contribution by the Black Sea Fleet toward creating favorable conditions for the conduct of subsequent operations of our ground forces in the Southwestern sector.

The security of our own shipping occupied an important place in the combat operations of the fleets throughout the entire course of the war. These shipments acquired vast significance after the enemy cut the Murmansk railroad line. In the Black Sea they were vitally essential in the period of the defense of Odessa, Sevastopol, and of the Northern Caucasus, when conducting the Kerch-Feodosiya landing operation, in the Baltic during the defense and evacuation of Tallinn, Hanko, and the Moon Sound Islands, in reinforcing the groupings of our troops at the Oranienbaum beachhead, and in the subsequent liberation of the Baltic Republics.

Our fleets and flotillas executed extremely important missions in supporting troop shipments and shipments of national economic interest along water routes near the fronts, especially on Lake Ladoga when the difficult situation arose at Leningrad, and also along the Volga. In the war years more than 100 million tons of various types of goods, of which a considerable part were petroleum and petroleum products, were delivered along inland waterways. In addition, naval forces supported the shipment of 17 million tons of goods over external sea routes. Behind these figures are thousands of ship deployments and aircraft flights, hundreds of combat clashes with surface ships and submarines, the repulsing of enemy air attacks, and the surmounting of thick minefields.

However, the activity of our fleets was not limited to battling the enemy at sea, although the execution of this mission required great daily efforts by the forces. Our fleets had to simultaneously execute the important mission of cooperating with the coastal units of the Soviet Army defensively and offensively in support of the stability of the strategic flanks of a vast front

---

[1] The Second World War. 1939–1945, Voyenizdat, 1958, p. 567.

stretching from the Black Sea to the Arctic Ocean. And the more complex the situation became on land, the more crucial and active operations by the fleets became in carrying out this strategic mission and also in defending major coastal administrative and political centers, naval bases, and ports.

It is difficult to overestimate the role of the Black Sea Fleet in defending the more important ports and in giving stability to the southern flank of the ground front. The successful and prolonged resistance deep in the enemy's rear by the Odessa defensive region, whose garrison included many navymen, was possible only owing to constant aid from the sea by warships and the uninterrupted delivery of everything necessary to the besieged city. The heroic defense of Odessa, by tying up the entire Romanian Army for more than two months, held up the progress of the southern flank of the "Southern" group of armies and disrupted the strategic plans of the Hitler command.

In September 1941, a real threat arose of an enemy breakthrough into the Crimea, and on 30 September the General Headquarters of the Supreme High Command issued a directive which stated its decision to evacuate the Odessa region and to reinforce the defense of the Crimean peninsula with its troops.

In carrying out the orders of the General Headquarters, the Black Sea Fleet delivered the troops defending Odessa to the Crimea without losses where they took part in the defense of Sevastopol.

The defense of Sevastopol tied up a 300,000-man enemy grouping for eight months and did not permit it to engage in the offensive in the south. Moreover, the retention of Sevastopol in our hands eliminated the possibility of the Fascists using the sea route to feed the southern group of armies and prevented them from breaking through to the ports of the Northern Caucasus.

In a telegram of 12 June 1942 the Supreme Commander in Chief gave the following appraisal of the actions of the forces defending Sevastopol: "The selfless struggle of the people of Sevastopol serves as an example of heroism for the entire Red Army and the Soviet people."

A communication by the Soviet Information Bureau in connection with the evacuation of Sevastopol said: "The military and political importance of the defense of Sevastopol in the Great Patriotic War is very great to the Soviet people. By tying up a large number of German and Romanian troops, the defenders of the city confused and shattered the plans of the German command. The iron tenacity of the people of Sevastopol was one of the most important causes for the failure of the notorious German 'Spring offensive.' The Germans lost time and momentum, and suffered great manpower losses. Sevastopol was evacuated by the Soviet troops, but the defense of Sevastopol will go down as one of the brightest pages in the history of the Great Patriotic War. The utter courage, the fury in battle with the enemy, and the selflessness of the defenders of Sevastopol inspired the Soviet patriots on to further heroic feats in the struggle against the hated invaders." [2]

The Fascist offensive in the Caucasus harbored the real threat that they would seize this most important region and alter the military-political situation in the Black Sea theater as related to the possible entry of Turkey (who was then biding her time) on the side of Hitler Germany. The Black Sea Fleet's existence depended on our Army's holding the Caucasian coast. Yet the stability of the ground forces defending the littoral areas of the Caucasus area, in turn, was also supported by naval operations. Through the combined efforts of the Army and Black Sea Fleet, the battle for the Caucasus was won.

In reviewing this battle, Marshal of the Soviet Union A. A. Grechko writes: "In the defensive stage of the battle for the Caucasus, of the nine defensive operations conducted by Soviet troops from July to December 1942, the Black Sea Fleet and the Azov Flotilla directly participated in six. . . . The Black Sea Fleet and the Azov Naval Flotilla, by acting closely in concert with ground troops, rendered them a great deal of aid in the defense against and defeat of the Hitlerites in the Caucasus. . . . The Black Sea Fleet and the Azov Flotilla also rendered considerable support to the ground forces in the offensive period. By landing landing parties of naval forces the troops were aided in breaking through the powerful permanent defense of the enemy. . . . The most important task handed the Black Sea Fleet in the period of the battle of the Caucasus was the reliable support of our sea communications along the Caucasian coast, and it was successfully carried out. The Caspian Flotilla . . . provided the defense of sea routes which were extremely important to the entire country. . . . The Black Sea Fleet and the Azov and Caspian Flotillas carried out their assigned missions in the battle for the Caucasus with honor." [3]

In the period of the Hitler offensive against Leningrad, the Red Banner Baltic Fleet rendered Red Army units extremely great aid. In defending Liepaja, Tallinn, the Moon Sound Islands, and the Hanko naval base together with our ground troops, it tied up a 100,000-man grouping of enemy forces. The stability of the defense of Leningrad, especially at the beginning

---

[2] *Pravda,* 4 July, 1942.

[3] A. A. Grechko. *Bitva za Kavkaz.* (The Battle for the Caucasus), Voyenizdat, 1969, pp. 466–467.

of its siege, was determined to a great degree by the vigorous actions of the Baltic Fleet forces. Throughout the war it retained the Oranienbaum beachhead and diverted major enemy forces toward itself. The Red Banner Baltic Fleet sent more than 83,000 nonrated and rated men, and officers to fight the enemy on land. At Leningrad there was not a single division in which a Baltic Fleet man was not fighting. The powerful guns of the Fleet served as a firm fire shield and the foundation of the defense of the close approaches to the heroic city. Its striking power was supplemented by the unprecedented support and irresistibility of naval infantry attacks.

Through attacks by its ships and planes on groupings of German Fascist troops pushing toward Murmansk, by landing landing parties and naval infantry operations, and by hindering the enemy's shipping, the Northern Fleet played a decisive role in disrupting his offensive on the right flank of the Soviet-German front. And only because the Northern Fleet sent everything it had to the ground front to aid our troops, which amounted to a little more than one rifle division in strength, did they succeed in stopping the offensive of the German mountain corps on the approaches to Murmansk. More than 9,000 officers and men of the Northern Fleet were fighting on land at that time. The retention of the ice-free port of Murmansk and the Polyarnoye naval base was of extremely important operational-strategic significance: throughout the entire course of the war it permitted using the shortest sea route connecting the Soviet Union with its allies of that time, the successful execution of missions in defense of its communications, the disruption of the enemy's shipping, and it permitted concerted actions with the ground troops defensively and later also offensively.

In the war years the Navy sent a total of more than 400,000 nonrated and rated men and officers to the ground fronts. More than 40 brigades of naval infantry and naval rifle brigades, six individual regiments, and a large number of individual battalions and detachments were formed from these men. These forces and units were distinguished by their exceptionally high combat qualities and therefore were employed by the Army command on the more important sectors of the front. Seven naval rifle brigades were in action in the most intense period of the battle for Moscow as a part of the troops of the Western Front.

In addition, some 100,000 naval infantrymen who remained within the fleets and flotillas carried out the land defense of the naval bases and islands and participated in amphibious landings which also rendered real aid to units of the Soviet Army.

After the Soviet Armed Forces had gained the strategic initiative, cooperation with the coastal groupings of troops remained one of the basic missions of the Navy, although the content of the mission had significantly changed, the operational scales had increased, and the conditions for carrying them out had become even more complicated due to the losses of individual basing areas. Yet despite this, the fleets successfully handled all of the missions with which they were charged.

For the Red Banner Baltic Fleet this was expressed in the participation of the air force, the long-range artillery, and brigades of naval infantry in breaking through the blockade of Leningrad, in transporting troops to the Oranienbaum beachhead, in landing landing parties, in supporting our troops ashore with gunfire and air strikes, in increasing the scope of operations against sea communications, and in the destruction of the enemy troops being evacuated by sea from Liepaja, Memel (Klaipeda), Danzig (Gdansk), Swinemuende (Swinoujscie), and other ports.

By the Novorossiysk landing operation the Black Sea Fleet began the liquidation of the Taman beachhead of the enemy, supported the crossing in force of the Kerch Strait by our troops, and seized a beachhead in the Crimea. Follow-up operations by our Fleet hindered the evacuation of the German troops from the Crimea, and the landing of a landing party hastened the liberation of the southern regions of the country and also of Bulgaria and Rumania.

The Northern Fleet also played an important role in the defeat of the enemy on the extreme right flank and in the liberation of the Pechenga Oblast and of Northern Norway.

By using naval ships and merchant ships poorly suited for landing troops, the fleets landed more than 110 landing parties with a total strength of 250,000 men in the course of defensive and offensive operations in the coastal areas. At the same time active naval operations did not permit the enemy to land a single landing party on our shore, although he had specially designed landing ships at his disposal and had experience in the successful conduct of such operations in the Western European theater of military operations.

The Azov, Ladoga, Onega, White Sea, Volga, Danube, and other Flotillas which were created on the internal seas, large rivers, and lakes operated successfully. They rendered direct and important aid to the ground troops both defensively and offensively. The White Sea Flotilla, for example, executed missions associated with the use of the sea routes in the Arctic areas and the transit of combatants and convoys via the Northern Sea Route. The Caspian Flotilla reliably defended our main petroleum line in the Caspian Sea. The Ladoga Naval Flotilla supported the functioning

Sailors of the Black Sea Fleet came ashore as reinforcements for the beleaguered ground troops at Sevastapol and, although the city itself was ultimately evacuated after a 250-day siege (October 1941 to July 1942), the Russians inflicted enormous losses on the German and Romanian armies.

of the "Lifeline", the solitary route connecting besieged Leningrad with the country. The Danube Flotilla covered more than 2,000 kilometers with intensive fighting along the Danube River and participated in the liberation of six European states from the Fascist yoke. Marshal of the Soviet Union V. Chuykov gives a vivid appraisal of the operations of the Volga Naval Flotilla in the battle of Stalingrad: "Let me briefly tell of the role of the navymen of the Flotilla and of their feats: if they had not been there, it is possible that the 62nd Army would have perished without ammunition and without food and would not have been able to carry out its mission." [4] Navymen of the Pinsk Naval Flotilla heroically fought alongside units of the Red Army in the most serious period of the Great Patriotic War. In bloody defensive battles on river banks its ships supported the ground forces and participated in the defense of Kiev. The Dnepr Flotilla, which was revived in 1943, participated in the Berlin operation and concluded its combat path on the Spree River.

The short, but intensive combat operations of the

[4] *V. I. Chuykov. Nachalo puti* (The Start of the My Route), Voyenizdat, 1962, p. 182.

Pacific Fleet and the Northern Pacific and Amur Naval Flotillas played an important role by their offensive operations in the rapid occupation of the southern part of Sakhalin Island, the Kurile Islands, and the ports of Korea, and in the rapid advance of Soviet troops into the depths of Manchuria. Owing to their swift landing operations the men of the Pacific Fleet severed the communications of the Japanese Kwantung Army with the home country and completed its full encirclement.

Thus, the Navy, throughout the entire war, successfully carried out the missions with which it was charged in accordance with the needs of the armed struggle in the main theater where its outcome was decided. The operational and strategic employment of naval forces was determined by the need to closely relate their operational plans to the plans of the Army, and above all to defeat the main forces of the enemy on land. The Soviet Navy made a significant contribution to achieving a victory over a strong enemy, providing stability to the strategic flanks of the ground front and comprehensive support of our troops defensively and offensively. In this most difficult of wars the Navy fully justified the hopes placed in it and the great trust of the Soviet people, and did its duty for the Motherland to the end.

The experience of the Great Patriotic War once more affirmed the correctness of the basic thesis of our military doctrine that victory over a strong enemy can be won only through the coordinated actions of all branches of the Armed Forces which have been developed in harmony, well trained, prudently deployed, and supported in every way.

From the very outbreak of war many major problems arose for our Navy on the technical and operational and tactical plane. It was necessary in the shortest possible time in the context of an intense armed struggle to eliminate defects in peacetime combat training which were revealed in the course of the struggle and to solve pressing problems connected with the conduct of combat operations under unforeseen conditions. And it must be acknowledged that the career personnel of our Navy rose to the occasion: optimal ways were found of employing forces in operations in concert with ground troops defensively and offensively. In the course of the war a Soviet school of amphibious operations was formed with a specific organization and operational methods for them. Submarine and air force tactics were developed which were modern for that period, and questions of the defense of bases from land, the organization of concerted actions and control of forces, and the support of their operations which arose in the course of the struggle were solved.

Soviet industry delivered a sufficient amount of combat and technical equipment for the needs of the Navy. The replacement of losses in ship inventory was very difficult in connection with our loss of a series of shipyards and with the changing over of considerable capacity of the shipbuilding industry to the construction of tanks and other armament for the Army. Therefore in the course of the war mainly small combatants and patrol boats were built. Despite these difficulties, during the Great Patriotic War the Navy received two light cruisers, 25 destroyers, escort ships, and minesweepers, 52 submarines, 15 large submarine chasers, and 873 different patrol boats from industry.

The quality of the Navy's armament and combat and technical equipment improved. Radar appeared aboard combatants. New models of influence mine weaponry appeared. The Naval Air Force grew quantitatively and qualitatively; the number of torpedo-carrying aircraft more than tripled.

In the course of the war the Soviet Navy had to carry out two groups of missions concurrently: first, to battle a strong enemy at sea who was steadfastly striving to seize the initiative and destroy our naval forces, and second, to support the stability of the strategic flanks of the front and act in concert with the ground troops offensively and defensively. This employment of the naval forces in the war was the only correct employment because it was fully appropriate for the situation.

Due to the particular features of the context of the armed struggle with Hitler Germany, the main load lay on the shoulders of the Soviet Army. All other branches of the Armed Forces, including the Navy, acted in concert with the ground troops on whose operational success the outcome of the war depended. Our Navy carried out their own missions under more difficult conditions than the navies of other states, which, as a rule did not have to aid their troops in the coastal areas daily, and protect their bases and important coastal points from attacks by the enemy from the land side. Yet under these difficult conditions our Navy showed itself to be an active and powerful striking force capable of changing the situation both in the sea areas and in the coastal strip of operations of the ground troops.

From the very first hours of the war, the Navy, as was noted above, went over to resolute operations against the naval foe and conducted them uninterruptedly right up to the capitulation of Hitler Germany. These operations were the disruption of enemy sea communications, the delivery of strikes from the sea against naval bases, ports, and military-industrial objectives of the enemy, the destruction of his surface ships and submarines at sea, the blockading from the sea of areas which were more important to the enemy for combat operations, active mine-laying, and numerous landings of landing parties.

The losses of the enemy fleet attest to the high intensity of the war at sea which demanded thousands of combat warship cruises and aircraft sorties, and the conduct of numerous naval battles and operations. This struggle, continuing from day to day, in itself demanded extremely great efforts by the forces, but, indeed, in addition to this, the Navy still had to constantly participate in the direct support of the ground troops, which aided the achievement of victory on the Soviet-German front. Moreover, in delivering strikes

In 1944, Admiral Gorshkov assumed command of the newly
formed Danube Flotilla, which included the Azov Flotilla
he had commanded after the victory of Stalingrad. He and
the men he is seen inspecting in these photographs distinguished
themselves in the landing on Kerch Peninsula and helped
liberate the Ukraine, Romania, Bulgaria, and Hungary.

against bases and sea communications and against
enemy ship groupings, the Soviet Navy rendered support to the navies of our former allies, i.e., it made
a weighty contribution to the general efforts of the
anti-Hitler coalition in combatting the enemy's Navy
in the oceanic theaters. Due to the activity of the Soviet
Navy, the German command was forced not only to
retain significant forces of its own Navy allocated to
battling the Soviet Navy, but also to systematically
reinforce them with ships and aircraft from the Atlantic
Ocean and the Mediterranean and North Seas. Even

in the most intense periods of the "Battle for the
Atlantic," in 1941–1944, of the 141 submarines fit for
combat operations, 29 were kept in the Black, Baltic,
and Barents Seas.[5]

The German command, not considering the "Battle
for the Atlantic" the main area in the Second World
War, concentrated almost all of its forces, including
considerable naval forces, on the Soviet-German Front.

[5]Yeremeyev, L. M. and A. P. Shergin. *Podvodnyye lodki inostrannykh flotov
vo vtoroy mirovoy voyne* (Submarines of foreign navies in WW II), Voyenizdat, 1962, pp. 43.

Proof of this is Hitler's statement in January 1943: "We must clearly understand that this submarine warfare will be useless if we are unable to defeat Russia in the East."[6]

Only owing to the Soviet Armed Forces, which themselves tied down the largest and best part of the armed forces of Hitler Germany, were the U.S.A. and England able to win the "Battle for the Atlantic," and also to construct a new giant merchant fleet, which was twice as large as the tonnage lost on the sea lanes, and to create vast forces to combat the German submarines, i.e., 133 convoy aircraft carriers, 1,500 destroyers, frigates, and corvettes, 1,900 submarine chasers, 1,000 minesweepers, and several thousand aircraft.[7]

Thus, the Soviet Navy played an important role in the Great Patriotic War and, consequently, in the Second World War as a whole. Its dogged, resolute opposition to the powerful naval foe and the retention of the initiative at sea in combat operations throughout the entire war created conditions which ruled out the employment by the enemy of such forms of armed combat as landing and antilanding operations. The German Fascist Navy was limited in the employment of sea communications, even at the moment of hottest

battles on the decisive ground fronts, and was unable to support its own troops in situations which were critical for them. This was highly inspirational aid to the Soviet Army's troops, who were freed from the need to defend the long coastal expanse, and, because of this, were able to strengthen the force of their attacks in the main and decisive areas.

Another and no less important mission and a task which, in essence, became the main component part of the Navy's effort, was its direct participation in the defense and liberation of the coastal cities, ports, and naval bases, its constant support by its own forces of coastal units of ground troops defensively and offensively, and also the active participation of naval personnel in the decisive battles on the ground fronts. This was a very weighty contribution to gaining the victory.

The Soviet Navy, having stood up to a strong enemy in a savage struggle, and having fulfilled all missions assigned to it, emerged from the war strengthened and hardened, firmly maintaining its superiority in all naval theaters in the arena of the struggle. By their steadfastness in carrying out the assigned mission, by massive heroism of the personnel, and by fearless and unwavering belief in victory, the navymen demonstrated in the flames of the war their fidelity to their people, and an infinite devotion to the Communist Party and to the cause of Communism.

[6]S. Morrison. The Battle for the Atlantic Won. Voyenizdat, 1959, p. 80.
[7]Potapov, I. N. *Razvitiye voyenno-morskikh flotov v poslevoyennyy period* (The development of navies in the postwar period), Voyenizdat, 1971, pp. 23–31.

Commentary

By Arleigh Burke

After graduation from the U. S. Naval Academy in 1923, Admiral Burke served five years in the USS *Arizona*. He then attended the Navy PG School and the University of Michigan, earning an MS degree. After various staff tours, he served as XO of the destroyer *Craven* from 1937 to 1939 and then commanded, for a year, the USS *Mugford*. During World War II he commanded, successively, DesDivs 43 and 44, and then in 1943, DesRon 23. In 1944 he became C/S and aide to ComCarDivThree, later TF 58. During the Korean conflict, while commanding CruDivFive in 1951, he also served as a member of the Military Armistice Commission. From December 1951 until 1954 he directed the CNO's Strategic Plans Division and then commanded CruDivSix (1954) and Destroyer Force, Atlantic Fleet (1955). From August 1955 until his retirement in August 1961, he served an unprecedented three terms as CNO.

Like all the articles in this revealing series, this discussion of the role of the Soviet Navy in World War II asserts that the interests of the State require a strong, effective Navy. Indirectly he acknowledges that the Soviet Navy during that difficult war was primarily a coastal defense force whose main missions were to protect the seaward flanks of the Soviet Army and to transport supplies on internal waterways for the Army, and that mostly under Army direction.

What he says is true enough. The Soviet Navy did supply to the Army over 400,000 men to fight as naval infantry. Another 100,000 naval infantrymen defended naval installations and conducted some amphibious landings under naval command. Most of this article is devoted to the tremendous support the

Soviet Navy gave to the ground forces and to the excellent cooperation among the Soviet services. This was the Soviet Navy's then-assigned mission, and he lauds the "doctrine of coordinated action of all branches of the Armed Forces" and of employing Naval Forces "in operations in concert with ground troops defensively and offensively."

In no place in this article is Admiral Gorshkov critical of the type of navy the Soviets had or the manner in which it was employed during World War II. He applauds what was done and the way it was done without intimating in any way that the Soviet Navy might have contributed much more to the defeat of their enemies had the Navy operated more at sea on the offensive and so perhaps prevented their enemies from advancing as far as they did.

Yet, after the war the Soviets studied carefully operations of both their allies and their enemies to determine the causes of success or failure of those operations. The study of this war, as well as other wars, caused them to realize that naval power was essential for a major power to be successful in war. Although in this article Admiral Gorshkov merely mentions the activities of the fleets of the United States and Britain in keeping control of the sea—thereby able to support the Soviets with supplies as well as keep the major portions of the enemies' naval forces quite well occupied—the Soviets concluded that their Navy needed to be re-oriented toward a high seas fleet. They had learned the hard way the limitations of a coastal defense fleet, and they embarked on an extensive naval building program of World War II-type ships. But after they developed that fleet, they still operated in waters close to their own shores and did not get the much-needed experience in operating for long periods at sea. They developed guided missiles and, when nuclear power came along, they increased their already heavy emphasis on submarines. Technically, they were doing pretty well, but it was not until the missile crises in 1962 that they fully comprehended what it took to control the sea, or to deny its use to the enemy. From that experience they learned that the first essential element of an effective navy is an officer corps experienced at sea and skillful in the operations of their ships and weapons systems, plus the equally important element of having ships that could perform their tasks wherever those tasks had to be performed. By 1966 it was apparent that the Soviets were starting to operate on the high seas, and now, today, it is apparent that they are trying to build ships, aircraft, and equipment that can be effective in war and influential in peace.

So, although it is evident that the type, composition, and operational procedures of the Soviet Navy have changed radically from those in existence during World War II, and while it is equally evident that these changes have come about largely from experience in that war, Admiral Gorshkov does not even allude to it. That is significant in itself and bears out the contention of other commentators that Admiral Gorshkov is having some difficulty in obtaining approval of the Soviet hierarchy for the building, support, and operation of the Navy he envisages and, hence, has written his extensive series in a manner which will generate as little antagonism as possible. What is past is finished and cannot be changed, so he is starting from where he is now to try to convince his associates that his proposals are sound and needed by the U.S.S.R.

Throughout the series Admiral Gorshkov has used every opportunity to recount the excellent performance of duty of Soviet Navy men on every occasion. He recites the personal characteristics that enabled men in the past to perform extraordinarily well. He emphasizes the utter courage, initiative, aggressiveness, tremendous effort, stamina, willingness to bear hardship, persistence, selflessness, heroic defense, iron tenacity, fury in battle, cooperation, obedience, devotion to duty, skill, and all the other qualities that every combat unit must instill in its personnel if that unit is to perform at maximum effectiveness. He is building pride of past performance in his naval people and he is doing it extremely well.

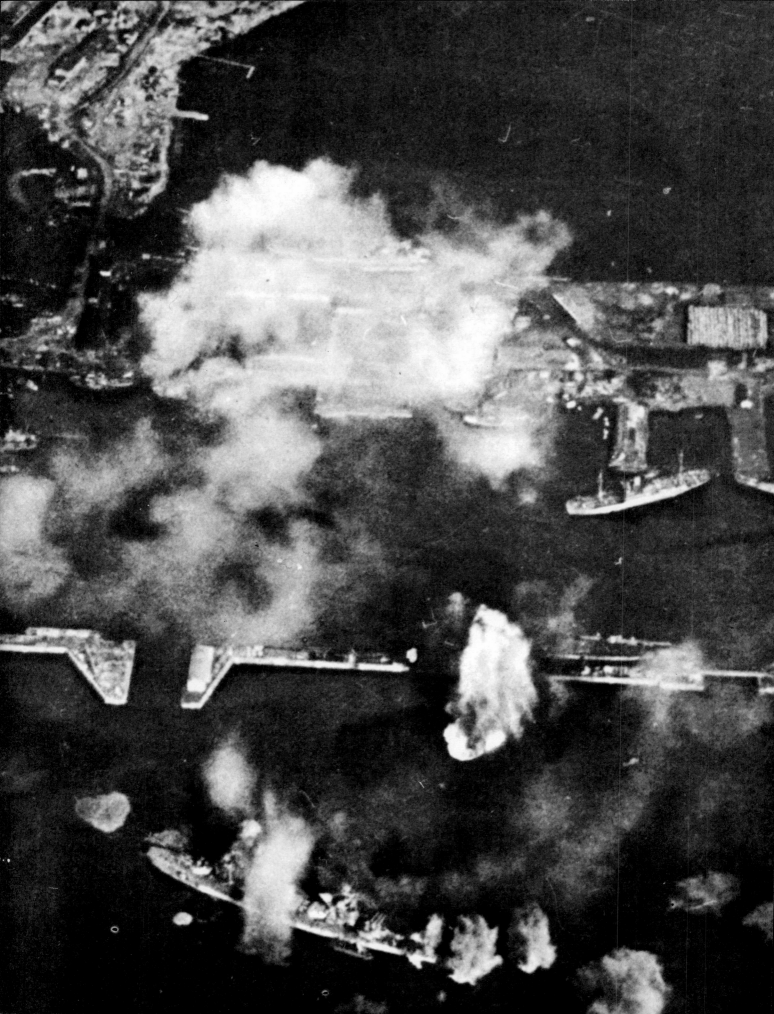

Analysis of Navies in the Second World War

With Commentary following the article by
Rear Admiral J. C. Wylie, U. S. Navy (Retired)

EDITOR'S NOTE: *In the following chapter, cleared for publication in the Soviet Union on 2 November 1972, the admiral analyzes the struggle for Atlantic and Pacific Ocean communications in which vast naval forces were employed. He concludes that the disruption of sea shipping to a great degree weakened the economies of the belligerents and had a definite influence on the course of the military operations in what he considers to be the "secondary theaters," but was not the decisive factor that determined the outcome of the war.*

The Second World War was basically a continental war, since its main goals were achieved by armed combat on the ground fronts. However, certain strategic missions could not have been executed without the participation of navies (especially in the Pacific Theater); for example, sea and ocean communications were disrupted almost exclusively by naval forces. Consequently, combat operations at sea, although by nature generally subordinate to the strategic missions executed by the ground forces, nevertheless had a significant effect on the course of the war as a whole.

Three months before Pearl Harbor, German bombers caught the Baltic Fleet's only two battleships, the Marat, *foreground, and the* October Revolution, *at Kronstadt. Because of the battleship's vulnerability to air attack, she was replaced as a serious threat—says the author—by the submarine.*

In our view, in the Second World War, navies were charged with the following missions: to disrupt the sea and ocean communications of the enemy in order to undermine his military-economic potential; to protect own communications; to cooperate with own ground forces in defensive and offensive operations, and, above all, in the opening of new areas of military operations on land and in increasing the rate of the offensive operations of own ground forces in the coastal areas by carrying out amphibious operations of various scales; and also to destroy groupings of hostile naval forces.

The communications battle extended to all sea and oceanic theaters, although its importance in the overall volume of military operations at sea differed in different theaters. The greatest weight in this battle fell in the Atlantic theater, and the cutting off of shipping to

England was the main mission of all Fascist German naval activity. In analyzing the situation, the heads of the allied states who gathered in Casablanca in 1943 recognized the necessity of directing the main efforts of the allied nations primarily toward combatting the German U-boats. Churchill, for example, frankly stated that the only thing he was really afraid of in the course of the entire war was the German U-boats.

In the course of World War II some special features of naval operations against sea communications emerged, occasioned by the growth of shipping and the poor preparedness of the belligerents for this type of operation. Initially, to disrupt sea communications the navies devoted insufficient forces which were capable of achieving only comparatively small results. Only as these forces were increased and acquired experience, and also with an increase in the volume of shipping did the scale and activity in sea communications battle gradually increase.

Fascist Germany was late in developing the struggle against sea communications in the Atlantic on a widespread scale. In this connection, the events on the main, Soviet-German front had a great influence on these events. Germany's attack on the Soviet Union required the concentration of all of its possible forces on the Eastern front of the armed struggle; therefore, Germany conducted operations against communications in the Atlantic practically only with submarines, without the support of other types of forces (especially without aircraft which could have operated not only against ships at sea but also against ports, industry, and accumulated stores of supplies). The diversion of the main German efforts to the East permitted the British and Americans to expand mass construction of escort ships to protect communications from U-boat attacks, and to initiate the rebuilding of the merchant fleet. As a result, the effectiveness of the Fascist German Navy and its influence on the British economy and on the level of the condition of the British armed forces (which, by the way, did not play a decisive role either in the war as a whole or even in its concluding stage) were reduced. The influence of the struggle in the Atlantic theater on the course and outcome of the war, although it was significant, was not decisive.

The integrated employment of various types of naval forces, and also of new forms of weaponry and combat equipment created during the course of the war, such as radar, sonar, homing torpedoes, the snorkel, etc., were characteristic of the battle of communications. The change in the combat characteristics of armament naturally evoked a change in the employment of forces. Thus, mass employment of forces and means became possible, the boundary between the conduct of day and night-time operations was erased, and the focus of attacks on ports and bases as the key points in sea communications increased many times over.

Moreover, despite the exceptional threat to submarines by ASW forces, the German naval command did not conduct a single operation or other specially organized combat actions directed at destroying these forces, which doubtlessly reduced the intensity of the communications battle.

As is well known, different types of naval forces played far from the same role in the battle of sea communications. Thus, of the total number of destroyed transports, submarines sank more than 65%, aircraft about 20%, surface ships 6%, and 8% perished on mines.[1] However, these figures are not enough to determine the place of forces in the battle of communications; we need an in-depth analysis of their operations.

Despite the considerable growth in opposition by ASW forces, in World War II submarines fully revealed their combat capabilities which had been brought out as early as World War I. In particular, they attacked not only transports, but also the combatants supporting them, and operated successfully against enemy submarines.

During this war, Fascist Germany sank 5,150 ships, whereby 68% of the destroyed tonnage was accounted for by submarines.[2] Their most effective operations were from 1939 to 1942, when they sank 2,177 transports. Beginning with 1943, the effectiveness of submarine operations began to drop. In the second half of the war they succeeded in sinking only 651 transports despite the increase in the number of German submarines at sea.[3]

In the last war, the Americans sank 2,143 Japanese ships, and 62.1% of the tonnage was accounted for by submarines.[4] In this case the success of the operations grew steadily. Thus, in 1942 they sank 134 ships, in 1943, 308, and 549 ships were sunk in 1944.[5] This is explained by the weakness of the Japanese naval opposition, the completely unorganized ASW defense, and the increase in numerical strength of the American submarine forces participating in the disruption of Japan's shipping.

According to American figures, during the war Japanese submarines sank 147 ships (according to French figures, 170) with a total tonnage of 776,000 tons. The submarine forces of the Italian Navy destroyed (accord-

---

[1] S. N. Maksimov, and K. V. Penzin. *Voyenno-morskoye iskusstvo flotov kapitalisticheskikh gosudarstv vo vtoroy mirovoy voyne* (The Naval Art of the Navies of the Capitalist States in World War II), Leningrad, 1962, p. 166.

[2] *Op. cit.* Belli, V. A., et al. p. 614.

[3] *Op cit.* Yeremeyev, L. M., and A. P. Shergin. pp. 66–69.

[4] *Ibid,* p. 391.

[5] *Ibid.*

ing to German figures) 105 ships with a total tonnage of some one million tons.

From the cited statistics it follows that in World War II submarines were actually the main force in the battle with enemy shipping, although their effectiveness varied noticeably according to the period of the war. This was mainly due to the course of the armed conflict on the Soviet-German front, which directly affected the character of events in all of the other theaters. Thus, the turning point in this struggle, which occurred as a result of the victory of the Soviet Armed Forces, forced Hitler Germany to concentrate all of her attention on the Eastern Front and to weaken her attention to the Atlantic Theater. Moreover, the German military command decided to transfer from the Atlantic Theater aircraft and a considerable part of the surface ship forces to the Soviet-German Front, and to send part of the submarines operating in the Atlantic to the Norwegian and Barents Seas. The appropriations allocated to the German Navy were reduced from 12.1% in 1942 to 5.6% in 1944 (of the total sum allocated to the armed forces).[6]

Taking advantage of the weakness of the Germans in the Western Theater, our former allies made amphibious landings in North Africa, on the island of Sicily, and on the Apennine Peninsula, which forced Italy to capitulate. All of this reduced Germany's submarine basing capabilities, narrowed the area of their operations, and permitted the British and Americans to transfer considerable naval forces from the Mediterranean to the Atlantic.

The ASW forces of England and the U.S.A. also had an important role in checking the operations of the German U-boats. Soon after Germany's attack on the Soviet Union, more than 2,000 British and American ASW combatants and specially configured merchantmen and several thousand aircraft were in operation against the German U-boats in the Atlantic Theater. For each German U-boat, there were 25 British and U. S. warships and 100 aircraft, and for every German submariner at sea there were 100 British and American antisubmariners. A total of six million men were thrown into the antisubmarine war.

One can hardly find a similar ratio of attacking to defending forces among all of the other branches of the armed forces!

Yet, nevertheless, this significant numerical superiority of defenders was insufficient to force the attackers to fully curtail their active operations. Therefore, the question of the ratio of submarine to antisubmarine forces is of great interest even under present-day conditions, since if ASW forces, which were so numerous and technically up to date (for that time), possessing a vast superiority, turned out to be capable of only partially limiting the operations of diesel submarines, then what must this superiority be today in order to counter nuclear-powered submarines, whose combat capabilities cannot be compared with the capabilities of World War II-era submarines.

Although the ASW forces pressed the submarines considerably, they were unable to discredit them and knock them out as was the case, for example, with battleships, which the growing capabilities of attack aircraft caused to leave the arena. The submarines turned out to be very much alive: of all the armed forces of Fascist Germany they alone represented a serious threat to British and U. S. shipping right up to the very last day of the war. "The submarine war" was concluded only after German territory was taken by the anti-Hitler coalition.

The slowness of the technical improvement of submarines and also the insufficient level of training of the German submariners also had a great effect on the struggle between the submarine and ASW forces. However the accelerated construction which was begun in Germany of the new XXI series of submarines and the development of submarines with Walther propulsion plants, although late, clearly showed that there were great reserves for further upgrading performance characteristics of even the prenuclear-powered submarines.

The expanded construction of ships for the merchant marines in England and the U.S.A. also was of important significance in reducing the effectiveness of German U-boat operations against Atlantic communications. In the war years the Americans and British built transports with a total displacement of 42.5 million tons, i.e., almost twice the tonnage that was sunk.[7] The transport fleets grew considerably during the war, despite losses from submarine and air attacks. In this connection, the U.S.A. moved into first place with respect to tonnage, overtaking England.

Aviation made a radical change in the character of naval warfare as a whole and the battle of sea communications in particular. However, for a series of reasons its capabilities were far from being utilized fully. One of the reasons was the frequent absence of aircraft within the composition of the fleets. Aviation units which were included within the fleet inventories operated significantly more effectively than those temporarily attached (this was the case, for example, with the Germans). In this connection, if aviation was only second in sinking transports, in the defense of own sea communications it was number one. For example,

---

[6] *Istoriya voyenno-morskogo iskusstva* (The History of the Naval Art), Voyenizdat, 1969, p. 521.

[7] *Op. cit.* V. A. Belli et al. p. 412.

the British and American air forces destroyed more than 40% of the submarines of the "axis" countries which were lost by them during the war.[8]

Surface ships were seldom used in combat operations for disrupting sea communications due to the fear of great losses from air and submarine attacks. Therefore, their role in the execution of this mission was not very great. However, they were the main force in the protection of their own sea communications: they destroyed more than 53% of the submarines of the Hitler coalition countries.[9] It should be stressed that as early as the First World War, surface ships began to carry aircraft. In World War II, aircraft carriers became widely used and were first among the forces protecting ocean communications.

From all that has been said, it is clear that in World War II submarines were the main means of combatting enemy shipping, and they are even more important in today's context.

In examining the struggle for sea communications in World War II, it is impossible not to dwell in somewhat more detail on the so called "Battle for the Atlantic," which our former allies try to represent as the most important event of the Second World War, nearly leading to the destruction of Hitler Germany.

The entire course of the war clearly showed that the Atlantic Theater and the role of the military operations in it in World War II were much less significant than in World War I. And here is why.

First, the naval blockade of Germany lost its former significance due to the fact that the Hitlerites succeeded in seizing and putting at the service of their own military machine the economies and vast natural resources of almost all of the Western European countries. Therefore German industry did not experience serious difficulties due to the naval blockade prosecuted by the allied navies, and the state and military leaders of Germany (in contrast to those of England) were not even conscious of the very concept of the "Battle for the Atlantic."[10]

Second, the leadership of Hitler Germany, in preparing for the implementation of the "Barbarossa Plan" (the attack on the Soviet Union), was forced to call off operation "Sea Lion" (the invasion of the British Isles), converting it into a series of deceptive measures, and was also forced to cease the "air offensive" against England and sharply reduce (and subsequently to completely cease) the employment of aircraft to disrupt shipping to England in connection with the transfer of Goering's Air Force squadrons to the east.

Third, after the attack on the Soviet Union, Hitler Germany, in reducing her operations in the Atlantic still further, turned over the execution of the task of disrupting England's oceanic communications in this secondary theater exclusively to the submarine forces. A significant part of the combatants, including submarines too, were directed to cooperate with their own troops on the Eastern Front. Thus, the German naval forces which had been operating in the Atlantic were weakened and were incapable of fully executing the mission with which they were charged.

Fourth, the war with the Soviet Union required extreme efforts by the German economy, which did not permit it to take effective measures to build up forces in the Atlantic Theater (this was borne out particularly by the reduction in expenditures for the Navy which in 1944 were less than half of those in 1942).

Fifth, Great Britain and the U.S.A. taking advantage of the diversion of German Fascist forces to the Eastern Front and their weakening operations against England's industry and communications, directed a considerable share of their economies toward the construction and development of forces and means to support their shipping. For this reason the rates of growth of British and American forces and means of conducting combat operations in the Atlantic exceeded the rates of construction and introduction into service of German submarines several times over. Thus, by the end of 1942 the British already had about 1,200 minesweepers in their naval inventory, and by the fall of 1943 the allies had put about 3,000 surface ships and 2,000 aircraft into operation to combat German U-boats in the Atlantic Theater.[11] The sharp change in the relative strength of the opposing forces naturally led to a reduction in the operational efficiency of the German U-boats against the Atlantic communications of the enemy and to an increase in their losses.

Thus, there is no basis to believe that the "Battle for the Atlantic" had a decisive effect on the course and outcome of World War II. With respect to results and with respect to the composition of the participants on both sides, the "Battle for the Atlantic" represented combat operations of a complementary nature in a secondary theater. Thus, the entire course of the battle of Atlantic communications directly depended on the events on the main front of the war—the Soviet-German front—where the fate of the peoples of the world, including the English and American people, was decided.

For the second time in her history, Germany was

---

[8] *Op cit.* L. M. Yeremeyev and A. P. Shergin. p. 428.

[9] *Ibid.*

[10] K. Donets. German U-boats in the Second World War. Translation from the German. Voyenizdat, 1964, p. 136.

[11] *Op cit.* V. A. Belli, et al. p. 465–466.

forced during the course of the war to make a cardinal change in the employment of naval forces and belatedly to change over to the mass construction of submarines to hinder British sea shipping. Yet despite this, during World War II, Germany, having built 1,131 submarines[12] (not counting "midget" submarines), inflicted great losses on Britain's merchant marine, destroying up to 60% of its prewar inventory. Yet she was unable to achieve any more. One of the main reasons for this was that the submarines did not receive support from other forces, and above all from the Air Force, which would have been able both to carry out the reconnaissance for the submarines and destroy ASW forces, as well as to operate against the enemy's economy by attacking his ports and targets in the shipbuilding industry, not to mention attacks against ships at sea. The effectiveness of German submarine employment in disrupting the enemy's shipping in the Atlantic was considerably reduced for these reasons.

The battle of Japan's Pacific Ocean communications was of an entirely different nature. At the outbreak of war Japan possessed a 6.4 million-ton merchant marine, and she captured ships of other countries with a total displacement of more than 800,000 tons.[13] However, her capabilities for replacing the lost tonnage were negligible, and the strength and quality of the forces protecting the transports were clearly inadequate to defend her own ocean communications. As a result, as strange as it may seem, the Japanese Navy, the Navy of an insular power, turned out to be completely unprepared to defend her own sea communications.

The Americans employed submarines, aircraft, and surface ships to combat Japanese shipping. In addition, they planted mines in Japanese waters (mainly with aircraft). The monthly average of American submarines operating against Japanese shipping was: 10 in 1942, 17 in 1943, 28 in 1944, and 14 in 1945.[14] Clearly the American submarine forces handled the mission assigned to them without any special effort and sank more than 80% of the Japanese merchant fleet, which attests to the simple and favorable conditions under which American submariners operated.

The emerging situation and the relative strength of naval forces permitted the Americans to seize control of the communications connecting Japan with the areas of the South Seas. However, the Americans did not put up any opposition to the sea communications connecting Japan with such important (from an economic point of view) areas as Korea, Manchuria, and Northern China. And indeed it was precisely from these areas that Japan imported in 1941, for example, about 80% of the iron ore, and more than six million tons of coking coal needed for the industries of the home country and a large part of the lead, zinc, chrome, molybdenum, and tungsten required by Japanese industry.[15]

Thus, the results of the opposition of the American Navy to the enemy's shipping, despite their impressiveness, turned out to be entirely insufficient to force Japan to capitulate.

Japanese armed forces located in Korea, Manchuria, and China were not even subjected to opposition by the Americans. The strongest grouping of Japanese ground forces, the Kwantung Army, located on the Asiatic mainland, like the communications connecting it with the mainland, was also totally unopposed by the Americans.

What was this—an underestimation of the importance of communications for Japan, or a deliberate temporizing for a possible change in events and the preservation of the Japanese land armies for an attack on the Soviet Union in case of a favorable development of events for Germany on the Soviet-German front?

An analysis of the struggle for Atlantic and Pacific communications in which vast naval forces were employed permits the conclusion that the disruption of sea shipping to a great degree weakened the economies of the belligerents and had a definite influence on the course of the military operations in the secondary theaters, but was not the decisive factor determining the outcome of the war. On the other hand, the consequences of the operations against ocean communications were almost unfelt in the main sector of the armed struggle, on the Soviet-German Front.

This provides the basis to assert that under the conditions of the continental nature of World War II, operations against ocean communications, although they extended to almost all of the World Ocean and they drew into their sphere the main part of the naval forces of the belligerents, were only of secondary, local significance for the opposing sides. As for the Soviet Union, their effect was expressed only in a slight limitation of the delivery of strategic materials and armaments which arrived sporadically and with great irregularity through lend-lease from our allies of that day.

The landing of landing parties became an important mission of the belligerent countries in World War II. The number of these landings in this war turned out to be unexpected for many naval theoreticians and for the commands of the majority of the bourgeois navies.

[12]G. M. Gel'fond. *Istoriya voyenno-morskogo iskusstva* (The History of the Naval Art), Vol. III, Voyenizdat, 1963, p. 102.

[13]*Op. cit.* V. A. Belli, et al., p. 429.

[14]*Op. cit.* L. M. Yeremeyev, pp. 382–384.

[15]Ye. M. Zhukov, et al. *Yapanskiy militarism* (Japanese Militarism), Izd-vo Nauka, 1972, p. 185.

Gunboats of the Danube Flotilla, 1941

This occurred because, on the basis of the unsuccessful experience of the Dardanelles operation in 1915, during the period between the wars they overestimated the capabilities of antilanding defenses and underestimated the growing capabilities of armed forces to break through them and to expand their success ashore, and therefore they did not devote serious attention to landing operations. The only exception was Japan, who actively prepared herself to capture foreign territory separated from her by water expanses.

Some 600 amphibious landings on various scales were undertaken in all sea and oceanic theaters in the period of the Second World War.[16] As a rule, quantities of forces and equipment which were unheard of in any other form of naval warfare were marshalled to participate in them.

A high level of combat actions, heavy losses, and a vast expenditure of material and equipment were characteristic of amphibious operations. They were often accompanied by major battles having the goal of destroying the enemy's forces at sea. The outstanding characteristic of the amphibious operations of foreign navies was that they were conducted only in a favorable military-political situation in the course of a strategic offensive in a theater.

Drastic changes in the methods of landing landing

[16] *Op. cit.* The History of the Naval Art, p. 523.

forces took place during the war under the influence of the ever expanding employment of air power in naval warfare. Air superiority in the area of an operation became the indispensible condition for the successful conduct of it, even when the enemy had superiority in other forces. By the end of the war, airborne landing parties had become obligatory integral parts of amphibious operations.

Landing operations in World War II were very successful as a result of the considerable increase in the offensive capabilities of naval forces and of the troops being landed, their growing capability to break through the enemy's defense and to achieve the goals of the operations, and also due to the mass construction and employment of special landing party transport and landing craft. In the entire war only two landings of large scale landing parties failed—on Midway and at Port Moresby—and neither of the landing failures was of a strategic scale. This is explained by the overall military-political conditions which were favorable for the invading side, and also by the concentrations of landing forces, which were superior to the forces concentrated for antilanding defense. Moreover, in the entire war not a single antilanding operation was carried out in which powerful and consistent attacks were made against the landing party, beginning with the point at which the force was marshalled up to the area of its landing. This is explained by the delay of information on the preparation of the enemy landing party and by the insufficiency of assets to attack it in all stages of the operation.

As the analysis shows, landing operations occupied one of the leading roles in naval warfare in World War II. In some theaters, particularly in the Pacific where the ground forces of the belligerents did not come in direct contact, landing operations and the battles accompanying them and engagements of the naval forces made up the main content of the armed conflict between the belligerents. However, the effect of landing operations on the overall course of the war, although it was significant, was displayed only in the results of concerted actions in offensive operations with ground troops in coastal regions or in island areas.

The destruction of attack groupings of the enemy's naval forces was no less important a mission for navies in World War II. Yet whereas in World War I, the operations for carrying out this task were conducted apart from the other combat operations of the fleet, in World War II they were almost all integral parts of operations against communications or in support of landing parties. We must not fail to note that the importance of gunnery armament as the decisive means of destroying the enemy's ships at sea was drastically reduced in World War II. In connection with this, battleships,

the main bearers of large caliber guns, lost their leading position in the navies, since major naval engagements, as a rule, were conducted primarily by carrier aircraft forces, i.e., at ranges considerably exceeding the firing range of shipboard guns.

The destruction of naval forces at sea held an important place in the offensive and defensive operations of the adversaries. The achievement of success in this case not only ensured the prosecution of that operation within whose framework they were operating, but also had a considerable effect on the overall course of combat operations at sea.

The naval forces of the enemy were destroyed not only in major naval engagements, but also at their bases. An analysis of such operations makes it possible to draw a conclusion on the increase in their scale in World War II. Thus, whereas in World War I only five surface ships (about 1% of all the ships sunk) were destroyed in ports, in World War II, 87 surface ships and 71 submarines (8%) were destroyed, and aviation accounted for some 80% of the losses suffered by the enemy.[17] In many cases the destruction of surface ships was closely tied to the conduct of operations for disrupting shipping or the landing of an amphibious force.

Thus, even as World War II was being fought, the growing trend toward the threat of the destruction of ships in bases (primarily by attack aircraft) was becoming clearly defined, which engendered the need to disperse forces and craft in basing areas, and produced changes in methods of supporting them (including also support from the rear).

The war forced a re-examination of the importance of individual types of forces within the composition of navies and also of the role of navies within the system of a country's armed forces and their influence on the course of the armed conflict as a whole.

During the war, type forces of navies were converted into mixed forces permitting the execution of the more probable missions of naval warfare. Methods of joint opposition to the enemy through different types of forces and forms of weaponry in deeper and more open combat formations were developed and improved.

Naval combat activity revealed the growing necessity for a balancing of forces to the extent needed to execute the wide range of missions arising for the navies. Navies supporting the successful execution of various large scale and strategic-type missions turned out to be in a more favorable position. Fleets with a narrower mission (i.e., directed at executing one certain mission or another), occupied the role of defenders, since they were stripped of the possibility of actively opposing the enemy in new combat sectors, thereby yielding the

[17] *Op. cit.* B. A. Belli, et al. p. 609.

"The treacherous attack of Fascist Germany on the U.S.S.R., in which an overwhelming part of the armed forces of Germany and her satellites participated, determined the beginning of a new stage in the course of the world war, drastically changing the entire situation in the theaters of military operations. "Eastern Europe, where the fate of the entire Second World War was decided, became the main theater. It was precisely there where Germany and her satellites concentrated their main forces. All other theaters of military operations were transformed into secondary theaters. That is why the role of the navies in the war and their effect on its overall course cannot be regarded separately from the events on the Soviet-German front."

1

2

1. *Icebreaker* Alexander Sibiriakoff *which fought a losing action with the German pocket battleship* Admiral Scheer *in April, 1942.*

2. *Wreckage of the cruiser* Tchervonaya Ukraina *sunk by bombing at Sevastopol in 1942.*

3. *Torpedo-cruiser* Tashkent *after bombing attack in July 1942.*

4. *Landing operations at Feodosia in April 1944, were supported by cruisers, destroyers, and gunboats.*

5. *Malodki-Class submarine. These 200-ton craft were mass-produced and shipped to the coastal areas in sections.*

6. *The 2,900-ton destroyer* Bodri, *bombed at Sevastopol in June 1942.*

7. *A Fugas-type minesweeper driven ashore and captured by the Germans during landing operations in the Crimea, January 1942.*

3

4

5

6

7

initiative to him not only in the selection of the time and place of attack, but also in the development of own naval forces and means. An example of the most unbalanced navy was the Navy of Fascist Germany, whose employment was practically limited to the mission of disrupting England's ocean communications. The Navy of imperialist Japan, which possessed powerful attack forces, yet had almost no ASW forces, can also serve as an example of an unbalanced navy.

In the course of the war the importance of aircraft carriers rose, and the role of such traditional types of forces as battleships declined. Despite losses, the number of attack carriers almost doubled and their total number (including escort carriers) underwent an eight-fold increase. On the other hand, the number of major gunnery ships (battleships and cruisers) decreased by some 20%. The experience of combat operations at sea forced all states to curtail construction of new battleships and to take them out of the active fleet inventory after the war was over. Superiority among surface ships had completely shifted to aircraft carriers.

On the eve of World War II the opinion existed among bourgeois naval theoreticians that submarines were a weapon of the weak. The course of the war at sea totally refuted this. Moreover, submarines became the most important means of naval warfare. And while in some states their capabilities were underestimated in the prewar period, in the course of the war they had to make a reassessment of submarine forces. Thus, Hitler Germany, which in no way was among the weaker countries in a military respect, underestimated the importance of submarines in the prewar period, yet during the war built 1,131 submarines. Despite the furious development of enemy ASW forces and means, and considerable losses from opposition by them, the number of German submarines grew from 57 at the outbreak of war to 493 at the end (on 1 January 1945).

The U.S.A., which also had underestimated submarine forces in the prewar period, by the end of the war had increased their strength by a factor of almost 2.5. During the war submarines played an important role not only in combatting Japan's ocean shipping, but also in destroying her surface ships.

The other main imperialist states also constructed submarines intensively. During the war they built 1,669 units, i.e., almost four times the submarine inventory at the outbreak of war. And despite the vast losses in submarines—1,123 units—their number by the end of the war had more than doubled as compared with the prewar level.[18]

Naval aviation, both carrier and land-based, was furiously developed in the war years. Not only a mani-fold numerical increase in aircraft occurred, but they were also divided into torpedo, bombing, ASW, and reconnaissance aircraft forces. In World War I, the capabilities of aviation as a combat arm of the navy were only outlined, while in the course of World War II it was transformed into a type of naval force directly and actively participating in almost all of the combat operations at sea, and firmly occupying one of the leading places in the navies of all countries.

The construction of antisubmarine ships grew rapidly during the war: the U.S.A. and England alone built about 4,500 of these ships.[19] By mid-1945 their specific weight within the naval inventories had increased several times over the prewar level. At the same time there was mass construction of special escort and landing ships, and minesweepers, the constant participants in almost all of the main naval operations. The fact that the U.S.A. alone from 1 July 1940 to 31 August 1945 built more than 82,000 landing ships and landing craft vividly attests to the importance and scale of the construction of special landing ships and craft for various missions. Having fully justified their employment, they remained within the inventory of all navies even after the war.

Based on what has been said, we may conclude that the navies of the belligerent states played a significant role in World War II, which had a clearly expressed continental nature. The activity of the navies to a great degree was goal-oriented toward cooperation with the ground fronts and toward supporting their needs, i.e., it stemmed from the nature of the armed combat in the main theater of the war where the most decisive events in the struggle of the main forces of the opposing coalitions took place.

The activity of the navies in the secondary theaters of the war was very important, since it considerably affected the economic level of the belligerents and supported the execution of strategic missions by their armed forces.

Of particular significance was the fact that, having herself received an attack by the main part of the armed forces of Fascist Germany and her satellites and later containing them and destroying them, the Soviet Union presented the allied states the opportunity to develop their military-economic potentials, to mobilize armed forces, and to initiate widespread mass construction of fleets in response to the nature of the armed combat at sea practically without hindrance.

Taking advantage of the occupation of the main striking forces of Hitler Germany on the Soviet-German front and the favorable conditions which arose in connection with this, the British and U. S. Navies

[18]*Op cit.* L. M. Yeremeyev, et al. p. 421.

[19]*Op. cit.* S. N. Maksimov. p. 215.

realized the military-economic potentials of their countries in the battle of the Atlantic communications and also in Africa and Western Europe. To an equal degree, the American Navy realized the capabilities of the U. S. economy in operations against Japan.

Nevertheless, the superiority of the American Navy over the Japanese turned out to be insufficient to overwhelm Japan and force her to capitulate (even after the barbaric nuclear bombings of Hiroshima and Nagasaki). By not having actually hurt the economic potential of Korea, China, and the other countries of Southeast Asia, and by having preserved the integrity of the ground forces and their main nucleus, the Kwantung Army, the U.S.A. therefore preserved conditions in Japan for the prolonged continuation of the war. Only the defeat of the Kwantung Army by Soviet troops and the capture by them of Japan's economic

employing electronics, nuclear power, etc. The military-technical revolution became imminent, and, on the threshold of this, each of the great powers strove to ensure decisive superiority for their navies over the fleets of potential aggressors.

The imperialist countries strove to use scientific discoveries and technical gains primarily for military aims and especially to develop their navies. Scientific investigations and technical research related to the creation of qualitatively new means of armed combat, including also naval warfare, were widely developed. New concepts of the employment of navies appeared, and then began a period of re-examination of naval doctrines and their applicability to the presence of new forms of weaponry and to the new forms of armed combat. Naturally, this brought about changes in the role and missions of the navies.

base on the continent—Korea and Manchuria—led the country of the rising sun to military failure and forced her to capitulate.

After the end of World War II, in which nuclear weaponry was used for the first time, the possibilities of employing it as well as other new combat means in naval warfare began to be revealed. Thus, all of the leading imperialist countries turned their attention to missiles as a promising means of delivering nuclear warheads against strategic and operational targets of attack. At the same time, intensive quests were begun for possibilities of expanding the spheres and ways of

The author contends that Germany "underestimated the importance of submarines in the prewar period, yet during the war built 1,131 submarines." One of these, the U-123, seen during her commissioning on 30 May 1940, made Germany's first thrust into American waters since 1918; she sank nine ships totaling 52,586 tons.

Commentary

By Rear Admiral J. C. Wylie, U. S. Navy (Retired)

 Rear Admiral Wylie graduated from the U. S. Naval Academy in 1932. After three years service on board the *Augusta,* flagship of the Asiatic Fleet, he served on the West Coast. He was serving on convoy duty in the North Atlantic when the U. S. entered World War II. He served as XO of the USS *Fletcher* in the South Pacific and then commanded the USS *Trevor* and the USS *Ault* with the Third and Fifth Fleets in 1944 and 1945. Two tours with the Naval War College and one with ONR were followed by command of the USS *Arneb* in the early 50s. After another tour in Washington he commanded the USS *Macon.* Command of a cruiser division and then a cruiser-destroyer flotilla in the Far East was followed by three years in Washington and then, in 1966, he became Deputy CinCNavEur. He retired in 1972 after a tour as Commandant First Naval District. Admiral Wylie is now the President of the USS *Constitution* Museum Foundation.

By the time this comment is published, quite a few men will have read these articles and will have based their judgments, both published and private, on quite different points of view. The historians, the political analysts, the budget analysts, the strategists, will have had their say; and of them all I suspect the historians will have had the most fun because these articles are, by and large, rather myopic and selective history.

But the facet that caught my attention is that, in this series of articles by Admiral Gorshkov, we have a rare glimpse into the mind of a very important man. It is not a complete psycho-intellectual analysis, not a blueprint, but a glimpse into a mind. It may turn out, when enough people have formed their opinions, to be a rather useful one because the most important element of intelligence in any adversary situation—in the courtroom, in the market place, or in armed conflict—is some degree of insight into the mind of the opponent.

Addressing this particular article, the ninth in the series, it seems to me that some useful benchmarks can be brought out from the mind of one possible adversary. We can get glimpses of how he thinks, and why he thinks that way. And since he has been the chief of his service for so long, and so success-fully, he is probably a good indicator of how most Soviet naval officers think. What follows are a few illustrations of this, none of them notably surprising or markedly out of pattern, but most of them fairly good cues as to how he or his successors might think in the future, and thus cues as to how these men might act if action were called for.

First, and to the surprise of no one, Admiral Gorshkov is very strong on submarines as the pre-dominant weapon system for upsetting the other fel-low's maritime commerce, his economy, and his war support capability. ". . . submarines were the main means of combatting enemy shipping, and they are even more important in today's context." But he is not nearly so keen on ASW. "One can hardly find a similar ratio of attacking to defending forces among all the other branches of the armed forces. . . . Yet this significant numerical superiority (of ASW forces in World War II) was insufficient . . . what must this superiority be today to counter nuclear powered submarines." With this point of view, combined with the relative internal self-sufficiency of the Soviet Union in terms of resources, we can see very good reason for the size of the Soviet submarine fleet to-day, and we can infer that the prospects look good for continuation of the attention given to these ships. On the other hand, I suspect we can look forward to something considerably less than that in the allocation of Soviet effort to ASW. The ASW effort will probably be carefully limited. Such a conclusion with respect to ASW effort might help to put in perspective whatever technical intelligence we may have on this matter.

Admiral Gorshkov recognizes clearly that submarines alone are not enough to meet the responsibilities of a major navy. "The most unbalanced fleet was the fleet of Fascist Germany" and "the (German) submarines did not receive support from the other forces, and above all from the air force . . . these reasons considerably reduced the effectiveness of German submarine employment. . . ." If we add to these thoughts his pointed comment on a knotty command problem "aviation units which were included within the composition of the fleets operated significantly more effectively than those temporarily attached . . .", we have a fairly solid cue not only as to how he wants his navy organized and equipped but also as to how he would use it if ever it were put to action.

With respect to the amphibious role of navies, he seems, at least superficially, somewhat ambivalent. As far as World War II is concerned, he appears to classify amphibious efforts as peripheral and not really germane to the central problem of massed armies meeting in a climactic blood bath (and perhaps he is right); but there are clear indications that he does see the amphibious capability as a useful asset in the military support of political aims in a situation less than massive war itself. Speaking of landing operations, he twice mentions that they were made only in favorable military-political situations. It makes little difference whether we agree with him; what is important is his consistent linking of the political with the military in these cases. This could be a cue to the reason-for-being of the modest but efficient Soviet naval landing forces. Then he mentions that "not a single anti-landing operation was carried out in which powerful and consistent attacks were made against the landing party, beginning with the point at which the force was marshalled . . ." It is a reasonable inference that he would not be guilty of this omission if he were defending, a conclusion that might, some time, lead to prudent precautions by any of his opponents.

Above these few specific comments, the thing that comes out most clearly to me, as an observer, is his clear sensing of Soviet vital interests. All his judgments are keyed to this. There are no exceptions.

At first reading, some of his assertions may seem to us to be way off the mark. "The 'Battle for the Atlantic' represented combat operations of a complementary nature in a secondary theater." Or ". . . operations against ocean communications . . . were only of a secondary, local significance. . . ." Or, on another subject, after inferring that the United States preserved the Japanese army in China for possible later operations against the Soviet Union, "Only the defeat of the Kwangtung Army by Soviet troops and the capture by them of Japan's economic base on the continent . . . led (Japan) to military failure and forced her to capitulate."

Most of us, almost intuitively, would rise to rebut these assertions. But every one of these, and others like them, grows from a clear and consistent sensitivity to the vital interests of his nation. There is no question in his mind but that the main war was fought inside the Soviet Union against the Germans. That is where the Soviet vital interests were most sorely threatened and nearly lost. All else was secondary. As for the other end of his continent, Japan's navy was no threat to Soviet vital interests, nor were the several small islands of the Japanese homeland. But the Kwangtung Army was a threat and, having in mind the long and vulnerable southern border of Siberia, that Kwangtung Army was crucial. By his lights, when that army was defeated, and not until then, the war was won.

This matter of perception of vital interests has, I think, too little been considered. I suggest that the Soviets are far more sensitive to this than are we on this side of the Atlantic. I suggest, too, that the behavior of the Soviets (and, in passing, the Chinese and, among the nations of the western world, the French) is far more predictable than we have realized. They simply do not hazard their vital interests nor, turning the coin over, do they waste their substance on issues they do not consider vital.

I wish that we, on our side of the Atlantic, had always been as hard-headed in our perception of our vital interests as they have been in theirs. I rather suspect that some (not all) of our own major policy readjustments of the past few years do reflect an increased influence of our vital national interests in the formulation of our policies.

I believe this sort of sensitivity to national vital interests is consistently evident in Admiral Gorshkov's article, and I believe, too, that we can count on this in assessing what he and his navy and nation may do in the future. I suggest that strategically and, if it ever comes to that, tactically, our first planning task should be to set out for examination our appreciation of our own vital interests alongside those of our adversaries. Then, based on that judgment of what our own needs may be and of how our adversary is thinking, we can set our own courses toward our own attainable ends. This, to me, is the principal lesson of these fascinating Gorshkov papers—the support and defense of vital interests.

We have gotten a glimpse into a very important mind at work. We should profit by it.

Navies as Instruments of Peacetime Imperialism

With Commentary following the article by
Admiral D. L. McDonald, U. S. Navy (Retired)

EDITOR'S NOTE: *In the following chapter, cleared for publication in the Soviet Union on 8 December 1972, the admiral selectively quotes American writers and publications to portray the United States as a jingoistic nation whose imperialistic aspirations have been held in check only because the Soviet Union and other Socialist countries "have stood as an immovable force in the path of these aspirations."*

Armed forces have always been one of the effective means of state policy. In our day, proof of this is evident at every step. For example, the U. S. attempts immediately after the end of the Second World War to take upon itself the mission of "representing" the interests of all mankind, while having a monopoly at that time on nuclear weapons, is still fresh in everyone's minds. Thus, in one of his speeches, U. S. President Truman asserted that "The U. S. today is the strongest power. . . . While possessing this power we must assume the responsibility for the leadership of the world."[1] American policy and strategy, in aiming at one goal—the achievement of rule over the entire world by American monopolistic capital—at that time reduced its own entire state policy and diplomacy to a nuclear policy and diplomacy. The creation and testing of nuclear weapons in our country was the sole factor which forced the latter-day pretenders to world supremacy to restrain their aggressive zeal.

As a result of the intensive efforts of the Soviet people and of Soviet scientists in creating their own nuclear weaponry, in the early 1950s the American nuclear monopoly was dashed, the world Socialist system received its own shield, and the imperialist powers lost the material basis for conducting a policy of nu-

The author hopes that this African sentry and all of his countrymen will welcome this call by a Soviet combatant as a neighborly display of Russian technology, friendship, and resolution to thwart U. S. imperialism. Conversely, a visit by a U. S. warship should be regarded as saber-rattling.

[1] Yu. N. Listvinov. *Pervyy udar.* (*Nekotoroyye tendentsii razvitii amerikanskikh kontseptsiy "total'noy sily"*) (First Strike) (Some Trends in the Development of American Concepts of "Total Power") International Relations Publishing House, 1971, p. 12.

clear blackmail, the "from a position of strength" policy vis à vis the Socialist countries.

The U. S. pretensions to world supremacy were not curtailed even after the loss of the monopoly on nuclear weapons. The longing for world domination has been rather openly proclaimed by the idealogues of American imperialism; they have mainly counted on nuclear weapons, aviation, and later also on the Navy. The journal "Military Review," for example, noted: "Nuclear power plus naval superiority gives our country such a freedom of action that it could easily implement its God given right to lead the whole world."[2] An active proponent of the establishment of U. S. world supremacy is Colonel George C. Reinhardt, U.S.A. (Ret.) who, in stressing in his book "American Strategy in the Nuclear Age" that nuclear weapons are the key to the establishment of world supremacy, wrote: "Technology, in making the world smaller, is for the first time in history creating conditions which permit effective rule over the entire world by a single government."[3]

However, the U.S.S.R. and the other Socialist countries have stood as an immovable force in the path of these aspirations of American imperialism. And the fact that, despite all threats to destroy Communism, imperialism has not decided to unleash a new world war is explained primarily by the enormous growth of the might of the U.S.S.R., which has altered the relative strength of the forces in the world arena. This serves as convincing proof of the fact that only the vast economic and defensive might, the unprecedented political unity of the Soviet people, and their devotion to the ideals of the Communist Party have a sobering effect on the aggressively oriented circles of the imperialist camp, which has not given up its shameful ideas of crushing the countries of the Socialist community, and above all the U.S.S.R.

The leaders of the U.S.A. themselves have been forced to recognize this situation. Thus, as early as 1959 the Senate Foreign Relations Committee noted in its report that the end of the American nuclear monopoly and the growth of the strategic capabilities of the Soviet Union have increased the difficulties associated with supporting a military posture necessary to achieve established American goals.[4] This awareness by bourgeois figures means a great deal, especially if you consider that the imperialists provide acknowledgement of one achievement or another of the Socialist

countries only when life itself forces them to do so.

The economic might and defensive strength of the Soviet Union ensures the security of all the countries of the Socialist community and is altering the fundamental form of the relationship of forces in the world arena in favor of revolutionary progress and universal peace. This was stressed with the utmost force at the 1969 meeting of Communist and workers' parties by representatives of many fraternal countries.

Among the main means supporting the high defensive capability of the Motherland we must cite above all the Strategic Rocket Troops and the Navy, which incorporates as many means of armed combat as practical of those which the other branches of the armed forces have at their disposal. The Air Force, the Ground Forces, and the other branches of our glorious Armed Forces, which we shall not examine here since our main attention is being devoted to the Navy, to a great degree are an instrument of deterrence to the aggressive acts of the imperialists.

Policy, as V. I. Lenin taught, is a concentrated expression of the economy, whose condition determines the power of that most important weapon of policy, the armed forces of a country, whose condition is a reflection of the economic might of the state. A navy is a graphic indicator of the level of development of a country's economy.

"A modern warship is not merely a product of major industry, but at the same time is a sample of it . . . ," F. Engels pointed out. "The country with the more developed major industry enjoys almost a monopoly on the construction of these ships . . . Political power at sea, based on modern warships, is not at all wielded 'directly,' but just the opposite, it is exerted *indirectly* through economic strength."[5] This thesis remains true even today. With further development, the Navy, as well as the other branches of the armed forces, ever increasingly is embodying the latest achievements of science, technology, and production.

Actually a high level of development in all sectors of industry and science is needed to build a modern warship. As a rule, several hundred industrial enterprises take part in the construction of a combatant. Only a state with a well developed economy is capable of creating a Navy as a whole, with an inventory sufficient to carry out the missions with which it is charged and with all the support means necessary for its normal functioning.

The long periods of construction of the main ship types (in comparison with other branches of armed forces) and the relatively short service life, due to rapid

[2] Cited in Z. M. Solontsov's book *Diplomaticheskaya bor'ba SSLA za gospodstro na mope* (The U S Diplomatic Struggle for Domination of the Sea), Foreign Relations Publishing House, 1962, p. 385.

[3] Yearbook of World Affairs, Washington, 1958, p. 5.

[4] See the book *Voyennaya strategiya* (Military strategy) edited by Marshal of the Soviet Union V. D. Sokolovskiy (Voyenizdat, 1968, p. 71).

[5] F. Engels. *Izbrannyye voyennyye proizvedeniye* (Selected Military Works), Voyenizdat, 1957, pp. 17–18.

obsolescence, make especially great demands on science, which determines the path of naval construction, anticipating it by years or even decades. This is why throughout the course of history the navy, to a greater degree than the other branches of the armed forces, by concentrating in itself the latest achievements of science and technology, has reflected the level of economic and scientific-technical development of a state. This thesis permits the navy to be regarded as a unique indicator of the development and economic might of a country, and as one of the factors of its ability to firmly hold a definite place among the other powers.

Owing to the high mobility and endurance of its combatants, the Navy possesses the capability to vividly demonstrate the economic and military might of a country beyond its borders during peacetime. This quality is normally used by the political leadership of the imperialist states to show their readiness for decisive actions, to deter or suppress the intentions of potential enemies, as well as to support "friendly states."

It should be noted that the arsenal of instruments of such demonstrations is constantly being expanded. In recent years, as is well known, this has included displays of missile weaponry, combat aircraft, and diverse military equipment conducted on an international scale. Such propagandistic measures by the imperialist states are aimed at a clearly evident goal: to surprise probable enemies with the perfection of the equipment being exhibited, to affect their morale, to intimidate them right up to the outbreak of war, and to suggest to them in advance the hopelessness of fighting the aggressor. However, this far from always leads to the desired goal, primarily because all countries demonstrating the means for waging war appear only as a potential threat to peoples.

In contrast to the displays of missile weaponry, combat aircraft, and military equipment, warships of the imperialist powers which appear directly off foreign shores represent a real threat of immediate operations. And whereas in the past, the threat was rather great in scale when its dimensions were characterized by the firing range of smoothbore guns, and later by rifled shipboard guns, today it has grown even further, since today's combatants carry not only guns, but also nuclear-missile weaponry and aircraft, whose operating ranges can cover the entire territory of a foreign state. Therefore, the capability of navies to suddenly appear close to the shores of different countries and immediately proceed to carry out their assigned missions has been used for ages by various aggressive states as an important weapon of diplomacy and policy in peacetime, which in many cases has permitted the achievement of political goals without resorting to military operations by merely threatening to initiate them.

Consequently, the role of a navy is not limited to the execution of important missions in armed combat. While representing a formidable force in war, it has always been an instrument of policy of the imperialist states and an important support for diplomacy in peacetime owing to its inherent qualities which permit it to a greater degree than other branches of the armed forces to exert pressure on potential enemies without the direct employment of weaponry.

And today the imperialists are striving to use the quality of navies, such as the capability of making a visible demonstration of force, to put political pressure on other states and to support the diplomatic moves of one's own country in order to threaten potential enemies.

Many examples are known when the presence alone of a powerful navy in one area or another has permitted the achievement of political goals.

As early as the 17th century it was believed among the major sea powers that a fleet was capable of threatening a potential aggressor by the very fact of its existence and by its readiness for immediate and decisive actions. This thesis was recognized by all capitalist powers and, essentially, transformed navies into a diplomatic threat and deterrent force, and raised naval construction to the level of one of the most important problems of the political and ideological struggle in the international arena. For example, England took economic, military, diplomatic, and propagandistic measures in order to ensure the primacy of her Navy over the navies of other states. This permitted her to create the strongest navy of that day which supported Britannia's unpunished seizure and plundering of colonies, her enrichment by imperialistic robbery, and the acceleration of her rate of industrialization. A vivid characterization of the fact that England's policy was supported by the power of the Navy was the credo of her bourgeoisie: "God and the Navy—the two foundations of the wealth, security, and greatness of Britannia." As for the first foundation, God, his significance was more evident to the British; however, the Navy actually played the main role in achieving the goals of British policy, not only in wars, but also in peacetime, and it fostered the transformation of England into the greatest colonial power.

Navies also made it possible for other imperialist states to extend their supremacy to new areas and to maintain colonial rule in them. So-called "Gunboat diplomacy" arose in accordance with these aims, when the naval forces of the imperialist countries, in moving along the seacoast and penetrating up rivers into the depth of the area being colonialized, put down the freedom movement of the oppressed peoples and aided in plundering them.

The diplomatic significance of navies in peacetime is confirmed by many examples from the history of maritime states, including also Russia. Thus, evidence of the influence of the Navy on the growth of the international weight of Russia during the lifetime of Peter I is the report of the French ambassador to his king in which he said: "Russia, who has never had much of a name, now has become an object of attention of a majority of the European powers which are seeking her friendship, either being afraid of her hostile attitude toward their interests, or hoping to gain from an alliance with her."[6] The French ambassador explained the main cause of these changes was that many "had already seen how he (Peter I) had crossed the Baltic Sea with these ships and was able in a very short time to transport a significant army to conquer his neighbors."[7]

The use of the Russian Navy in peacetime as a political instrument is of no little interest. Thus, in 1780, Russia, owing to the growing might of her Navy, emerged as the initiator of a declaration on freedom of neutral maritime commerce. All of the main sea powers joined in it (except for England) which fostered the development of world sea trade and was a blow to England's unfounded pretensions to her sole right to conduct sea trade and to ship only in English bottoms.

In 1863, the international situation was fraught with the possibility of war between Russia and England and France due to the so-called "Polish question." In the same period relations worsened between the U.S.A. and England, leading to armed conflict against ocean communications. Under these conditions, Russia felt it expedient, not expecting the outbreak of military actions, to move her squadrons to the trade routes to the Atlantic and Pacific Oceans to put pressure on her enemies in order to obtain a peaceful solution to the conflict which had arisen. Admiral Lesovskiy's ships secretly crossed the Atlantic and put into New York harbor. At the same time, Admiral Popov's squadron appeared off the Pacific coast of America. The surprise arrival in U. S. ports of two Russian squadrons capable of cutting the vitally important oceanic communications of the English and French made a strong impression on the leaders of England and France and forced them to change their political position.

The special significance of navies to states as an instrument of policy in peacetime is confirmed by a series of acts regulating international relations. Thus, under the Treaty of Paris of 1856, which concluded the Crimean War, Russia was prevented from having a fleet in the Black Sea. And only in 1871 did Russian diplomacy succeed in achieving the lifting of the humiliating restrictions on the sovereign rights of the Russian state. The Anglo-Japanese Treaty of 1902 specially stipulated the need to retain a combined fleet in the Pacific Ocean exceeding Russia's Fleet there. In discussing the draft of the Portsmouth Peace Treaty in August 1905 after the Russo-Japanese War, Japan tried to include in it a demand to limit the composition of the Russian Fleet in the Pacific. However, the demand was not met because England, France, the U.S.A. and other countries were afraid of the excessive strength of Japan.

The important diplomatic significance of navies is also attested to by the fact that in the peace treaties concluded after World War I and World War II special attention was devoted to limiting the naval forces of the defeated states (the characteristic earmark of the treaties was the requirement to completely destroy submarines and the unconditional prohibition against these countries building or acquiring them). Moreover, the victors deprived the vanquished of the fleets remaining after the war. Thus, in the Berlin Conference (July–August 1945) the three great powers, the U.S.S.R., U.S.A., and Great Britain, determined the procedure for dividing up the Navy of Fascist Germany. They divided all of her surface ships (including those under construction and being repaired) equally among themselves, and destroyed the submarines (except for 30 submarines which also were divided equally). In addition to the warships, all of the stores of the German Navy were turned over to the conquering countries.

The division of the Japanese Navy took place according to the same principle after her capitulation.

The special role of navies in the policy of the major imperialist states is also attested to by the repeated attempts in the period 1922–1935 to limit and regulate the construction of warships, undertaken at specially convened international conferences. True, they fulfilled only a delaying function in the naval construction of the largest states and then only up to the mid-1930s (thereafter the naval arms race proceeded without any sort of limitations.) It is interesting that no such attempts were undertaken until our day with respect to the other branches of the armed forces. Even today, when the arms limitation talks have become a reality and ways of solving this problem have been defined, arms control is still only being extended to strategic missiles, including also those belonging to the navies.

The role of navies as an instrument of policy of states is also evident when examining the events which led to the weakening of England who, for a long time, was the leader of the capitalist world. We would note

---

[6] Cited in Ye. V. Tarle's book *Sochineniye* (Works), Izdvo AN SSSR, 1962, Vol. 12, pp. 184–185.

[7] Ye. V. Tarle. *Russkiy flot i vneshnyaya politika Petra I* (The Russian Fleet and the Foreign Policy of Peter I), Voyenizdat, 1949, p. 100.

that her ally—the U.S.A.—has evicted England from the throne of "Mistress of the Seas." In this connection, the Americans succeeded without a war in achieving what Germany could not achieve in two world wars.

The weakening of England began as early as the First World War and became evident immediately after its completion, when the "Mistress of the Seas" was forced to drop the "Two Power Standard" and to agree to an equality of forces between her own and the American Navy.[8] In the course of World War II, the decline of England as a great sea power accelerated, which was due to the effect of the law of the nonuniformity of development of capitalist countries and also to the revolutionary and national freedom movements embracing the entire world. One manifestation of this law is the change in the power of navies. The fact of the matter is that the U. S. Navy operated not only against the navies of the Hitler coalition, it also simultaneously ousted the navy of its old imperialist competitor from the oceans. The U.S.A. followed this policy over a long period of time, but especially in the second half of World War II and after its completion. The Americans succeeded in ousting the British from the ocean areas contiguous to the American continent, and in liquidating her former power in the Western hemisphere, in the Mediterranean Sea and Indian Ocean, in the Far East, and in the Pacific Ocean basin.

As a result of British payments to the Americans for the aid rendered them in World War II, the entire gold reserves of England migrated across the Atlantic Ocean. Moreover, in the most difficult period of the war the U.S.A. posed the question to England about the withdrawal of her fleet to American bases in case of the threat of capture of the ships by the Germans. Along with this, the U.S.A., taking advantage of the inaccessibility of her territory to attacks by the enemy and her economic might, furiously expanded naval construction. As a result, the American Navy was twice as strong as the British Navy after the end of World War II.

The growth of naval forces has permitted the Americans to expand widely in countries overseas, including also in the colonies of the British empire. The U.S.A., and not England, became the center of a system of postwar aggressive blocs. In this case, it is the American Navy which is the element binding these blocs together. The role of suppressor of the national freedom movement of peoples who are freeing themselves of the colonialist yoke finally was transferred from

England to the U.S.A. Not the British, but the U.S. Sixth Fleet is today constantly in the Mediterranean Sea, the traditional region of the former supremacy of Great Britain.

This was one aspect of the role of naval forces in the policy of bourgeois states which was clearly manifested in the course of World War II and after its end. It is evident that, in addition to the economic potential, the naval forces played a significant role in advancing the U.S.A. among the leaders of imperialism. The conditions which arose during the war and a powerful economy permitted the Americans to direct their main efforts toward the development of their Navy and to build tens of thousands of various warships during the war. By the end of the war, with respect to number, the main ship types of the U. S. Navy were equal to the navies of all of the other capitalist states taken together. The U. S. Navy also exceeded the navies of the other imperialist powers with respect to quality. In 1945, this was the most modern Navy in whose inventory more than 75% of the warships of the main types were less than five years old.[9]

American naval leaders have strived to convince world opinion that under peacetime conditions and in a possible future war, the U. S. Navy will remain the main power. At the same time U. S. ruling circles are widely using the Navy as an instrument of imperialist policy. It is precisely for this purpose that the American Sixth Fleet, which is constantly in the Mediterranean Sea, far from its home shores, is putting political pressure on the Mediterranean states. By its presence it is supporting a reaction in the struggle against progressive democratic forces on Cyprus, in Italy and Greece, and against the national freedom movement of the Arab peoples, is inspiring the aggressive actions of Israel, the henchman of the American monopolies in the Near East, and is supporting economic expansion in a series of states of Europe, Africa, and Asia.

The U. S. Seventh Fleet, which is in the waters of Southeast Asia, is an instrument of American policy in the struggle against the national freedom movement, democracy, and progress in Korea, Vietnam, Laos, and Cambodia. This Fleet, the leading grouping of the imperialist armed forces, has repeatedly acted as the instrument for unleashing wars in this area of the world, including also the barbaric war against the progressive forces of the young states of Indochina.

It would be difficult to find an area on our planet where U. S. leaders have not used their pet instrument of foreign policy—the Navy—against the progressive forces of the peoples of various countries. It imple-

---

[8] The 1922 Washington Conference of five powers—the U.S.A., England, Japan, France, and Italy—officially established the ratio of the total tonnage of the capital ships of these countries as 5:5:3:1.75:1.75, respectively (*Istoriya voyenno-morskogo iskusstva* [The History of the Naval Art], Voyenizdat, 1969, p. 179).

[9] Potapov, I. N. *Razvitiye voyenno-morskikh flotov v poslevoyennyy period* (The Development of Navies in the Postwar Period), Voyenizdat, 1971, p. 24.

mented a blockade of revolutionary Cuba, landed counterrevolutionary bands on its territory, put down the democratic movement in the Dominican Republic, etc.

Like the U.S. politicians, the British imperialists, using their Navy, have taken reprisals against the inhabitants of the British Isles who are trying to free themselves from the colonial yoke, and also have supported reactionary regimes on the coast and islands of the Persian Gulf.

After the war, the U.S.A. became the organizer of a system of military alliances of the imperialist states. The American Navy, as the most powerful in the imperialist camp, is the most important element cementing this system together. It is also being used in pacts to pressure its own allied partners who have relatively weak forces at sea. In this connection, not only direct pressure is used but also a unique flattering bribery. Thus, each time tension rises due to interimperialist contradictions within the military alliances, U. S. politicians advance plans to create various groupings, so called "combined forces," thereby trying to impart a semblance of equality among the pact members. For example, in 1962, Secretary of State Dean Rusk proposed creating "multinational naval nuclear forces." Later it was proposed to organize a surface nuclear fleet of 25 ships with crews consisting of members of the pact countries. However, the U.S.A. was unable to go any further than the creation of a symbolic Atlantic squadron of three to five ASW ships of different NATO-member countries. Later, they widely used their own fleet to put political pressure on the participants of the military alliances who displayed "centrifugal" intentions.

Times are changing and the methods of employing the navies of capitalist states as an instrument of policy in peacetime are also changing. Thus, in the postwar years in the antagonistic struggle between systems, the leading circles of imperialistic countries are resorting to more and more refined methods of demonstrating force, not stopping even short of crimes against mankind in order to retain or restore their supremacy over the peoples of former colonies and countries who had extricated themselves from the vice of capitalist exploitation.

Demonstrations of naval force by the leading capitalist sea powers have been employed more than once to put pressure on the Soviet Union and the countries of the Socialist community. The U. S. Navy has especially distinguished itself by special activity in these operations. In the initial postwar years, it was handed the role of a connecting link in a chain of bridgeheads and military bases created by American imperialists around the perimeter of the borders of our country. The American Navy with its attack groups of nuclear forces was supposed to fill in the gaps of this "ring of fire" from the direction of the sea. The aggressive, openly anti-Soviet trend of deployment of the naval forces and the formation from them of various types of NATO strike forces, carrier strike forces, and later also squadrons of nuclear-powered guided-missile submarines, were employed for numerous threats to our country in the speeches of military leaders, served as an instrument of nuclear blackmail, and were the foundation of their military doctrines. It was precisely for this purpose that the patrols of the nuclear-powered submarines in different areas of the World Ocean were widely advertised, demonstrative operations by aircraft carriers in seas contiguous to our country were undertaken, systematic overflights of our combatants and auxiliaries were carried out by aircraft, and demonstration visits were made by American ships in the Black, Baltic, and Japanese Seas. Up until the signing in 1972 of the Soviet-American Incidents at Sea Treaty, there were numerous attempts at provocative clashes by American and British ships with our ships, etc. All of these actions received definite opposition on the part of the U.S.S.R. and the other Socialist countries and did not achieve those goals at which the organizers and executers were aiming; they merely exposed their initiators.

The collision between the Soviet destroyer Besslednyi, *right, and the USS* Walker (DD-517) *in the Sea of Japan on 10 May 1967 was one of a series of what the author terms "provocative clashes" on the high seas, all of which ended with the signing in 1972 of the Soviet-American Incidents at Sea Treaty.*

The Soviet Armed Forces, including also the Navy, have emerged as one of the instruments of U.S.S.R. policy. However, the goals and methods of employing them in this capacity in the international arena differs fundamentally from the goals and methods of the political employment of the armed forces of the imperialist powers in peacetime. The Soviet Army and Navy are the instrument of a policy of peace and friendship of peoples, a deterrent to military adventurists, and a resolute opposition to the threats to the security of peace-loving peoples on the part of imperialist powers.

In realistically appraising the growing threat to the security of our country, the CPSU Central Committee and the Soviet government have seen that the way out of the situation which has been created lies in opposing the forces of aggression on the World Ocean with strategic defensive counterforces whose foundation is made up of the Strategic Missile Forces and an ocean-going Navy.

The creation at the will of the Party of a new Soviet Navy and its emergence onto the ocean expanses have fundamentally altered the relative strength of forces and the situation in this sphere of contention. In the person of our modern Navy, the Soviet Armed Forces have acquired a powerful means of defense in the oceanic areas, a formidable force for the deterrence of aggression, which is constantly ready to deliver punishing retaliatory blows and to disrupt the plans of the imperialists. And the Navy, along with the other branches of the Soviet Armed Forces, is successfully fulfilling its main mission—the defense of the country from attacks by aggressors from the direction of the ocean. The warships of our Navy are a threat to no one, but they are always ready to decisively repulse any aggressor who dares to infringe upon the security of the Motherland.

Thus, the inspirers of the arms race and of the preparation for a new world war, in counting on speeding up the development of their own naval forces and the creation of new problems which are difficult for the defense of the Soviet Union to resolve, have themselves been faced with even more complex problems with the strengthening of our Navy on the oceans. The former inaccessibility of the continents, which permitted them in the past to count on impunity for aggression, has now become ancient history.

But there is still another side to the question.

With the emergence of the Soviet Navy onto the ocean expanses, our warships are calling with continually greater frequency at foreign ports, fulfilling the role of "plenipotentiaries" of the Socialist countries. In the last three years alone, some 1,000 Soviet combatants and auxiliaries have visited the ports of 60 countries

in Europe, Asia, Africa, and Latin America. More than 200,000 of our officers and rated and nonrated men have visited the shores of foreign states.

All of these calls are visits of the most representative delegations of Soviet people. Indeed, aboard every combatant and auxiliary serve men of various professions—workers, collective farmers, and engineers. All of them are representatives of different *oblasti* and *rayony* of the country, of different republics, of different nationalities—Russians, Ukrainians, Uzbeks, Belorussians, Azerbaydzhanians, Georgians, Armenians, Jews, Tatars, Latvians, Estonians, and other equal members of the friendly family of peoples of our multinationality Motherland.

The friendly visits of Soviet navymen make it possible for the peoples of many countries to become convinced with their own eyes of the creativity of the ideas of Communism, and of the genuine equality of all nationalities in the Soviet state, and to gain a concept of the level of development and culture of representatives of the most varied regions of our immense Motherland. They see warships embodying the achievements of Soviet science, technology, and industry, and establish friendly contacts with representatives of the most diverse strata of population of our country. Soviet navymen, from admirals down to seamen, are bearing the truth about the first Socialist country in the world, about Communist ideology and culture, and about the Soviet way of life to the masses of peoples of other states. They are clearly and convincingly spreading the ideas of the Leninist peaceloving policy of the Communist Party and the Soviet government through many countries of the world. It is impossible to overestimate the significance of this ideological influence.

In turn, Soviet navymen, in visiting the ports of various states, are also seeing for themselves the achievements of the peoples of countries who are friendly to us and who have won the right to govern their own fate, and to see the results of centuries of rule by the colonializers, and the social contrasts of capitalist society, which bourgeois propaganda so thoroughly conceals.

Official visits and business calls of the warships of the Navy are making a significant contribution to improving mutual relations between states and peoples and to strengthening the international influence of the Soviet Union. This is convincingly confirmed by numerous examples of the display of warm feelings toward the country of Soviets by the inhabitants of those cities and countries which our navymen visit. Many official representatives of these countries warmly recall the visits of our ships. The statement by the Foreign Minister of Southern Yemen is characteristic of this: "For the first time in history, ships of a friendly country have visited our country. In the past many warships have arrived in Aden, but they did not carry the banner of friendship, but threats, force, and enslavement."[10]

The major OKEAN exercises conducted in April and May 1970 were completed with the calling of its ships at more than ten foreign ports of the different continents of the world. Normally, after major exercises, the forces participating in them are inspected. However, due to the global scale of these naval exercises, it was impossible to conduct such an inspection. Therefore the calls of Soviet ships at foreign ports was not only a unique inspection of the Soviet naval forces, but also a demonstration of the defensive might of the great Soviet power who is standing guard over the peace and security of peoples, fostering the strengthening of friendship with peoples of other countries, and the development of international ties between the Soviet Union and developing sovereign states. During these visits, Soviet navymen once more demonstrated a high

[10] *Al-Kifah al-Watani*, 10 May 1970.

degree of conscientiousness, orderliness, and culture and a deep respect for peoples, for national traits and customs of those countries which they managed to visit.

Soviet diplomatic representatives and officials of various states affirm that our navymen worthily represented their people abroad and, as always, greatly fostered the growth of sympathy and friendship toward the Soviet Union and its highly humanistic ideals. Thus, on 10 January 1969 the newspaper *Afro-American* wrote: "The Kenyans were surprised by the fact that the Soviet navymen, in contrast to the navymen of the American and British navies, did not leave the slightest trace of chaos behind them in port. . . Soviet navymen are so serious and conduct themselves in such a manner that it seems as though these men are from another planet."

From what has been said it quite clearly follows that navies, being one branch of the armed forces and the instrument of armed combat at sea, therefore, have played and are playing the role of an instrument of state policy in peacetime.

Commentary

By Admiral D. L. McDonald, U. S. Navy (Retired)

Admiral McDonald graduated from the U. S. Naval Academy in 1928 and became a naval aviator in 1931. His early service included duty in the battleships *Mississippi* and *Colorado*, in an air squadron on board the *Saratoga*, and with the aviation unit of the cruiser *Detroit*. Service with the Navy Rifle Team at the National Matches, and later as an instructor at NAS Pensacola was followed by a tour from 1938 to 1941 with PatRon 42 at Seattle and later in the Aleutian Islands. When the U. S. entered World War II, he was flag secretary to ComAirLant and then, from 1942 to 1944, he served as flight training officer at Jacksonville. During the latter part of the war he was operations officer, then XO of the *Essex* and, later, operations officer for ComAirPacFlt. After a tour in BuAer and as aide to the AsstSecNav (Air) and later, to the Under Secretary of the Navy, he commanded the carrier *Mindoro*. A tour as ACof S (Operations) at CinCPacFlt preceded command of the *Coral Sea*. Tours at the Office of CNO and at SHAPE were followed by command of CarDivSix. In 1961, Admiral McDonald became Commander Sixth Fleet. In April 1963 he became CinCNavEur and CinCNELM; in August of that year he became the CNO.

Although Admiral Gorshkov sometimes uses what might be termed "poetic license" in certain of his interpretations of historic events, he does indeed demonstrate a thorough knowledge of history and a great appreciation of the role navies have played throughout the years.

While reading those portions of his article which deal with the historical past and the influence of Western navies thereon, his remarks seemed to me to be tinged with both admiration and envy. He is, in effect, telling his Soviet naval officer readership, "Anything they can do, we can do better, but, of course, in our own humane way."

As we read this and other articles in this series, we ought to keep the thought of Admiral Gorshkov's *audience* clearly in mind. Perhaps he was writing with one eye on the 21st century's history books; perhaps, too, he chose this forum to speak, however obliquely, to his fellow members of the Central Committee of the Communist Party. But these are only speculations. We have been told, and thus we accept the explanation, that what the admiral says was intended specifically, if not solely, for Soviet naval officers.

It is not surprising, then, that much of this article, perhaps only slightly paraphrased, could have appeared in our own Navy League's magazine under the byline of one of their editors, or as a verbatim transcript of the testimony of one of our CNOs before an Armed Services Committee of the Congress.

I agree with Admiral Gorshkov that navies reflect the level of a State's economic and scientific-technical development to a greater degree than does any other branch of the Armed Services. Yet, it is not necessarily true, as he infers, that a country's navy is a graphic indicator of the level of development of a country's economy and, ipso facto, the more modern a country's navy, the more healthy its economy. Such a philosophy fails to take into consideration that there are countries—and Americans live in one of them—that are cantankerously unwilling in peacetime to permit their navies to benefit to the maximum extent possible from the country's economic and technical progress. While there is much to be said for frugality—an authentic American folk hero is the self-made millionaire who still rolls his own cigarettes—playing penny-wise with our defenses in this day and age is like issuing derringers to our police or buckets to our firemen.

No, the good admiral's argument is specious. Were he right, the Soviet Navy—which is considerably more up-to-date in certain respects and in some ways more modern on the whole than the U. S. Navy—would reflect a Soviet economy and technology that is superior to the United States. And our friends in the Kremlin who, from time to time, discover an earlier Russian inventor of the light bulb than Edison, or a hitherto unrecorded 13th century Russian circumnavigation, have always stopped short of claiming either economic or technical preeminence.

Still, if I was right earlier in detecting a note of envy in some things the admiral said, I must put that tight fitting shoe on my own foot and confess my envy of his navy's impressive progress—and my chagrin and sadness at our country's complacency. Moreover, he has emphasized the unique role of naval power in other than combat situations, and he has stressed its extreme effectiveness in such situations. No countryman of mine in recent years has been able to inculcate these universal truths for Americans with the vigor and singlemindedness of this tenacious Russian admiral.

But, before I say too many nice things about this man who is saying such terrible things about us, I must chide him for applying a double standard. On the one hand, he condemns the imperialistic navies for displaying naval weaponry, appearing off foreign shores, conducting operations on an international scale, making in-port visits for the purpose of propagandizing their capabilities and putting pressure on their hosts to support diplomatic moves, and exerting pressure on potential enemies without the direct employment of weaponry. Such reprehensible conduct, however, becomes immediately defensible if these activities are carried on by the Soviet Navy. They are then viewed as deterrents to the imperialistic military adventurists—a forthright opposition to the threats, by the West, to the security of "peace-loving peoples."

It would seem, then, as in the moral of the fable of the lawyer, the farmer, and the farmer's ox, that it does make a great deal of difference whose ox is being gored.

But for all that, there does seem to be a difference between the way Admiral Gorshkov views the peacetime activities of his navy and the way a modern U. S. Chief of Naval Operations might view his. And it seems to come down, not to where a navy will go and what it will do when it gets there but, rather, to the questions of why and how it will do what it does.

It seems to me—and, I sincerely believe, to most Americans—that the ultimate objective of each of our countries is to expand our respective political and commercial philosophies. We in the United States believe that if others see enough of us and our way of life they will want to adopt our form of political philosophy. Thus, it is our aim to afford peoples of all lands freedom of choice.

The Soviet Union, on the other hand, seems to be so sure that their philosophy is so much better for everyone than any other system that they have no hesitancy in imposing it on any "oppressed peoples," presumably for the good of those people.

When one stands back from the admiral's words and thinks only of his deeds—the superb navy he has fashioned ostensibly for the defense of the motherland—it seems very clear that the admiral is a firm believer in the axiom that a good offense is the best defense.

Finally, it is always difficult to determine what the leaders of States—either friendly or unfriendly—have in mind. It is particularly so of those leaders of a closed society whose political philosophy is so different from our own. Just why Admiral Groshkov chose to put so many of his thoughts on paper for distribution we may never know, but nevertheless he has and all of our citizens—especially those in whose hands the guidance of our Navy reposes—would do well to give careful consideration to his words.

Some Problems in Mastering the World Ocean

With Commentary following the article by
Vice Admiral Stansfield Turner, U. S. Navy (Retired)

Some problems in mastering the World Ocean. In analyzing the essence of imperialism, Vladimir Illich Lenin pointed out that financial capital, afraid of lagging behind in the furious struggle for the still underdeveloped parts of the world, is striving to seize as many different expanses of the globe as possible, assuming that they will later on become a source of raw materials. Areas of the earth which are unsuited for exploitation today, V. I. Lenin noted, may become suitable tomorrow in connection with the incredibly rapid growth of technical progress, which will permit

One dividend of a world-wide scientific effort occurred in July 1970 when the Soviet oceanographic research vessel Khariton Laptev, upper right, appeared off the Florida Coast just at the time the USS Observation Island, foreground, escorted by the USS Calcaterra (DER-390), was about to test-fire a Poseidon missile.

finding new methods of exploiting them and extracting profits.[1]

In the 18th and 19th centuries the efforts of the largest powers were directed toward the seizure of lands being opened up, their colonization, and later toward the development and redivision of them. At that time the seas and oceans were basically merely the arena for the struggle between enemy navies for control of communications, but were not objects of clashes of state interests.

In recent decades in the era of the exploitation of the resources of the World Ocean, an ever increasing struggle has begun between imperialist countries for the division of it for economic and military aims, since it is becoming an immediate objective of their expansion. It is quite evident that navies, as an instrument

[1] See V. I. Lenin. *Poln. Sobr. Soch.* (Complete Collected Works), Vol. 27, p. 381

of policy of the aggressive states, will not be able to take a back seat in this struggle.

The level and tempo of the development of science and technology in the context of today's scientific-technical revolution are creating vast possibilities for the study, mastery, and use of the World Ocean and its bottom for practical economic and military purposes. Therefore, attempts are already being made by certain capitalist states to usurp individual areas of it and to divide up spheres of influence in it. Thus, voices are being heard in the U. S. Congress calling on Americans to move to the East and by 1980 to occupy the Atlantic Ocean bottom up to the Mid-Atlantic Ridge, for, according to the authors of these statements, when it is a question of the ocean bottom, no one mentions borders: He who takes, is right. A highly alarming symptom is the practice by certain states of expanding the limits of their territorial sea up to 200 miles, which is nothing other than an attempt to seize great expanses of the ocean.

The main reason for the level of interest by states in the World Ocean is its truly inexhaustible resources, while the aggressive powers are attracted by its vast military significance.

As is well known, sea water contains all the elements of Mendeleyev's periodic system; the total amounts of these minerals reach fantastic figures. According to calculations by scientists the ocean water has some 10 million tons of gold, four billion tons of uranium, and 270 billion tons of heavy water. The reserves of metals, minerals, fuels (oil, gas, and coal), various chemical raw materials, nuclear material, power and food reserves, locked in the seabed, are so vast that there is no comparison whatsoever with the known reserves existing on land.

A considerable part of the seabed is covered with ore nodules consisting of iron, manganese, cobalt, nickel, copper, and rare earth elements. Geologists believe that great reserves of various natural resources lie in the seabed. Already major deposits of oil and gas are known today in the North Sea, in the Gulf of Mexico, in the Persian Gulf, off the coasts of Alaska and California, and in other areas. Moreover, it is postulated that the main deposits of oil and gas are located not on land but in the seabed. And although mankind will be able to utilize fully all of these riches only in the future, the importance of exploiting them is already increasing today. Prospecting for oil and gas reserves is being carried out in almost all of the areas of the continental shelf, and the output of "maritime" oil is approaching 20% of the entire petroleum output.

The truly inexhaustible energy resources of the ocean—its tides, currents, temperature gradients of the water, etc.—also are of vast economic interest.

The reserves of animal protein, i.e., fish, sea animals, plankton, etc., in the World Ocean (if measures are taken to restock them) make it possible to consider it to be one of the most important sources for solving the food problem for the growing population of the world. Today the catching of fish and other "gifts of the sea" is carried out only in a small part of the ocean surface, consisting of about 10% of it. The annual world catch of fish equals some 60 million tons, but in the near future it may reach 100 million tons or more.

The basic problem of "sea chemistry" arising in practice is the extraction of rare earth and trace elements from the waters. The problem of obtaining common salt, magnesium, bromine, potassium, iodine, and several other substances from sea water has been successfully solved from an economic and technical standpoint; ways have been found to obtain uranium, gold, and other valuable elements from sea water. The dimensions and scale of this work are such that in the near future major changes may be produced in the world economy.

The attack on the ocean is underway on an expanded front. Today man is capable of living and working at depths down to 200 meters and soon undersea stations will be lowered down to 700-1,000 meters. The bathyscaphe *Trieste* has already dived to a depth of 10,919 meters, reaching the bottom of the Mariana Trench, the deepest known trench in the World Ocean. In the coming decades, a fuller, economically effective utilization of all the resources of the World Ocean, supported by technology, will be realized.

The scale of exploitation of the ocean is characterized by the following data published in the American journal *Foreign Affairs;* in 1956, U. S. expenditures on oceanographic work were 25 million dollars, in 1968 they were 448 million dollars, and in 1970 they increased to 900 million dollars.

The growth in appropriations for these goals, which is being observed on an international scale, is explained by the economic interest of all states in a more complete utilization of the riches of the oceans. Today this is one of the most important international and national problems entering the world political sphere. Just as in the 19th century the question of the division of land into spheres of influence became particularly acute, at the present time the intentions of several capitalist countries to establish spheres of influence in the World Ocean is becoming no less acute. The imperialist states are no longer restricting themselves by their own laws concerning the exploitation of the natural resources of the continental shelf: they are striving to extend their national jurisdiction to the open waters of seas and oceans located vast distances from their shores.

Attempts at usurping certain areas of the seabed by

individual bourgeois countries are becoming an increasingly blatant and widespread practice, subjugating certain fields of politics, economics, production, and science. And inevitably contradictions and crisis situations arise here. Thus, some countries, in carrying out the development and surveying of the continental shelf, are already raising the question of prohibiting freedom of navigation and the cruising of naval ships in the waters over the locations of undersea work, the question of a significant expansion of the territorial sea, etc. The posing of this question in this way is having a definite effect on the status of the high seas and freedom of navigation, which are the main legal instruments ensuring the regulation of the mutual relations between sovereign states whose interests come into contact with one another in the international waters of the World Ocean.

The CPSU program calls for not only the utilization of known natural resources, but also prospecting for new ones. The World Ocean is assuming extreme importance in connection with this. The study of it and utilization of resources is becoming one of the most major state problems aimed at supporting the economic might of the Soviet Union. A great deal of attention was paid to this in the documents of the 24th CPSU Congress and in the speeches of the delegates. In a report to the 24th Party Congress, Secretary General of the CPSU Central Committee L. I. Brezhnev said: "Our country is ready to participate together with other interested states in the solution of such problems as . . . the study and mastery of space and of the World Ocean."[2]

However, this is possible only if the bottom of the seas and oceans remains a sphere of peaceful cooperation and if it will not be seized by the imperialists and transformed into a bridgehead for the emplacement of new forms of weapons.

Scientific technical progress has permitted man to master parts of the planet, the sea and ocean bottoms, which until recently were inaccessible. Yet at the same time this process also created the prerequisites for positioning of nuclear and other forms of mass destruction weapons there by aggressors. This is why peaceloving states, headed by the Soviet Union, are waging a struggle against a new arms race, so that the seabed will remain a sphere of peaceful international cooperation.

The treaty prohibiting the locating of nuclear or other forms of mass destruction weapons on or under the seabed, concluded at the initiative of the Soviet Union, has become the first, but important, step on

the path to solving this question. This treaty encompasses all areas of the World Ocean located beyond the 12-mile limit of the coastal zone of the territorial sea. The treaty, which was signed by more than 90 states, went into force on 18 May 1972.

A definite impact on the division of the ocean was made by the signing in 1958 of the Geneva Convention on the Continental Shelf according to which all littoral states were granted the right of ownership of the resources of the seabed in their own sections of the shelf down to a depth of 200 meters or beyond this limit to a point at which the water depth permits exploitation of the resources of this area. A defect in the Convention is the absence of a clear-cut wording concerning the outer limits of the continental shelf of the littoral states. This vagueness makes it possible for certain capitalist states to seek ways of seizing vast areas beyond the limits of the shelf.

Today the serious threat of a further division of the World Ocean exists. Therefore, it is not by chance that many countries and a great number of international organizations, beginning with the U.N. and ending with dozens of different types of intragovernmental and nongovernmental organizations and organs, are engaged with questions of the legal regime and with the development of new norms regulating the use of the World Ocean. The most characteristic feature in their work in the current stage is the fact that several Afro-Asian and Latin American developing countries are insisting on a review of all existing standards, regulating the use of the World Ocean, based on the fact that they did not participate in their exploitation. In particular, they assert that current international maritime law is outmoded and does not reflect changes which have occurred in the world since 1958. Representatives of these countries put their position on the plane of a struggle between the poor and rich, the backward and the industrially developed countries, which, according to their assertions, are putting national interests first.

The delegations of the U.S.S.R. of other Socialist countries have sharply criticized such extremist views at the United Nations, pointing out that such a non-class-oriented approach, i.e., the simple division of people into rich and poor, was not only unjust, but also was deeply in error and insulting to the peoples of Socialist countries. They have created their own wealth themselves, without exploiting anyone, while the imperialist powers have profited from the exploitation of colonial peoples. That is why they must be required to return at least a part of what was stolen to the developing countries.

In order to prepare proposals concerning many problems of international maritime law, an expanded U.N.

---

[2] L. I. Brezhnev. *Otchetnyy doklad Tsentral'nogo Komieta KPSS XXIV s"yezdu Kommunisticheskoy partii Sovetskogo Soyuza* (Summary Report of the CPSU Central Committee to the 24th Congress of the Communist Party of the Soviet Union), Politizdat, 1971, p. 37.

Committee on the Peaceful Use of the Seabed Beyond the Limits of National Jurisdiction was created and is in operation. In accordance with General Assembly Resolution 2750c (XXV) of 17 December 1970, it was transformed into an organ for preparing for an international conference on maritime law. At the 27th Session of the U.N. General Assembly a resolution was adopted concerning the holding of two sessions of the conference in 1973–1974. Various legal aspects of the use of the World Ocean will be examined in the course of the Committee's work. In connection with this, several countries raised the question of a complete review of the existing legal regime of the World Ocean and of the violation of all existing regulations of international maritime law. There are also statements against even freedom of the high seas on the ground that this principle is outmoded and is being used by the imperialists to the detriment of the interests of the developing countries. Our position on this question is very clear. The imperialists' violation of the legal norms attests not to the insufficient effectiveness of these norms, but rather to the strengthened aggressiveness of imperialism itself, which is stressed in the decisions of the 24th CPSU Congress. Therefore, it is not the norms themselves which must be changed but, above all, cooperation must be achieved between peaceloving forces in order to force the imperialists to strictly observe existing regulations.

Several developing countries are steadily promoting the idea of developing a convention on the seabed regime and on creating an international organ with very extensive powers which would become, essentially, a supranational organ and would control all exploitation of the seabed conducted by different countries. It is quite evident that such an approach is not very realistic, since it actually envisions an institution of some sort of international consortium in which inevitably, due to the objective laws of the capitalist market, the largest imperialist monopolies would play the main role. Therefore, regardless of the good intentions of the authors of this idea, the power in the organization would belong to precisely those forces which its creation is supposed to protect against.

The attention of international organs concerned with the use of the World Ocean is riveted today on the question of the breadth of the territorial sea.

Experience has shown the viability of a 12-mile limit for the breadth of the territorial sea. Presently 54 states have 12-mile territorial seas, 26 have 3-mile limits, 10 states have 4- and 6-mile seas, four states have 30-mile limits, two have 80-mile territorial seas, there are single states with 10, 18, 100, and 130 mile territorial seas. Eight Latin American and one African state have 200-mile territorial seas. Experts have calculated that

if all countries declared a 200-mile territorial sea, then of the 360 million square kilometers of water on our planet, about 140-150 million square kilometers would be appropriated by the coastal states. Almost all of the seas would be transformed into their territorial seas and, in particular, the Mediterranean would turn out to be completely divided up.

The key to the solution of this question is the strict establishment of limitations on the breadths of territorial seas, since a further extension could create the danger of an actual division of the high seas. Such a danger is already taking shape today, if you consider scientific technical progress and the modern means and practical capabilities which states presently have at their disposal. Based on existing practice, and on a sensible combination of interests of the coastal states with the principles of the freedom of the high seas, it would seem completely acceptable to limit the breadth of the territorial sea to limits of up to 12 miles.

The problem of the innocent passage of combatants and auxiliaries and aircraft overflights through international straits is also a subject of discussion. A considerable number of U.N. delegations believe that freedom of the high seas is unthinkable without freedom of navigation through international straits connecting the high seas and oceans which have long served mankind as important peaceful waterways.

Many sea powers, and also countries not having access to the sea, are expressing concern that even with the adoption of a 12-mile limit for the breadth of the territorial sea, more than 110 straits being used for international shipping will turn out to be closed territorial seas of littoral states. It is evident that this may have a considerable effect on the legal status of those straits which until now have been part of the high seas and which have been used for navigation without any sort of limitations. Therefore, in those straits which connect the open seas and are used for international shipping, all transitting ships (and in the wider straits also aircraft flying overhead) must be accorded equal freedom of transit and overflight.

Concrete proposals were introduced on freedom of navigation in straits by the Soviet Union at the fourth session of the U.N. Committee on the Seabed. In particular it is envisaged that in narrow straits, littoral states will be able to establish appropriate corridors for the transit of ships through straits and for aircraft overflights of the straits. These proposals do not affect the legal regime of those straits through which passage is regulated by special international agreements.

And there is one more problem provoking sharp discussions—the definition of the outer limit of the continental shelf. The positions of states on this question are extremely diverse. Thus, the U.S.A. is advo-

cating the concept of a 200-meter depth for the outer limit of the shelf. However, this concept is not finding widespread support from a majority of the developed and developing countries. Indonesia and Cyprus are expressing concern with regard to the fact that the establishment of a single criterion for determining the outer limit of the shelf would lead to injustice and inequality between states: one would have a large shelf, and others would not have one at all. Therefore, they propose defining the limit of the shelf taking into account both depth and distance from shore. Mexico and Australia, for example, consider the regulations of the 1958 Convention on the Continental Shelf completely sufficient. There are also other proposals, however; an analysis of them shows that a more realistic limit would be one which would be established taking into account the criteria of depth and distance from shore.

Many countries are insisting on a rapid determination of the shelf limit, since the danger exists of certain states declaring vast areas of the seabed to be their own shelf, and many countries are coming out for adoption of criteria for establishing shelf limits acceptable to all states.

In December 1973, scientists of the Azerbaijan branch of the Soviet Research Institute of Geophysical Methods of Prospecting created seismic waves, not with explosives, but with this battery of gas detonators. Submerged and detonated with no danger to any aquatic species, these devices permit the study of the relief of the bottom of the Caspian Sea and can detect the presence of oil and gas in the strata.

The above questions far from cover the list of problems connected with the use of the World Ocean attracting the attention of practically all states and constantly in the realm of international negotiations being conducted on different levels by different departments. The number of such problems is not decreasing and continues to grow. One of them raised by the Soviet Union and other Socialist countries is the prohibition of using the seabed for military purposes. This was raised because of the fact that in several capitalist countries, development of programs for building undersea equipment for the militarization of the ocean bottom at great depths is proceeding on a broad front.

The statements of a prominent figure in the U. S. military circles published in the journal *Foreign Affairs* attest to the true intentions of the American imperialists in regard to the World Ocean: "In ten years or so we shall begin to carve out sections of the ocean far from shore which will be important to us from the point of view of our national defense. And we shall prohibit access by any other country to the areas staked out by us." [3]

Everything that has been said above attests to the importance of the treaty prohibiting the placing of dangerous forms of weaponry on the seabed or under it, signed on 11 February 1971. Moreover, it is difficult to overestimate the significance of this treaty both as a measure to limit the expansionist desires of individual states, and as a first step on the path toward complete demilitarization of the seabed leading to the cessation of the ruinous and wasteful arms race.

The problems of a modern Navy. In taking into account the importance of questions related to the strengthening of the country's defense from the direction of the sea, the Soviet Union, in cooperation with the other Warsaw Pact member nations, is constantly strengthening her own sea power, including several necessary components.

In order to exploit the World Ocean and to utilize its resources, it is essential to have detailed and comprehensive knowledge of the hydrosphere of the Earth, to understand the processes occurring in it, and its effect on the land and the atmosphere, and on the formation of weather. Knowledge ensuring navigational safety in the oceans and seas and flights over them is also needed. Moreover, reliable information on the various resources existing in the hydrosphere and on possible methods of exploiting them is necessary. Special expeditionary, research oceanographic ships, scientific organizations, equipment, and, of course, the appropriate personnel are required to understand the seas and oceans. All of this is one component of the sea power of a country.

Our country, its scientists, and navymen have written many glorious pages in the history of geographic discoveries and seafaring, and in the ocean sciences. We are presently conducting a large volume of research on the hydrosphere. Yet the World Ocean still remains the least studied section of the globe, and the scale of work on trying to understand it must and will be expanded in the future.

An important integral part of sea power is the equipment and personnel which make possible the practical utilization of the oceans and seas as transport routes connecting continents, countries, and peoples. For this it is essential to have a merchant marine, a network of ports and services supporting its operation, and a developed shipbuilding and ship repair industry.

In 1972, the Soviet Merchant Marine, which is growing at a rapid rate, was sixth among the merchant fleets of the world. A majority of its ships have been built in recent years and are among the more technically advanced ships.

The next component of sea power is the ships, technical equipment, and personnel needed for the practical exploitation and utilization of the resources of the World Ocean, i.e., the fishing fleet. Today our country has the strongest fishing fleet in the world at its disposal. The sea and ocean fishing industry will be developed even further, will exploit new areas, and will expand the assortment of products of the sea being caught. The broadest prospects are opening up in the creation of equipment for extracting mineral resources from the water, from the sea bottom, and from beneath it.

However we must consider the most important component of the sea power of the state to be the Navy, whose mission is to protect state interests on the seas and oceans and to defend the country from possible attacks from the direction of the seas and oceans.

Through the efforts of the people in the Soviet Union a nuclear-missile, technically advanced Navy has been created as a indispensable integral part of the Soviet Armed Forces.

The need to have a powerful Navy corresponding both to the geographical position of our country and to its political importance as a great world power has already long been understood, as we have said above. However, this question became particularly acute in the postwar years, when as a result of the alignment of forces in the world arena, the U.S.S.R. and other Socialist countries found themselves surrounded on all sides by a hostile coalition of maritime states posing the serious threat of a nuclear-missile attack from the direction of the sea.

At the same time the imperialists, headed by the U.S.A., having created a situation for the Socialist countries in which they were surrounded from the direction of the sea, did not experience a similar danger. Could the Soviet Union reconcile itself to such a situation? Could it agree to an age-long domination of the seas and oceans by the traditional western sea powers, especially under the conditions when vast areas of the oceans had become launching pads for nuclear-missile weaponry?

Of course not!

The Communist Party and the Soviet government

---

[3] *Foreign Affairs.* No. 7, p. 31.

fully appreciated both the threat to our country which is arising from the oceans, and the need to deter the aggressive aspirations of the enemy through the construction of a new, ocean-going Navy. And this need is being answered.

While continuing a policy of peaceful coexistance between different social systems and of prevention of a new world war, our Party and government are taking serious steps to ensure the security of the Socialist countries. The chief measure was the building up of powerful modern Armed Forces, including the Navy, capable of opposing any enemy plots, also including those in the oceanic sectors, where the mere presence of our Fleet presents a potential aggressor with the need to solve those same problems himself which he had hoped to create for our Armed Forces.

The need to build a powerful ocean-going Navy, which stemmed from the situation which arose on the oceans in the postwar period, from the policy of the U.S.S.R., and from her military doctrine, was backed up and is being backed up by the vast capabilities of the military-economic potential of the Soviet state and by the achievements of our science and technology.

In speaking of the military-economic potential of our country, it should be noted that it possesses vast, practically inexhaustible energy, raw material, and fuel resources. The high, stable rate of growth of the economic power of the U.S.S.R., observed throughout its entire history, confirms the stability, planned nature, and harmoniousness of the process of development of the Soviet state.

The utilization of the achievements of science and industry together with the introduction of scientific methods in determining the more valuable mix of weapons and equipment characteristics, taking into account economic factors, has made it possible for naval development to approximate the Navy's vital needs to the maximum degree, without copying naval construction in the Western countries and following our own national path which best corresponds to the specific tasks facing the Navy and the conditions for carrying them out.

The operational combat qualities of the new weaponry, of the means for depicting the situation, and of

Soviet trawlers, more numerous than the fish visible in this photograph of a Soviet fisherman unloading his catch, fish in all the world's oceans. The range of the Soviet fishing fleet, the value of its harvest, and the differing territorial claims of other nations are all seen as compelling reasons for a strong Navy.

SOVFOTO

power plants, have been an important precondition determining the development of the Soviet Navy. Here, nuclear weaponry, which has permitted the Navy's submarine forces to become a part of the country's strategic nuclear forces, should be considered the decisive factor.

The ballistic missiles of submarines have ensured the capability of destroying strategic targets of the enemy deep in his territory from different directions.

Cruise missiles have become a most important weapon for destroying surface targets. Their appearance has introduced radical changes in the organization of a naval engagement and permits the delivery of powerful and accurate attacks from great ranges against the enemy's major surface ships.

Shipboard sea-to-air missiles together with automatic antiaircraft guns are the main means of ship air defense.

Electronics have had a great influence on the trend of naval construction. The employment of electronics has increased ship and aircraft capabilities to destroy surface targets. The use of electronics has sharply improved the efficiency of air reconnaissance, has opened up great possibilities for increasing the depth of the air defense system for surface ships, and supports their effective employment of surface-to-air missiles for self-defense.

Nuclear power, being an inexhaustible power source for long range ship cruises, is greatly increasing their combat capabilities. However, these qualities, which are new in principle, are being imparted only to submarines, which are being transformed into genuine undersea warships, incorporating in themselves such basic earmarks of sea power as maneuverability, hitting power, and concealment. Submarines are also becoming valuable antisubmarine combatants, capable of detecting and destroying the enemy's missile-carrying submarines.

The equipping of submarines with nuclear power plants has made possible a sharp increase in the speed and range of their underwater navigation. And this is understandable, since the power-to-weight ratio of submarines with a nuclear-power plant considerably surpasses that of diesel submarines.

The above-cited qualities of the new weaponry, means for depicting the situation, and nuclear power are greatly increasing the combat capabilities of all the forces of the Navy. They are objectively fostering the advance of submarines and aviation into the forefront of these forces. This also accounts for the general priority development of submarines and aviation within the navies of the great powers.

Military geographical conditions, which even today the imperialists strive to utilize primarily in order to surround the Socialist countries with a ring of their naval and air bases and also with groupings of naval forces, have always had an important influence on naval development. In peacetime, the imperialists have deployed these groupings in combat patrol areas ready to deliver a surprise attack against land objectives located on the territory of the Soviet Union and of the countries of the Socialist community. According to the testimony of the Americans themselves, the U.S.A. alone has 3,429 military bases, and supply and administrative points manned by 1.7 million men in various countries outside its national borders.

The process of the approach of U. S. bases toward the borders of the U.S.S.R. is continuing, despite the measures taken by the Soviet government to ease international tensions and despite the SALT talks. We cannot be indifferent to the creation of a new naval base for the Sixth Fleet in Greece—in direct proximity to the territory of the People's Republic of Bulgaria and within carrier aircraft range of the central regions of the Soviet Union. We also cannot remain indifferent to the expansion of the basing of U. S. nuclear-powered submarines and carrier forces on the Japanese islands, in Italy (Maddalena Island), in the Indian Ocean, and in other areas of the World Ocean, for all of this powerful and widely dispersed military organization is directed against the U.S.S.R. and the countries of the Socialist community.

Naturally these circumstances—and the military-geographical conditions and operational combat qualities of the new weapons and equipment—have had an effect on the building of our Navy, whose combatants, both with respect to design and with respect to armament, differ significantly from the warships of the Western states.

As is well known, through the will of the CPSU Central Committee a course has been charted in our country toward the construction of an ocean-going Navy whose base consists of nuclear-powered submarines of various types. It is precisely these forces, combining in themselves the latest achievements of scientific-technical progress, which are characterized by such qualities as great endurance and high combat capabilities.

However, a modern navy, whose mission is to conduct combat operations against a strong enemy, cannot be only an undersea navy. The underestimation of the need to support submarine operations with aircraft and surface ships cost the German high command dearly in the last two wars. In particular, we have already pointed out above that one of the reasons for the failure of the "unlimited submarine war" prosecuted by the Germans was the absence of such support for the submarines, which forced them to operate alone without the support of other forces.

Therefore, we, while giving priority to the development of submarine forces, believe that we have a need not only for submarines, but also for various types of surface ships. The latter, in addition to giving combat stability to the submarines, are intended to accomplish a wide range of missions both in peacetime and in war. The diversity of the tasks confronting us has evoked the need to build numerous types of surface ships with a specific armament for each of them. It is characteristic that the attempts which have been made in many countries to build general-purpose combatants to carry out all (or many) missions have been unsuccessful. Therefore surface ships continue to remain the most numerous (with respect to type) of naval forces.

The foreign and domestic preconditions cited above which determined the development of the Navy in the postwar period have had a considerable effect on the formation of views on its role in modern warfare. Thus, in connection with the equipping of the Navy with strategic nuclear weapons, the Navy is objectively acquiring the capability not only of participating in the crushing of the enemy's military economic potential, but also in becoming a most important factor in deterring his nuclear attack.

In this connection, missile-carrying submarines, owing to their great survivability in comparison with land-based launch installations, are an even more effective means of deterrence. They represent a constant threat to an aggressor who, by comprehending the inevitability of nuclear retaliation from the direction of the oceans, can be faced with the necessity of renouncing the unleashing of a nuclear war.

Only our powerful Armed Forces capable of blocking the unrestrained expansionism displayed today all over the world by imperialism can deter its aggressiveness. In addition, of course, to the Strategic Missile Troops, it is the Navy which is this kind of force, capable in peacetime of visibly demonstrating to the peoples of friendly and hostile countries not only the power of military equipment and the perfection of the naval ships, embodying the technical and economic might of the state, but also its readiness to use this force in defense of state interests of our nation or for the security of the Socialist countries.

Naturally, the question arises: What must a Navy be in terms of quality and quantity for this?

Today, in the context of the possible use of new means of combat in naval warfare, and above all of nuclear-missile weaponry with various types of carriers, the relative strength of naval forces cannot be measured in numbers of combatants or their total displacements, just as one cannot measure their combat might by the weight of the gun projectile salvoes or by the quantity of torpedoes or missiles being launched.

Today the criterion of comparability of naval capabilities is the relative strength of their combat might calculated by the method of mathematical analysis, by solving a system of multicriterial problems for various variants of the situation and different combinations of heterogeneous forces and means. This kind of objective analysis permits the determination of the necessary and sufficient composition of forces and the more rational combination of them which we call balanced forces.

Under today's conditions the basic mission of navies of the great powers in a world-wide nuclear war is their participation in the attacks of the country's strategic nuclear forces, the blunting of the nuclear attacks by the enemy navy from the direction of the oceans, and participation in the operations conducted by ground forces in the continental theaters of military operations. In this instance, navies will perform a large number of complex and major missions.

Important missions in protecting the interests of the Soviet state and the countries of the Socialist community confront the Navy in peacetime too.

This latter point is particularly important because local wars, which imperialism is waging practically uninterruptedly, invariably remain within the sphere of imperialist policy. Today these wars can be regarded as a special form of the manifestation of the "flexible response" strategy. By seizing individual areas of the globe and interfering in the internal affairs of countries, the imperialists are striving to gain new advantageous strategic positions in the world arena which they need for the struggle with Socialism and in order to facilitate carrying out missions in the struggle with the developing national freedom movement. Therefore local wars can be regarded as a manifestation of the more determined imperialist methods for acting against the movement for national independence and progress. Under certain circumstances such actions carry with them the threat of escalation into a world war.

The constant upgrading of its readiness for immediate combat operations in the most complex situation is a most important precondition determining the development of the Navy. At the present time, when in a matter of minutes it is possible to reach major strategic targets and even to accomplish particular missions of the war in certain areas, the need is objectively arising to maintain the highest readiness for naval forces and weaponry. This is a consequence of the effect of the development of naval equipment and weaponry and also of the conditions in which navies have to carry out missions.

In light of what has been said above, the old well known formula—"the battle for the first salvo"—is taking on a special meaning in naval battle under present-day conditions (conditions including the possible employment of combat means of colossal power). Delay in the employment of weapons in a naval battle or operation inevitably will be fraught with the most serious and even fatal consequences, regardless of where the fleet is located, at sea or in port.

The new requirements for forces and for the means to support them are also determined by the particular features of the employment of navies in the nuclear era. Therefore these special features can be regarded as still another important precondition having an effect on the trend of development of modern navies.

From this stems such requirements for the development of modern navies as *long cruising ranges for ships at high speeds, a great operating range for aircraft, and the introduction into submarines of nuclear power plants.*

Long oceanic cruises require that ships have great

SOVFOTO

A growing oceanographic research effort and the world's largest fishing fleet would seem to be justification enough for a strong Soviet navy. But Admiral Gorshkov completes the troika *by reminding his countrymen that there is yet another* sine qua non *of seapower—a modern merchant marine with its network of ports and services, and a developed shipbuilding and ship repair industry.*

endurance and good sea-keeping ability. This in turn has a considerable effect on the dimensions and displacement of combatants, especially of surface ships. The greater the endurance of ships, the longer every grouping can stay out in the ocean and the fewer the ships needed in the fleet inventory.

In addition, the long stay of ships at sea, when the machinery, systems, and propulsion plants are forced to run at high speeds is related to *increasing their service life and reliability.*

The long stay of ships in the ocean, frequently under extreme climatic conditions, is being achieved through habitability standards which permit the officers and men to retain a high combat capability as long as necessary.

It goes without saying that diverse technical equipment plays a leading role in keeping up the crew's physical condition and morale. Yet we must not forget the efficient organization of ship replenishment at sea and of their communications with the Motherland, relatives, close ones, friends, etc.

Long ocean cruises by naval ships present new increased demands on rear services support. The campaign to prolong the endurance of ships without returning to port, ship repairing, and aiding damaged ships at sea is being carried out by powerful mobile rear services, including tenders, repair ships, replenishment ships, oilers, and salvage ships.

Thus, the new form of utilizing naval forces is one of the most important factors in determining technical policy in developing modern naval forces.

Yet, however technically advanced a navy may be, and however powerful the weapons it receives are, the foundation of naval forces will always be man—the master of all means of combat. And the role of man in armed combat, of the specialist masterfully controlling weaponry, machinery, instruments, and apparatus, who is capable of utilizing their capabilities fully, will grow as the Navy develops further. Therefore, men, educated by the Party and devoted to the Socialist Motherland, have always been, are, and will remain the main might of our Navy.

The question of training and forming cadres of Soviet navymen and of tempering them morally and politically is becoming particularly acute and taking on special significance now that the Navy has become completely different, and indeed also since the conditions for cruising have changed in connection with its emergence onto the expanses of the World Ocean. Our ships are at sea for long periods close to the imperialist fleets, and have the opportunity to really evaluate their strong and weak points and to observe not only their actions but also reactions to the change in the international situation.

In this connection, the daily service of naval officers is taking on a qualitatively new character. The conditions under which the daily activities of naval officers proceed are immeasurably more complex, and special responsibility is demanded of them for the performance of missions when cruising far from our own ports, for maintaining ships in constant combat readiness, for training reliable personnel, for inculcating personnel with high morale and combat qualities, and tenacity in overcoming the difficulties of sea duty. In this connection, it should be taken into account that not only has the equipment changed and the ships become more complex than several years ago, but also the activity itself of the Navy has considerably expanded.

The Soviet officer bears a special responsibility to the Party and people for the education and conduct of his subordinates, and for their performance of great and difficult missions on long ocean cruises with high military skill and self-assurance. The success of these cruises is determined not only by the reliability of the equipment and weapons built by Socialist industry, but above all by the outstanding schooling of the crews embodying in themselves a deep conviction of the righteousness of our great cause and a high awareness of their filial duty to the Motherland and to the Communist Party.

This is only a part of the considerably more versatile nature of the Soviet naval officer. The successful cruises of our warships in all areas of the World Ocean serve to confirm that the officers of the Navy possess these qualities.

However these successes would be unthinkable without the daily purposeful leadership of the Navy on the part of the Communist Party and without properly organized Party-political work. It is not accidental that our military leaders, officers of all ranks, being deeply aware of and piously carrying out the precepts of V. I. Lenin, consider political work a powerful searchlight lighting the way to victory for the soldier and general, the seaman and admiral. Political work is a special weapon of the Party ensuring the boosting of the combat readiness of the armed forces, including also the Navy, inspiring fighting men to feats, and more than ever it is one of the decisive factors of victory.

The current situation demands increased vigilance and readiness for the selfless defense of Socialism by the Soviet armed forces and the fraternal armies of the Socialist countries. Constant high combat readiness is primarily determined by exemplary order in the units and forces, and by our naval forces being in a technical condition permitting them to go into action without delay. In the Navy it requires even more outstanding nautical and special training, complete knowledge of the combat capabilities of the equipment, and the ability to employ it masterfully under any climatic conditions and in various sea states.

All of these qualities do not occur spontaneously. In order to shape them, educational work and intensive training is underway the entire year round in the fleets. Navymen acquire comprehensive knowledge and the ability to control machinery and systems and complex modern weaponry in training classrooms, on training ranges, and in trainers, aboard ships and in units. Ocean cruises, long deployments, serve as the highest stage of training, the best and only school capable of strengthening the obtained knowledge and skills, and developing them to the level of mastery.

With the emergence of our ships into the oceans, the Navy acquired the capability of not only completely eliminating arbitrary conditions in combat training and of conducting it under conditions close to actual conditions, but also to thoroughly study that specific feature of the situation in which he will have to perform missions in war, should the aggressors unleash it.

Ocean cruises are a school of moral-political and psychological training of personnel for modern warfare. Indeed, it is not as easy as it may seem at first glance in the training process to educate officers, petty officers, and nonrated men in tenacity in achieving goals, initiative, and self-control. These qualities cannot be developed behind a school desk—steadfast, purposeful work is needed on ocean cruises where navymen are taught to perform their duties in storms and amid the elements, in cold and heat, in fog, and in foul and clear weather. They gain confidence in the reliability of combat equipment and skills in the best employment of it. Long cruises and exercises permit developing the teamwork of the entire crew of the ship, upgrading its schooling, and making sure that the actions of each member of the crew are automatic.

Propaganda concerning revolutionary and combat traditions greatly aids the education of skillful and courageous navymen. From examples of the military feats, bravery, and courage of the heroes of the Revolution, and the Civil and Great Patriotic Wars, the fighting men learn military skills, the overcoming of difficulties and adversity, and the ability to successfully carry out assigned missions under any conditions, and they are taught to strive to imitate the heroes of past battles and cruises, and develop the desire to repeat their feats today.

The rich experience of the Great Patriotic War and the postwar long cruises attest to the fact that the Soviet navyman, inspired by the high ideals of Communism, is capable of overcoming all hardships on cruises and in battle. More than once he has given his life without hesitation for an idea, for in the moment when the heat of the struggle is greatest, ideas have been placed above everything for him, above any hardships. There is no doubt that also in the decisive moments in the future the Soviet navyman will act precisely as the interests of the Motherland and the interests of the victory of Socialism and Communism demand.

In conclusion, we must say the following.

In order to ensure the defense of a country and the accomplishment of military-political missions, states have always strived to have armed forces appropriate to these aims, including naval forces, and to maintain them at a modern level. Within the armed forces of a country navies fulfill an important role as one of the instruments of state policy in peacetime, and are a powerful means of achieving the political goals of an armed struggle in wartime.

History shows that the creation of major navies is feasible only for maritime states having the necessary resources and a developed economy at their disposal. In this connection, a policy taking into account the country's need for sea power is an important factor determining the nature of naval construction, promoting the mobilization of its capabilities for the indicated goal, and is an indispensible condition of the development of sea power.

An analysis of the alignment of forces in the international arena today and the sharp increase in the capabilities of modern navies to have a decisive effect on all fronts of an armed struggle provide the basis to assert that the absolute and relative importance of naval warfare in the overall course of a war has indisputedly grown.

It has been essential in all stages of its history, for our state—a great continental world power—to have a mighty Navy as an indispensible integral part of the armed forces. Today our armed forces have a fully modern Navy equipped with everything necessary for the successful performance of all missions levied upon it on the expanses of the World Ocean.

We must once more stress the fundamental difference in the goals for which the naval forces of the imperialist states, on one hand, and those of the Soviet Union, on the other, have been built and exist. While the navies of the imperialist states are an instrument of aggression and neocolonialism, the Soviet Navy is a powerful factor in the creation of favorable conditions for the building of Socialism and Communism, for the active defense of peace, and for strengthening international security.

The Central Committee of the Communist Party and the Soviet government, in bringing to life the precepts of V. I. Lenin on strengthening the defense of the country, are displaying unwavering attention to boosting the defensive might of the state, to strengthening its armed forces, to increasing its sea power, and to the harmonious, balanced development of the forces of an ocean-going Navy meeting today's needs, and capable of carrying out the tasks confronting them. L. I. Brezhnev firmly and confidently stated this at the 24th CPSU Congress: "Everything that the people have created must be reliably protected. It is imperative to strengthen the Soviet state—this means strengthening its *Armed Forces,* and increasing the defensive capability of our Motherland in every way. And so long as we live in an unsettled world, this task will remain one of the most primary tasks."[4]

Soviet navymen consider their highest duty to be the maintenance of a high state of readiness of all naval forces to carry out tasks of defending the state from the direction of the sea, and in every way to improve skills of employing combat equipment under any climatic and weather conditions. All of this must support the protection of the state interests of the Motherland and be a reliable shield from enemy attacks from the sea and a real warning of the inevitability of retaliation for aggression.

The concern of the Communist Party and the Soviet people for the valiant armed forces of the country, including the Navy, serves as a true guarantee of the fact that the Soviet Union will also in the future remain not only one of the strongest continental powers, but also a mighty sea power, a faithful guardian of peace in the world.

[4] L. I. Brezhnev. *Otchetnyy doklad Tsentral'nogo Komiteta KPSS XXIV s"yezdu Kommunisticheskoy partii Sovetskogo Soyuza* (Summary Report of the CPSU Central Committee to the 24th Congress of the CPSU), p. 100.

Commentary

By Vice Admiral Stansfield Turner, U. S. Navy

Vice Admiral Turner graduated from the U. S. Naval Academy in 1946 and then served a year at sea before entering Oxford University where his studies as a Rhodes Scholar led to a Master's Degree. After Oxford, he held a variety of sea assignments, including command of a minesweeper, a destroyer, and a guided missile frigate which he placed in commission. His shore duties included the Politico-Military Policy Division in the Office of the Chief of Naval Operations, the Office of the Assistant Secretary of Defense for Systems Analysis, the Advanced Management Program at the Harvard Business School, and Executive Assistant and Naval Aide to the Secretary of the Navy. In 1970, he assumed command of a Carrier Task Group of the Sixth Fleet. After that and just prior to his present assignment as President of the Naval War College, he served as Director of the Systems Analysis Division of the Office of the Chief of Naval Operations.

In this eleventh and final article of his series, Admiral Gorshkov ties the threads together and places his view of the position of the Soviet Navy in perspective. First and foremost, he makes his case for why the Soviet Union requires a large Navy. Next he describes his rationale for the kind of naval forces he wants. The manner in which he presents these concluding arguments on force size and structure can be very instructive to professionals in the U. S. Navy. After all, we must argue these same two cases for our Navy. Even though our arena of debate is quite different, seeing how Gorshkov presents his cases can be helpful.

Interestingly, he approaches the issue of why the Soviet Union needs a large Navy from three generalized, almost abstract, viewpoints. The first is an extensive dissertation on the growing importance of the oceans to mankind. He stresses to the point of exaggeration the potential for extracting food and minerals from the oceans. He extends Mahan well past the use of the seas primarily as highways for commerce. He expresses great concern at possible curtailments of freedom of movement on the ocean highways. With this he describes the elements of sea power as including oceanographic research, a merchant marine, a fishing industry, and a Navy. He clearly implies that an increasing importance of the seas dictates increased attention to all of these elements, but particularly to the Navy. His second foundation for a Navy builds on the historical analyses which have preceded this article. He contends that the great powers of the world have been sea powers and that in the past the Soviet Union has failed to capitalize on opportunities when she has turned her back on the Navy. Finally, one theme permeates this article: that the Navy is unique in its ability to be an adjunct to diplomacy in peacetime.

Gorshkov treats as obvious the specifics of how naval presence in peacetime contributes to national purpose, why a great power requires a seagoing capability, and just why increasing development of the seabeds demands more naval power. It appears to me that, in contrast, we have fallen into the trap of having to explain why we need a Navy in overly specific terms. Perhaps we should study Gorshkov's example. Quantitative systems analysis has carried over too far into strategic concepts. We have become too dependent upon scenarios and hypothetical campaign analyses to justify every force level, e.g., a NATO campaign of 90 days, a ground war in Asia, a so-called "unilateral" war in the Mideast, etc. We have fallen into this trap from a lack of vision and because we have failed to articulate the purposes and historical perspectives of naval power.

Gorshkov does describe in varying degrees of detail the four missions of his Navy, though not defining specific scenarios. These are:

▶ *Strategic Offense.* The marriage of nuclear powered submarines to ballistic missiles places Navies in the forefront here, he contends.

▶ *Strategic Defense.* The defensive orientation of the Soviet Navy is longstanding. Although not explicitly stated, it is clear that Gorshkov means that the Soviet Navy must be able to deny us the use of the seas in those areas from which our submarines or attack carriers could launch weapons against the Soviet Union.

▶ *Support of Ground Operations.* Gorshkov is not specific on how his Navy will support ground operations. It is possible only to infer that he contemplates sea denial to interrupt our lines of resupply to the land campaign. He never discusses what we call the mission of the Projection of Power Ashore wherein naval forces provide direct support to ground forces by means of tactical air, amphibious assault, or naval bombardment. There is no clue in this article, or in the other ten, to whether the new *Kiev* class carriers will have an air attack capability or only be employed to provide air cover or ASW for sea control purposes. In the amphibious field, this series of articles would leave the impression that Gorshkov sees expansion in that direction, but there is no clear indicator that he expects to go as far as a global intervention capability.

▶ *Naval Presence.* As mentioned above, there is particular emphasis on this mission.

Overall, this review enables us to compare in the chart what Gorshkov says about the missions of his Navy, with what we have published about ours:

United States	USSR
Strategic Deterrence	Yes-with added emphasis on Strategic Defense. As a by-product to their war fighting capability.
Sea Control	
A. Denial to others	Yes-clearly in home waters, very probably in general interdiction.
B. Asserting own use	Yes-under shore based air umbrella. Beyond that, dependent on what direction Kiev carrier employment proceeds.
Projection of Power Ashore	
A. Tactical Air	Unclear-Depends on evolving carrier capability.
B. Amphibious	Unclear-Depends on extent of build-up.
C. Bombardment	Yes.
Naval Presence	Yes.

The second underlying theme of this eleventh article is a description of the kind of naval forces Gorshkov feels are appropriate to his circumstances. This argumentation also can be quite instructive to us. To begin with, he points out that relative naval strength cannot be measured simply by counting numbers of ships, total displacement, or any other simple conventional index. The tools of systems analysis, including quantitative techniques and cost comparisons, are demanded here, though the Admiral emphasizes that one must examine a wide range of possible scenarios and differing combinations of forces. He also stresses that imitating other navies is not the way to go. He points out that a Navy must chart its own course in light of its own intended employment and its particular circumstances.

Well we might keep these two basic philosophies for force structuring in mind. How often do we protest our shortages by recounting how many like units the Soviets possess? How often do we overlook some of our advantages over the Soviets, a number of which Gorshkov mentions? How often do we accept what technology will produce, not what analysis says our missions demand? Lastly, is there an incipient tendency today for us to imitate the Soviet Navy and justify this or that weapon system because the Soviets have one?

Gorshkov does become more specific in developing the needs of his navy when it comes to submarines and aviation. Clearly he sees these weapon systems as the backbone of his Navy's strength. He does not tell us, however, whether his concept of naval aviation is for the projection of power ashore or for the exercise of sea control. The writing is too terse for us to divine just how much his emphasis on submarines is for strategic war fighting and deterrence, how much for antisubmarine operations in asserting one's use of the seas, and how much for anti-shipping sea denial operations. Next, there is a strong emphasis on the need for surface forces to complement and balance submarines and aviation, and to carry the load of peacetime presence operations. With this he stresses the need for coordinated tactics among all three branches. He specifically points out that the Germans suffered in both world wars because their submarines operated without the support of surface forces. Gorshkov seems to be saying that, when an enemy can concentrate his efforts on defeating a single weapon system or tactic, he can usually succeed. When he must divide his forces, research effort, and tactical talent among a number of threats and permutations of tactical and force combinations, outcomes are not so predictable.

There is much in this approach that we in the U. S. Navy should consider deeply. Many trends in our development of forces and tactics have been leading in the opposite direction, toward independent, uncoordinated operations, e.g., submarines or mines in barriers, VP aircraft in open area search operations, destroyers as the sole anti-submarine defense of attack carriers, and so forth.

Gorshkov also discusses some of the Soviet Navy's present shortcomings. One of these is staying power. He regrets not having overseas bases. He stresses endurance, replenishment capability, reliability, habitability, seakeeping, and communications in his ships. He talks in turn of the importance of extended deployments. He discusses in surprising detail the hardships these present to the crews: cold, heat, fog, length of time away from home, complexity of duties, heavy responsibilities, and rough seas. There is an extended exhortation, presumably to his officers and men, to perceive a noble purpose to all this, founded in the Communist Party's ideology. It would appear that morale and reenlistments may well be an issue for Admiral Gorshkov, just as for ourselves. It would also appear that these questions of staying power and the necessity of deployments point clearly to a global intent he wishes for the Soviet Navy in the years ahead.

Does Admiral Gorshkov appreciate the effort and distance that he has to go in obtaining the staying capability to which he aspires? Can we read anything between the many lines of discussion of habitability and hardships, readiness and reliability? Is Gorshkov implying that Soviet combatants are deficient in these respects today, ships of limited capability for more than a first salvo? Are we planning our strategy and tactics to take advantage of any edge here? Similarly, are we devising ways to benefit from the other areas of Soviet naval inferiority which Gorshkov mentions or fails to mention? Our amphibious capability, our integral tactical air for defense and offense, our superior expertise in antisubmarine warfare, our more extensive training, our greater familiarity with the world's oceans, our allies, and our tradition and record of success at sea are all factors Gorshkov, and we, must weigh. How much we can weigh them against the missions and purposes which Gorshkov has outlined in this series is difficult to know.

Even if this published view is an accurate portrayal of Gorshkov's thinking, it may change, especially as Soviet naval capabilities evolve with time. Still, having his articles as a benchmark can be useful to us. It can encourage us to look for evidence that he was duping us or that things have changed. For instance, we must observe closely the use to which they put the *Kiev* carriers.

This series, and the Naval Institute's foresight in publishing it, should accent to all of us the importance of keeping abreast of the open literature from the Soviet military sector. The United States Air Force has recently undertaken to translate and publish several hundred works by Soviet writers on military affairs. Perhaps the Institute could make some pertinent article or excerpt from Soviet writings a regular monthly feature. Beyond that, I would urge all commanding officers to encourage discussion of the Gorshkov series. We all need to gain the fullest appreciation of the difficult task which lies ahead. Admiral Gorshkov has told us that the competition will be stiff. To meet it, we need to understand it. We can be grateful to the Naval Institute *Proceedings* for starting us in that direction.

Conclusion

By Admiral Elmo R. Zumwalt, Jr., U. S. Navy (Ret.)

In reading Admiral Gorshkov's brilliant series on "Navies in War and Peace," I could not help but reflect on the fact that when I graduated from the U. S. Naval Academy, Gorshkov was already serving as a rear admiral in the Soviet Navy. The experience of his 33 years as a flag officer has served him well. In the publication of this series, Admiral Gorshkov emerges as a 20th century Russian Mahan, an articulate advocate of seapower as a vital—indeed indispensable—attribute of great power status.

The parallels between Gorshkov and Mahan go beyond their roles as advocates of seapower. Both were perceptive strategic thinkers who were able to appreciate new technology, and to discern its relevance to the changing art of naval warfare. Mahan wrote in 1890, following the authorization of our first iron-clad, big-gun steam warship in 1883. A technological revolution of comparable dimension took place in the Soviet Navy in the 1950s, with the application of nuclear power to submarine propulsion, and development of the cruise missile. And now, almost 20 years later, we see Gorshkov, like Mahan, weaving his perceptions of naval history into a major treatise on seapower.

Both Gorshkov and Mahan view a strong navy as essential for any nation which would be a world power. Both subscribe to the strategy of meeting your enemy while he is still well distant from your shores. Both also hold that their respective nations require a fleet large enough not only to defeat its strongest adversary, but adequate to deal successfully with any combination of hostile navies.

But Gorshkov is much more than a historian or seapower advocate. He is the architect of today's Soviet Navy—the world's most modern naval force. Not only has he been a flag officer for more than 30 years; but he has been commander-in-chief of the Soviet Navy for almost 20 of those years. This continuity is unparalleled in any modern navy; and the Soviet Navy has clearly benefited from it.

Gorshkov inherited the Soviet Navy when it was at a particularly critical crossroad. Stalin, in the early postwar period, had authorized the construction of a large surface fleet—a pre-war Soviet goal which had been interrupted by World War II. After Stalin's death, the value of a surface navy was called into question; and building programs which were then underway were cancelled.

In Khrushchev's eyes, the future of the Soviet Navy lay in a large submarine force, supplemented by landbased air, with surface ships relegated to a basically coastal role. These thoughts echoed a strain of thought which had periodically competed for predominance in the Soviet Navy prior to World War II, and which had eventually been rejected by Stalin in favor of proposals to build a balanced, seagoing navy. Stalin, like Gorshkov, appreciated the political value of a surface navy; and saw its utility as a vehicle to expand the U.S.S.R.'s worldwide influence.

The combination of Gorshkov's arrival in command, and Khrushchev's retirement from the political scene, turned the Soviet Navy once again in the direction of a balanced, oceanic force.

But Gorshkov had formidable obstacles to overcome before he could be sure of obtaining the necessary resources to achieve his grand design. The Soviet Union is a great land power, spanning the Eurasian continent. From earliest Czarist times the Army has held vast influence in the councils of the Russian Government. Although there were periods when Russia built up large navies and exhibited an interest in seapower, these efforts were intermittent; and in time of war, first thought always went to the army.

To this day, Army marshals dominate the Ministry of Defense and the General Staff. Soviet defense policy is predominantly the product of a land-oriented politico-military hierarchy. It is all the more remarkable, therefore, that Gorshkov was able to sell his case for "a navy second to none," and to obtain the resources necessary to achieve that goal.

His success was largely the product of changed historical circumstances, on which Gorshkov capitalized by the forceful advocacy of which the *Morskoi Sbornik* series is an example.

At the commencement of Gorshkov's tenure, the prestige of the Soviet Navy within the Soviet military establishment was low. A series of important political and technological developments ensued, however, which let Gorshkov make the case for greatly increased emphasis on seapower. With the development of the SSBN, Gorshkov ensured that the Navy would share in the Soviet strategic budget. With the Cuban missile crisis, he was able to demonstrate the requirement to project surface seapower over great distances, in strength sufficient to stand off a major naval adversary.

With the perfection of the antiship cruise missile, he was able to argue that the Soviet Navy could challenge the traditional supremacy of Western naval forces at times and places of its own choosing. During the Middle East crises of 1967, 1970, and again in 1973, Gorshkov succeeded in demonstrating the high political utility of projectable naval force in time of peace.

The cumulative effect of these individual developments has been to persuade Soviet leadership of the desirability of a large oceangoing navy.

Yet there is still another, and perhaps more important accomplishment to which Gorshkov can lay claim. He has taken his navy to sea. The Soviet Navy, which formerly seldom operated out of sight of land, has acquired a true oceangoing capability. Soviet warships are permanently stationed in the Mediterranean and Indian Oceans, regularly patrol off the west coast of Africa, have established a major (and politically significant) presence on NATO's northern flank, and are frequently seen conducting visits to the Caribbean. Admiral Gorshkov accurately boasts that the Soviet naval ensign flies over all the oceans of the world.

In the early chapters of his series, Admiral Gorshkov outlined the history of naval developments in Czarist and Communist Russia, and pointed—with something less than total accuracy—to the contributions which the navy has made to Russian history. In so doing he was not reluctant to emphasize the political opportunities which unenlightened Russian leaders missed owing to their failure to appreciate the value of seapower. He implicitly equates statesmanship with the support of naval programs by pointing out that the rise of great powers historically has been linked with their acceptance of a maritime strategy. Throughout his description of history it is clear that he is drawing analogies to today. To understand his interpretation of history is to understand his views with regard to the roles of the Soviet Navy in the contemporary world. His typically propagandized view of history makes interesting, albeit scarcely objective reading; but, more importantly, it allows us to see inside the mind of the Soviet naval leadership and appreciate its views of the world, and the relevance of Soviet naval power to it. This provides invaluable insights to current Soviet activity and to the likely shape of Soviet intentions for the future.

Throughout the series there is the constant repetition of ideological themes which one expects of all Soviet writing. Yet there are some fascinating undercurrents of great Russian chauvinism as well. Despite the facade of Communist ideology, basic Russian attitudes and desires come through which are unchanged from the attitudes and aspirations of the Czars. Gorshkov argues for access to warm water; Gorshkov argues for the need for acceptance of (Communist) Russia as a great world power; Gorshkov displays the almost messianic urge of Russians to export their view of the world—be it Orthodoxy or Communism. Had one of Gorshkov's illustrious predecessors—Admiral Ushakov—written these articles almost 200 years ago, many of these basic thoughts would have been the same.

Gorshkov's writings do not force us to do much reading between the lines. He spells out Soviet intentions for all to see—and therein lies one of the most important aspects of the articles. The theme which runs through the entire series is the requirement for a large, balanced Navy consisting of subsurface, surface, and air forces, capable of contesting control of the seas with the strongest naval powers of the day, either singly or in combination. Even a most cursory analysis of Gorshkov's writing leads to the conclusion that all elements of Soviet seapower will be expanded. This includes, of course, not only the Soviet Navy but also the Soviet merchant marine which has already outstripped ours and is one of the world's largest and most modern merchant fleets; the Soviet fishing fleet, to which Gorshkov points with pride as the world's largest; and the oceanographic and research ships required to support long-term Soviet goals for exploitation of the resources of the sea. The Navy's role in this expansion of Soviet seapower is to protect Soviet interests in, on, and at the bottom of the sea, as well as to advance the political, economic, and military interests of the Soviet Union in areas distant from the Eurasian landmass.

Since the publication of these articles, there has been some speculation in the West over the question of whether Gorshkov is announcing an approved strategy, or whether he is merely advocating such strategy in hopes of gaining its acceptance. The best information available to us indicates that the articles represent a "going public" of positions previously articulated in the more confidential forums within which major Soviet policy decisions are actually made. Had Gorshkov's arguments been rejected in their earlier presentation, it is most unlikely that they would subsequently appear in the carefully controlled Soviet unclassified press. In the Soviet system, such a series of articles by a member of the Central Committee and the Commander in Chief of the Soviet Navy would not appear if they failed to reflect basic Soviet policy. This conclusion is supported by other evidence as well, including the Soviet

shipbuilding programs which have taken place in the approximately three years since the articles were written. The first Soviet aircraft carrier is in the water. The second is under construction. New classes of bigger, more seaworthy guided missile cruisers have been launched and remain in series production. Other cruisers have been modified into command and control ships designed for support of fleet operations distant from the Soviet Union. Entire classes of underway replenishment vessels are in series production and the Soviet Delta class submarine, armed with a missile which the United States will not be able to match until the end of this decade, completes a picture of large capital expenditures indicative of strong governmental support for the powerful, well-rounded Navy which Gorshkov describes in his articles. Clearly the advocacy phase of Gorshkov's campaign for a navy "second to none" preceded the publication of his articles in the open literature; and that advocacy was effective indeed, witness the sustained high level of capital investment in Soviet naval forces which has characterized the last five years.

Gorshkov has announced that the Soviet Navy is going to sea. We scarcely need his announcement. With the passage of time, we see steadily increasing numbers of sophisticated Soviet naval units operating farther and farther away from their home waters. Already the Soviets have the largest presence of any non-littoral state in the Indian Ocean; and they have acquired a logistics infrastructure around the Ocean's littoral capable of supporting a much larger presence.

The Soviet Mediterranean Fleet, with its rapid surge capability, graphically demonstrated during the October 1973 Mideast crisis the ability to concentrate naval forces in an area of great strategic importance in support of political objectives. The pattern should not have surprised us; it was clearly presaged by Gorshkov's description of the Soviet Navy's peacetime role in advancing key Soviet politico-military goals outside the U.S.S.R.

In the future we can anticipate that wherever ships of the U. S. Navy operate we will see modern, highly capable, and sea-wise units of the Soviet fleet juxtaposed to our presence. In time of peace, their mission will be to provide active support to Soviet foreign policy, and to frustrate attainment of our own political objectives whenever those conflict with Soviet aims.

In time of war, their mission will be to contest control of the seas with the United States. Gorshkov makes clear that the Soviets' ultimate goal is the ability to win control of the seas in the principal theaters of operations. No longer will the interdiction of sea lines of communication and defense of the homeland be the main missions of the Navy. Throughout the series,

Gorshkov repeats the theme that the strategy of today's Soviet Navy must be an offensive, not a defensive strategy.

The asymmetries in the respective geographical positions of the United States and the U.S.S.R. give the Soviets great leverage from their employment of naval power.

To the Soviets, the use of the seas is a bonus. They are 90% self-sufficient in natural resources; and the preponderance of their profitable trade could be conducted with minimal resort to the sea. To the United States, however, seapower is a necessity. Our dependence on overseas supplies of raw materials was brought home during the recent Middle East war and the resultant energy crisis. A large segment of our economy is dependent on foreign trade, and our critical political and military alliances presuppose our ability to control the sea lanes to our allies. Were the Soviet Union to be deprived of its access to the sea, it would work a diplomatic and, to a lesser degree, an economic hardship; but it would not impact severely upon the survival of the Soviet Union. Were the United States to be deprived of free use of the seas, however, it could represent political, economic, and military disaster.

Our ability to utilize the sea in support of U. S. interests is dependent on our possession of the seapower required to ensure our independence from foreign threat—whether that threat takes the form of overt military challenge, or such action as a shipping boycott against the United States. The recent oil embargo highlighted the danger of dependence on the goodwill of other nations. Yet we have allowed ourselves to be dependent on the ships of other nations for much of our seaborne trade, and have seen our Navy shrink to the point that we are hard-pressed to meet even routine peacetime commitments.

The United States requires a total reawakening to the importance of seapower to the welfare of our nation; and a commitment to complete U. S. self-sufficiency with regard to our use of the high seas. As Gorshkov points out, the ocean bottom is a source of almost incalculable raw material wealth in a world of shrinking resources. The sea, as both Mahan and

Gorshkov observe, is the highway for commerce and intercourse among nations. The United States requires the large modern merchant marine which can successfully compete for world trade routes. We need a resuscitated fishing industry to exploit the natural resources off our shores. We need ocean mining and other resource exploitation capabilities, and we need the additional emphasis on hydrographic and oceanographic research which is required to support these industries. Along with this, of course, must come the revitalized shipbuilding industry needed to support a national reawakening to the need for seapower, and the Navy required to protect U. S. interests at sea and overseas.

But where does the United States stand at the moment? Our merchant marine is aging and non-competitive; our fishing fleets are disappearing from the world's ocean; other than offshore oil drilling, ocean resources are scarcely being touched; our shipyards are obsolescent and sometimes inefficient; our hydrographic and oceanographic research is modest; and our Navy is at its lowest ebb since before World War II. While the Soviet Union builds ships of all descriptions and announces its intention to utilize these in direct support of Communist policy, the United States of America—a nation with a true seafaring tradition—allows its seapower to atrophy.

Gorshkov has spelled out Soviet intentions for us. The issue is whether we are prepared to recognize the implicit threat in these intentions, and take the actions necessary to provide our nation with the wherewithal to counter and, in time, neutralize this threat; or whether we as a nation will persist in the hope that Soviet intentions can be rendered benign without the maintenance of countervailing U. S. strength. With Soviet intentions now a matter of record, I do not think we can take that chance.

"The flag of the Soviet Navy flies over the oceans of the world. Sooner or later the United States will have to understand it no longer has mastery of the seas."

Admiral Sergei G. Gorshkov
Commander in Chief,
Soviet Navy

Admiral Gorshkov: Architect of the Soviet Navy

By John G. Hibbits

W hen Admiral Sergei G. Gorshkov was formally appointed Commander-in-Chief of the Soviet Navy in June 1956 he was the youngest man ever to hold that post.[1] A year earlier Khrushchev had forced Admiral Nikolai G. Kuznetsov to resign. Thus Gorshkov, then First Deputy to Kuznetsov, became the de facto head of the navy.[2] For almost twenty years he has managed the affairs of the Navy in a manner that has pleased two political leaders—Khrushchev and Brezhnev. Who is this dynamic, durable leader who changed the Soviet Navy from a basically coastal defense force to a modern, blue-water fleet?

Sergei Gorshkov was born on 26 February 1910, in the city of Kamenets Podolski in the Ukraine. His parents were Russians who probably migrated to the Ukraine sometime before the turn of the century. As were most of the present leaders of the U.S.S.R., the highest admiral was born too late to play a role in Russia's Civil War. Since Gorshkov graduated from the four-year Frunze Higher Naval School in 1931,[3] it can be surmised that he was at least 17 when he entered the service. His first career assignment was as a navigation officer in the destroyer *Frunze* of the Black Sea Fleet,[4] after which he was transferred to the Pacific Fleet.

[1] Edward L. Crowley, et al., eds., *Prominent Personalities in the USSR* (Metuchen, N.J.: Scarecrow Press, 1968), compiled by the Institute for the Study of the USSR, Munich, p. 194.

[2] Thomas W. Wolfe, *Soviet Power and Europe* (Baltimore: The Johns Hopkins Press, 1970), p. 188.

[3] Heinrich Schulz and Stephen Taylor, *Who's Who in the USSR 1961/62* (Montreal: International Book and Publishing Co., Ltd., 1962), compiled by the Institute for the Study of the USSR, Munich, p. 260.

[4] Crowley, p. 194.

In 1937 Admiral Kuznetsov was appointed Commander-in-Chief of the relatively new Pacific Fleet where he claimed, "the best men were being sent."[5] In his memoirs, he identified Gorshkov as the commander of a surface ship in the Pacific in 1937. Sometime in that same year Gorshkov completed courses at a school for captains of destroyers.[6] By November 1938, just seven years after being commissioned, he was in command of a brigade of destroyers, which probably consisted of four ships, and must have been at least a captain second rank (equivalent to a commander in the U. S. Navy). Somehow he survived the extensive purge of military officers that took place between 1937 and 1938. Perhaps he was too junior to be noticed. In any case, the depletion of higher ranking officers must have helped him in his later advancement.

An embarrassing accident that occurred at the end of 1938 first brought Gorshkov's name to the attention of Stalin. Gorshkov was in charge of putting the new destroyer *Reshitelny* into commission. She was being towed to a fitting-out base when bad weather forced her on the rocks near Cape Zolotoi, in the Vladivostok area, and she split in two. One man was killed. When Admiral Kuznetsov went to Moscow to report the mishap, Stalin asked him "What sort of man is this Gorshkov?"[7] Kuznetsov defended Gorshkov and no punitive action seems to have been taken.

In 1939 Gorshkov returned to the Black Sea Fleet where he took command of a brigade of destroyers and then completed training for advanced senior officers at the Voroshilov Naval Academy, now the Order of Lenin and Ushakov Naval Academy. When war broke out with Germany in June 1941, he commanded a cruiser brigade under the Commander-in-Chief of the Black Sea Fleet,[8] Vice Admiral Oktyabrsky in Sevastopol. For the first three months of the war the defense of Odessa was the Soviet Navy's main concern in the Black Sea. When Odessa was cut off from the main Soviet forces of the Southern Front, a naval officer, Rear Admiral Zhukov, was put in charge of its defense. Stalin cabled Zhukov: "Do not abandon Odessa, defend it to the utmost, use the Black Sea Fleet to this end."[9]

During these critical stages of the defense of Odessa, Captain First Rank (equivalent to a captain in the U. S. Navy) Gorshkov[10] formed a naval landing force in Sevastopol.[11] At noon on the 21st of September 1941, the landing party boarded the cruisers *Krasnyy Kavkaz* and *Krasnyy Krym* and the destroyers *Bezuprechnyy* and *Boykiy* which, under the command of Gorshkov, set a course for the Odessa area.[12] The landing party was put ashore against supposedly heavy opposition in an area near Odessa. As a result of the successful landing operations, Rear Admiral Zhukov was able to contain the German offensive against Odessa without suffering devastating losses.[13] However, within two weeks the situation at Sevastopol had deteriorated seriously and the decision was made on 4 October to evacuate the troops from Odessa.[14]

In October 1941, having commanded the most successful Soviet naval landing operation of the war thus far, Gorshkov, after only ten years as a naval officer, was promoted to rear admiral (a one-star rank equivalent to a rear admiral, lower half, in the U. S. Navy) and placed in command of the Azov Flotilla, then a component of the Black Sea Fleet.[15] During the next three months he probably helped organize the Kerch landing of late December 1941 which was undertaken to alleviate pressure on Sevastopol. Ships of the Azov Flotilla under Gorshkov's command participated in the landing,[16] which was the largest land-sea operation undertaken by Russia during the war.[17] The 40,000 troops that landed relieved German pressure on Sevastopol, but the Russian High Command failed to continue the offensive. Consequently, a German counteroffensive, led by air attacks, forced the Russians to evacuate the Kerch Peninsula across the Kerch Strait in May 1942.[18] During the retreat to the Caucasus that followed, Gorshkov was apparently responsible for protecting the maritime flanks of the Red Army and for conducting amphibious attacks on the German rear forces.

By August 1942 the Azov Sea was controlled by the Germans. What remained of the Black Sea Fleet was to be found in Novorossiysk and other small ports in the extreme eastern part of the Black Sea.[19] Gorshkov was appointed a Deputy Commander for Naval Matters

[5] N. G. Kuznetsov, "Reminiscences," *International Affairs,* (Moscow), No. 9 (Sept. 1966), p. 91.
[6] Schulz and Taylor, p. 260.
[7] Kuznetsov, No. 8 (Aug. 1966), p. 98.
[8] "S. Gorshkov," *Bolshaya Sovetskaya Entsyklopedia,* (The Great Soviet Encyclopedia), 3rd ed., 1969, p. 396.
[9] Kuznetsov, No. 5 (May 1969), p. 110.
[10] Crowley, p. 194.
[11] Kuznetsov, No. 5 (May 1969), p. 111.
[12] S. A. Borzenko, "Landing Party Members," *Morskoy Sbornik* (Naval Digest), No. 5 (May 1970), p. 36.
[13] Donald W. Mitchell, *A History of Russian and Soviet Sea Power* (New York: Macmillan Publishing Co., Inc., 1974), p. 407.
[14] Kuznetsov, No. 55 (May 1969), p. 111.
[15] "S. Gorshkov," *Bolshaya Sovetskaya Entsyklopedia,* p. 396.
[16] Kuznetsov, No. 5 (May 1969), p. 111.
[17] A. Nikolayevich, et al., eds., *Istoriya Velikoy Otechestvennoy Voyny Sovetskogo Soyuza, 1941–45* (History of the Great Patriotic War of the Soviet Union, 1941–45) Vol. II (Moscow: Institute of Marxism-Leninism, 1965), p. 311.
[18] Alexander Werth, *Russia at War* (New York: Dutton Inc., 1964), pp. 387–388.
[19] Kuznetsov, No. 1 (Jan. 1970), p. 1.

and a Member of the Military Council of the Novoros-siysk Defense District.[20] This body was an integrated army and navy command whose main mission was to prevent the Germans from advancing to the Baku oilfields: included in it was the 47th Army headed by General A. A. Grechko, the present Defense Minister of the U.S.S.R.[21] At one point, for unknown reasons, Gorshkov assumed temporary command of Grechko's army. By September 1942 the Germans occupied Novorossiysk, except for a narrow strip of shore on the eastern side of the bay from which the Soviets could fire their artillery against shipping at almost any time. Consequently, the Germans could not use the harbor and were unable to advance farther. In February 1943, Soviet amphibious counterattacks, under the command of Gorshkov, began at Novorossiysk. They were not successful, however, until after the Battle of Kursk in midsummer, when many of the German troops in the south were forced to retreat. In September Gorshkov's forces finally succeeded in taking Novorossiysk.[22]

For the remainder of 1943 and early 1944 Gorshkov spent much of his time supporting landing operations on the Taman and Crimean peninsulas. He supervised the transporting of troops and safeguarding of goods across the Kerch Strait and attempted unsuccessfully to blockade the retreating German troops.[23] In April 1944 he assumed command of the Danube Flotilla which supported Marshal Malinovsky's troops in the "liberation" of the Ukraine, Rumania, Bulgaria, and Hungary.[24] As late as August 1944 Gorshkov was still referred to as a rear admiral.[25]

After the war, Gorshkov commanded a squadron of ships in the Black Sea Fleet until 1948, when he became the fleet's Chief of Staff. He was named commander of the same fleet and probably promoted to vice admiral in 1951, the same year that Admiral N. G. Kuznetsov was reappointed Commander-in-Chief of the Soviet Navy. Gorshkov was most likely promoted to full admiral shortly before he left the Black Sea Fleet to become the First Deputy Chief of the Soviet Navy in July 1955.[26]

By this time Nikita Khruschchev had been able to consolidate his power by replacing Malenkov with Bulganin as prime minister. Khruschchev's differences of opinion with Admiral Kuznetsov about the proper structure of the Soviet Navy were well known. The dynamic party secretary wanted to de-emphasize large surface ships[27] and build more submarines. This philosophy did not have the support of the head of the Navy, a strong proponent of a large surface navy, who had at one time been able to convince Stalin of the need for aircraft carriers.[28] Because of these differences Khrushchev probably went looking for a new man to lead his navy.

It is not clear whether Khrushchev brought Gorsh-kov to Moscow as Deputy Commander of the Navy, soon to replace Kuznetsov, or whether Kuznetsov appointed Gorshkov his deputy because he was a good friend. Kuznetsov and Gorshkov had served together in the Pacific and Black Sea fleets at one time or another. In any case Gorshkov was officially appointed Commander-in-Chief of the Soviet Navy in June 1956 and was obviously acceptable to other high-ranking Soviet authorities. He had served with civilian and military members of the influential "clique" that had fought on the southern front, and these people were now well advanced in the hierarchy: Malinovsky was returning from the Far East to be First Deputy Minister of Defense; Grechko was soon to be Commander of all Soviet Ground Forces; and Brezhnev had a power-ful position in the party leadership. The qualities of Gorshkov that probably appealed to Khrushchev in 1955 were his enthusiasm for missile technology, his record of political reliability,[29] and his Ukrainian back-ground.

It was only subsequent to his assumption of the leadership of the Soviet Navy in 1956 that Gorshkov's views on its role were somewhat reflected in a limited number of journals and in Navy Day speeches. Most of his statements of the late fifties and early sixties, however, echoed the hackneyed calls for defense of the maritime borders of the homeland.[30] In 1960 he was apparently still in the good graces of the leadership, since on his 50th birthday he was awarded the Order of Lenin for service to the state.[31] Two years later, Khrushchev during a visit to a Leningrad shipyard, specifically expressed his pleasure with the development of the Navy. In April of the same year, 1962, Gorshkov was promoted to fleet admiral.[32]

Although Gorshkov was a strong advocate of mod-ernizing the Navy, he was convinced of the continuing importance of large surface ships in the nuclear era.

[20] Sergei G. Gorshkov, "The Black Sea Fleet in the Battle of the Caucasus," *Voyenno-Istoricheskiy Zhurnal* (Military Historical Journal) Moscow, March 1974, p. 26.
[21] Ibid., p. 19.
[22] Ibid., pp. 18–26.
[23] Nikolayevich, Vol. IV, pp. 89, 91, and 451.
[24] "S. Gorshkov," *Bolshaya Sovetskaya Entsyklopedia*, p. 396.
[25] Nikolayevich, Vol. IV, p. 270.
[26] "S. Gorshkov," *Bolshaya Sovetskaya Entsyklopedia*, p. 396.

[27] "Khruschchev's Last Testament: Power and Peace," *Time*, May 6, 1974, p. 41.
[28] Robert W. Herrick, *Soviet Naval Strategy* (Annapolis, Md.: United States Naval Institute, 1968), pp. 63–64.
[29] David Fairhall, *Russian Sea Power* (Boston: Gambit, Inc., 1971), p. 184.
[30] *Krasnaya Zvezda*, February 20, 1958, p. 1.
[31] *Pravda*, February 26, 1960, p. 3.
[32] Herrick, p. 73.

He apparently prevailed on Khrushchev not to carry out his publicly announced intention of scrapping 90 per cent of the Soviet Navy's cruisers. Gorshkov most likely made cautious efforts over the next years to convince Khrushchev of the need for large ships.[33] He achieved a modicum of success by retaining most of the *Sverdlov*-class cruisers and by constructing large missile-equipped destroyers.[34]

By mid-1963, in the wake of the Cuban missile crisis, Admiral Gorshkov seemingly completed his surface-ship sales campaign with a general statement on the importance of such ships in the Soviet Navy: ". . . there must be other forces both for an active defense against any enemy within the limits of the defense zone of a maritime theatre and for the comprehensive support of the combat and operational activities of the main striking forces of the Navy. To such forces belong surface missile ships, warships and small craft."[35] Most of his other speeches and writings during the early sixties contained the usual party polemics against such symbols of Western aggression as U. S. reconnaissance planes, aircraft carriers, NATO, and the Multilateral Nuclear Force.[36]

The year 1965 seemed to hail Gorshkov's ascendancy in the Communist hierarchy. In the beginning of the year, on the 29th anniversary of the liberation of Budapest, Marshal Zakharov specifically honored him for his leadership of the Danube Flotilla.[37] In May the government paper *Izvestia* praised him for his World War II heroics.[38] In July his presence at official ceremonies with Brezhnev in Leningrad and with Kosygin in Riga was noted.[39] In October the leading party ideologue, M. Suslov, capped these praises in a speech honoring the "Gold Star" city of Odessa when he said; "The glorious amphibious forces of the Black Sea under command of Captain Gorshkov exhibited selfless courage and valor."[40] These praises are important because they came from the main forces of power in the Soviet Union; the party, government, ideologists, and even the Army—Gorshkov's primary foe in the battle for the defense ruble.

Perhaps reflecting the increased importance of the Navy's role in the Soviet armed forces, Gorshkov reached equality in rank with the Commanders of the Strategic Rocket Forces and the Ground forces in 1967 when he was promoted to the newly created rank of admiral of the fleet of the Soviet Union (a five-star rank similar to U. S. fleet admiral).[41] This was the same year that his wartime colleague Marshal Grechko was appointed Minister of Defense; the *Moskva*-class helicopter carrier and Y-class ballistic-missile submarine were introduced into the Navy; and the Israeli destroyer *Eilat* was sunk by missiles from a Soviet-made missile boat. Using *Morskoi Sbornik* and a Navy Day speech as his vehicles, Gorshkov began to emphasize a greater role for the Soviet Navy which is ". . . now constantly in different regions of the oceans where the ships vigilantly carry out their duty, protecting the state interests of the homeland."[42] He warned the Western powers that, sooner or later, they would be forced to acknowledge that their forces had lost supremacy at sea. He also repeated the standard Soviet criticism of aircraft carriers by noting their vulnerability to submarine and air forces.[43]

In speeches subsequent to 1967, Gorshkov has regularly described the expansion of the Soviet Navy and praised its great role in strengthening the state's power and international prestige; the Navy could now fulfill combat duties at great distances and strategic tasks of an offensive nature in any part of the world's oceans. The Navy's strength, he said, "was not determined by tonnage but by the presence of rockets and the quality of electronic warfare."[44]

Gorshkov's first article of the 1970s reviewed the Navy's role in the Great Patriotic War. He emphasized the importance of the 110 or more amphibious operations that the Soviets claimed to have carried out and praised the leaders of the armed forces, particularly Marshal Grechko, for the close coordination among services during World War II.[45] In his Navy Day speech of July 1971, Gorshkov reported that the "Ninth Five Year Plan would provide the Navy with still more improved ships."[46] Some of these improvements are now represented by the D-class ballistic-missile submarine and the *Kiev*-class antisubmarine-warfare carrier. Undoubtedly there will be additional new classes which were not initiated prior to the plan.

The unprecedented series of monthly installments bearing Gorshkov's name that appeared in *Morskoi Sbornik* beginning in February 1972 has been analyzed by various notable naval authorities in the U. S. Naval

[33] For a different view, *see* Michael MccGwire, "The Turning Points in Naval Policy Formations," as contained in Michael MccGwire, ed., *Soviet Naval Developments: Capability and Context* (Halifax: Centre for Foreign Policy Studies, 1972), p. 167.

[34] *Herrick, pp. 73–74.*

[35] *Morskoi Sbornik*, No. 7 (July 1963), pp. 9–18.

[36] *Pravda*, July 31, 1960, p. 3; February 26, 1960, p. 2; and February 2, 1962, pp. 1–2.

[37] *Pravda*, February 13, 1965.

[38] *Izvestia*, May 9, 1965, pp. 1–3.

[39] *Pravda*, July 9, p. 1 and July 11, pp. 1–2, 1965.

[40] *Pravda*, October 31, 1965, pp. 1–2.

[41] *Izvestia*, October 29, 1967, p. 2.

[42] *Pravda*, July 30, 1967, p. 2.

[43] *Morskoi Sbornik*, February 1967, pp. 9–21.

[44] *Pravda*, July 25, 1969, p. 2.

[45] *Morskoi Sbornik*, No. 5 (May 1970), pp. 3–12.

[46] *Pravda*, July 25, 1971, p. 2.

Institute *Proceedings,* the *Naval War College Review,* and other journals. Consequently, these articles will not be addressed at length here. Basically Gorshkov draws upon numerous historical examples, some misleading, to highlight the importance of seapower and he attempts to justify the U.S.S.R.'s desire for a "super" navy. The articles differ from his earlier writings in that they are much broader in scope; however, many of his previous themes remain unchanged. For example, he still does not advocate U.S.-type aircraft carriers although he strongly believes in a blue-water navy and is well aware of the need for air cover in distant areas. In addition, despite his extensive experience in amphibious warfare during World War II, he disdains large, modern, and sophisticated landing craft. This view is tangibly reflected in the limited number of such craft built for the Soviet Navy during his tenure.

It does not appear that Gorshkov was much interested in politics in the early stages of his career. There is no evidence that he was a member of the Communist Youth League (Komsomol) during his youth. In fact, it was not until 1942, after being promoted to flag rank, that he joined the Communist Party (CPSU). Thus, he appears to be more a pragmatist than an ideologist. Since 1952 he has been elected to every CPSU Congress. In 1954 he was a member of the Bureau of the Crimean Oblast and Sevastopol City Party committees, and became a member of the Ukrainian Communist Party. Elected a candidate member of the CPSU Central Committee in 1956, he was promoted to full membership in 1961. Since 1954 he has also been a Deputy to the U.S.S.R. Supreme Soviet from various electoral districts in Latvia,[47] where he probably maintains a residence.

In summary, Gorshkov's career has been remarkable. He rose to flag rank quicker than Lord Nelson did and has stayed at the top longer than Arleigh Burke. He is the architect of the new Soviet Navy whose accent is on sophisticated missile-armed submarines, ships, and aircraft. Now 64 years old he may be near the end of his spectacular career. Regardless of what his future plans may be, historians will surely judge Gorshkov as one of the most influential admirals of the twentieth century.

[47]"S. Gorshkov," *Deputaty Verkhovnogo Soveta USSR,* (Deputies of the Supreme Soviet of the USSR), Moscow: 1962, p. 108; 1966, p. 114; and 1970, p. 109.

Mr. Hibbits did his undergraduate work in economics at Fordham University and earned his M.A. in Russian Affairs from Georgetown University. Prior to becoming a Lieutenant Commander in the Naval Reserve, he had Russian language training at the Defense Language School in Washington, D.C., and served on the staff of the Commander, Naval Forces Japan. From 1969 to 1973 he was a civilian research analyst in the Office of the Chief of Naval Operations. He is presently doing research work on Soviet maritime affairs with the Central Intelligence Agency.

Index